Understanding Communication in Business and the Professions

Understanding Communication in Business and the Professions

Abné M. Eisenberg
Herbert H. Lehman College
City University of New York

Macmillan Publishing Co., Inc.
New York
Collier Macmillan Publishers
London

Printed in the United States of America

Macmillan Publishing Co., Inc.
866 Third Avenue, New York, New York 10022

Collier Macmillan Canada, Ltd.

ISBN 0-02-331850-3

PRINTING: 1 2 3 4 5 6 7 8 Year: 8 9 0 1 2 3 4

To my son Eric and daughter Danya. I wish the joy and meaning you both have given my life to every other parent on this planet.

Acknowledgment

If I had to call the roll of those people who played a vital part in the making of this book, outstanding among them would be Lloyd Chilton, Bruce Bumby, and Leo Malek. At Macmillan, they were friends as well as publishing colleagues. Each gave freely of his knowledge, experience, and counsel. To Marianna Ciraulo, who skillfully organized, edited, and typed the manuscript, I offer my profound gratitude. For screening the manuscript to determine its relevance to the college mind, I thank Cheryl Chrisohon, a graduating senior at Lehman College. And finally, I thank those many beautiful students whose interest and participation in my Oral Communication in Business and Industry course were largely responsible for the motivation from which I drew heavily while writing this text.

Contents

Briefing

There is no such thing as a business or profession, only people who, because of their mutual interests and training, have come together for some common purpose.

The purpose of this briefing is to give you some idea of what you are getting into, make you aware of the direction this book will be taking, and supply you with previews of what to expect in each of its chapters. It is most important that you understand at the outset that this is not a business text, but rather a book about how *people* in business communicate. It will have special appeal to students, apprentices, trainees, and assistants, as their needs are quite different from those of managers, supervisors, foremen and administrators. While the chapters of this work will not ignore management, their empathy lies heavily with those contemplating beginning, or working their way up in a given field of interest.

Another major point to be made in these pages is that *people are not things.* Ever since the Industrial Revolution put people in competition with machines, the distinction between human and machine has become less clearly defined. For example, have you ever had a job that made you feel like a nonperson, a piece of merchandise, a cog in a wheel? There are many organizations in which people feel this way. To combat this mechanistic tendency, people must be rediscovered in business.

A role in business originates with a decision—a career decision. Most career decisions, however, are not well thought out; they are often the result of whim or impulse. Advice on what you should do with your life comes in a variety of forms and from many different sources. The problem of figuring out which advice to follow and which to ignore can be frustrating. Suggestions from parents, teachers, relatives, friends, and occasionally complete strangers add to this frustration. What child has not at some time been asked, "What do you want to be when you grow up?"

Oddly enough, children have not always been asked this question. For most of history young men were never consulted about their futures. It was taken for granted that if their fathers were storekeepers, they too would be storekeepers; if their fathers were blacksmiths, they too would be blacksmiths, and so on. Young women had even more predetermined futures. It was automatically assumed that they would marry, have babies, and manage a household. Since the nineteenth century, however, questions concerning the future of a young woman or man have become more complicated. The element of *choice* has been added. Many parents do not want their children to follow in their footsteps—they want them to have better and easier lives. Young people whose fathers are farmers or factory workers dream of becoming doctors, lawyers, or even President of the United States.

Whether a decision about how you will earn a living is arrived at through intuition, inspiration, guidance, career planning, or aptitude testing, of one thing you can be sure—communication will play an important role in it. This brings to mind the answer a famous sculptor once gave when asked how he managed to create such magnificent statues. He said, "I just chip away the unimportant parts." Confused, the person who asked the question walked away mumbling. "But how does he know which are the unimportant parts?" Although you may not choose to become a sculptor, his words of wisdom should serve you well, no matter what you decide to do In the same spirit, I will make every effort to enhance the value of this text by chipping away its unimportant parts and by so doing, render its statement about the communication process more understandable. Traditional concepts about communication will not be presented in a separate chapter. Instead, they will be allowed to emerge naturally as they develops within the substance of the book.

Of no less importance is the fact that human communication has not always been recognized in the business world. "Only within recent years has management in the real sense discovered the instrument of communication, and that communication is one of its most powerful resources for operating success."*

Chapter Previews

Chapter 1 Intrapersonal Self-inventory.

Here you will be asked to take a close look at yourself from a number of different perspectives. Allowing yourself to be as open and honest as possible, you should be able to gain greater insight into both your good and bad

*Robert R. Aurner, "Communications impact: Power source for decision-makers," *Journal of Business Communication*, 5(2), 23–29 (1967).

points. Experience teaches that the more your physical and psychological characteristics are compatible with your career, the better your chances of succeeding in it. Materialistically speaking, in violation of the credo that people are not things, you are a product, of sorts–something that must be sold, not only sold to yourself, but to others as well. And, if you don't buy your own product, how can you expect others to buy it? Throughout this chapter, you will be looking at such things as your body type, grooming habits, moods, sense of humor, manner of speaking, perception, and body language, along with your attitudes, values, and beliefs. You will be making an intrapersonal self-inventory and as a result have a better concept of what you have going for you on the open market. From a practical standpoint, you will then know which of your qualities you should stress and which ones need improvement.

Chapter 2 Interpersonal Self-inventory.

In contrast with the preceding chapter, this one concentrates on how a person communciates with others. It is divided into two parts: (1) your silent self and (2) your speaking self. Each seeks to provide you with non-verbal and verbal insights that will be helpful on the job. Periodically, you will be invited to register your personal opinion on a variety of subjects.

Implicit in this chapter is the contention that most people have a distorted conception of themselves–of how they get along with others. Some, having the reputation of being bastards in an organization, have convinced themselves that they are model citizens and extremely easy to get along with. Others who are a pleasure to deal with needlessly torture themselves by believing that nobody likes them. In either instance, a reevaluation of the self is called for, a realistic appraisal made on the basis of real, not imagined facts. The content of this chapter makes such an appraisal possible.

Chapter 3 Investigating a Career.

Since few people know exactly what they want to do with their lives, this chapter offers those still undecided some valuable suggestions. Aside from checking want ads and having someone say, "Hey, why don't you look into . . .," the average person hasn't the foggiest inkling about how to investigate a specific job or career. Far too many consider landing a good job a matter of luck. To remedy the tendency to lean on "lady luck," this chapter will disclose where to look or write for information about a career, how to interpret a want ad; when, where, and how to advertise for a position; what questions to ask people already in a field; how to use the telephone when career-hunting; and how to analyze your personal motivation.

Finding out what you want to do with your life need not be an unpleasant chore. All it requires is a systematic approach, a stiff upper lip, and above all *patience.* There is no such thing as a negative experience.

Everything that happens to an individual in the pursuit of a career has value. The most unpleasant experience teaches something; i.e., that is, it alerts the person to whom it happened to be more prepared the next time. In short, the chapter encourages the reader to think about certain specific career-related factors that will make a decision easier. The process naturally involves communicating effectively with oneself and with others.

Chapter 4 Surviving an Interview.

According to Dr. Nathan Azrin, founder of Carbondale's Center for Human Development, "Employers make hiring choices on a skill-irrelevant basis." Whereas he certainly does not mean this in any absolute sense, he does mean that people are often hired for reasons other than their ability to do the job for which they were interviewed.

Also stressed is the fact that in any interview, you are your best ally. Attempts to deceive an interviewer into believing that you are something you are not usually backfire. And, since job interviews are difficult to avoid, the serious job-hunter cannot afford the luxury of being unprepared. In other words, the interviewee must be so prepared that no matter what an interviewer says or does, it comes as no surprise to the interviewee. To achieve this high degree of preparedness, the reader will not only have to understand the dynamics of an interview from both sides of the desk, but also those phases of it which go beyond words—nonverbal communication. Reasonable competence in these two areas should improve anyone's ability to survive an interview.

Chapter 5 Coping in Groups.

Because the age of rugged individualism is gone, learning how to communicate in a group on the job has become a necessity. These days, responsibility for the success or failure of a business seldom rests on the shoulders of a single person. Decisionmaking and carrying out responsibilities are tasks generally shared by several members of an organization. Because of increased specialization, effective communication in groups, committees, departments, teams, and sections has become a prerequisite for both personal and organizational growth. Recognizing this trend toward "groupness," the chapter closely examines what happens when people on the job come together and are expected to communicate in a meaningful way. "Job-talk," as this writer chooses to call it, is rapidly attracting the attention of management and labor. It is becoming progressively more difficult for people in organizational life to remain silent. As groups grow in size, number, and importance, greater demands will be made on their members to communicate with one another. This chapter reaches out to meet such demands.

Chapter 6 Listening, a Serious Business.

Despite being told by experts that good listening habits are indispensible to success in business, only a handful of courses in listening are presently being offered in our schools. This chapter pleads for an expanded interest in the listening aspect of communication. And, to support such a plea, it offers a broad-based discussion of the subject.

In addition to enlarging the reader's understanding of listening and the role it plays on the job, an effort is also made to dispel certain myths about listening that have cropped up through the years. For one, an overwhelming number of people believe that listening and hearing are the same thing. Identifying and correcting this mistake alone can improve one's interpersonal communication; together with other mistakes, a significant change in the reader's concept of listening may occur. If successful, listening will indeed have become a serious business.

Chapter 7 Negotiation: Disagreeing without Being Disagreeable

As its title suggest, this chapter deals with humanity's greatest achievment: the ability to negotiate differences over a conference table. But, as Ann Douglas claims, "A thinking person who takes the trouble to explore this field (negotiation) will be bound to wonder how it could have excaped the human discipline so long." Knowing what to do when confronted with differences of opinion, however, is a far cry from actually being able to do it. The ability to negotiate in a rational and productive manner is one of these paradoxes. Although we are able to propel ourselves through outer space and to transplant human hearts, we have yet to learn how to resolve our differences peacefully. Historically, on selected occasions, some leaders have been able to sit around a conference table and, through the art of negotiation, successfully resolve their differences. More often, to our discredit, we have resorted to settling our differences on the battle field.

Depending on the business or profession in question, communication can, at times, get rather sticky. The president of a large corporation who owes a great deal of money, the patient who requires major surgery, or the manufacturer who has been asked to take back a big shipment of defective merchandise from a customer all find themselves faced with the need to negotiate. In this chapter, the reader is urged to learn ways of disagreeing without being disagreeable with an "iron-fist-in-a-velvet-glove" approach to conflict resolution.

In a sense, every business consists of an endless chain of negotiations. And, as with the subject of interviewing, the negotiator who is vulnerable to surprises does so at great risk. Hence, to reduce such risk, this section of the book describes the various types of people who negotiate, their methods, shortcomings, and rationale. The result should be an added dimension of insight, understanding, and comprehension for the newcomer to the negotiating scene.

Chapter 8 Influencing Others

The importance of communication stressed throughout this text has come to represent the "backbone" of business. Communication, in turn, means "influencing others." That is what this chapter is all about—ways and means of influencing others verbally and nonverbally To achieve this end, the reader will discover why people believe what they do, the motives entertained by those who seek to influence others, how propaganda operates as a tool of influence, and methods of resisting the impact being influenced. In short, the chapter is designed to arm the reader with a working understanding of the dynamics of influence as it pertains to the world of business or, to the people who make up the world of business.

Chapter 9 Instructional Communication

On most jobs, someone is asked to either show or tell someone else how to do something. These instructional forms of communication may range from how to operate a switchboard, electron microscope, lathe, cash register or computer. If you have ever taught someone how to drive a car or have been taught yourself, you have some idea of the many things that can go wrong. Not only will the pitfalls associated with giving or taking instructions be discussed in this chapter, but also methods of avoiding them. Mention will also be made of the fact that, in special cases, faulty instructions could not only be costly, but dangerous. Examples of such danger might involve a mistake in writing or interpreting a prescription, negotiating a rather large deposit or withdrawal from a bank through a newly hired teller, or talking down a pilot attempting to land at a fogged-in airport. Each depends on words being translated into actions.

Aside from delivering a general discussion about oral and written instructions, forceful mention will be made of the fact that it is a woefully neglected area of interest in the field. While technical writers are specialists who perform their jobs with great competence, there is a large body of ill-defined, nontechnical writers who seriously lack any background in human communication. Among the latter, the prevailing belief is that anyone who knows the English language, understands how something is done, and has a knowledge of how a thing is constructed, can teach others to use it. To appreciate the validity of this claim, the reader is extended some invitations to participate in actual instruction-giving and instruction-taking exercises.

Chapter 10 Mistaken Meaning.

By focusing on breakdowns in communication, this chapter embraces the concepts and principles advanced in earlier chapters. The transition of theory to practice becomes visible. A serious reading of this chapter is crucial to an understanding of communication in business.

It is one thing to recognize a case of mistaken meaning but quite another to repair it. Whereas it is commonly agreed that every communication breakdown is caused by something (or someone), the greatest difficulty seems to settle on selecting the best method of getting at that cause. If two people are involved, chances are there will be at least two causes. If four people are involved, four causes, and so on. The number of causes of a communication breakdown appear to be proportional to the number of people involved in it.

In this chapter, the reader will be supplied with a checklist consisting of six checkpoints. Each checkpoint zeros in on one common cause of a typical breakdown in communication. Used as a diagnostic tool, it is suggested that the reader screen any breakdown according to this checklist. The value of this approach, on any level, is to preserve the accuracy of meaning and, by so doing, ensure the survival of both the individual and the organization served.

A final word about the chapters in this book. Each opens with a memo designed to provide you with a set of behavioral objectives–guidelines as to what should be learned from it. Each chapter closes with a Self-Examination Quiz to see whether you have indeed achieved these objectives.

Chapter 1

Intrapersonal Self-Inventory

The ability to accept blame and criticism without blaming and criticizing others is a reliable sign of intrapersonal growth.

MEMO

TO: Reader

FROM: Author

After reading this chapter, you should have a better understanding of:

1. Why it is important to make a distinction between people and things.

2. How awareness of your assets and liabilities can help you achieve personal growth as well as decide on a career.

3. How and why a prepared mind can increase your chances of achieving success.

4. How an honest and open self-inventory could be instrumental in aiming your life in a positive direction.

5. Why, more than any other single factor responsible for meaningful communication, your self-esteem ranks highest.

6. What differences emerge in a single-valued, two-valued, and multi-valued approach to living.

7. Where your thoughts and feelings come from.

8. Why a sense of humor is one of the greatest allies of communication.

9. How motivation shapes people's behavior in business and professional circles.

10. How certain items in your self-inventory can be altered to change the course of your future.

Chapter 1

The Difference Between Who and What You Are

In the briefing to this book, you were told that in certain business and professional organizations, people were treated as though they were "things" and not people. While you may find it convenient to say, "Well, that's the way it is, and we can't do much about it," such an attitude is argued against in this chapter. For you actually can do something about being treated as a "thing." It has to do with the difference between thinking of yourself as a *who* or a *what*.

Let's say someone were to ask you right now, "Who are you?" Place your response in the following space: ______________________________

____

____

____

Now, respond to the question, "What are you?" in the next space.

____

____

____

Most of you probably answered the *who* question by giving your name and, perhaps, your address, telephone number, and social security number. To the *what* question, you probably responded with the fact that you are a student and, perhaps, further qualified whether you are a freshman, sophomore, junior, or senior. The more analytical reader was probably put off by the question and first wanted to know under what circumstances the question was being asked. For example, being asked *who* you are while sitting in the school library might logically prompt the answer, "I'm a student." But if you were asked the same question on the street or in a bus terminal you might feel another type of answer was required. Obviously, if a police officer were to ask who you are, giving your name would seem appropriate. The entire issue of who and what you are appears to center on the way you see yourself. And, the way you see yourself may, in turn, depend on how you think others see you. To give you some idea of how you see yourself, try this rather interesting personal exercise: in the 10 spaces that follow, answer the question, "Who am I?" 10 separate times. Write whatever comes to your mind each time, and don't worry if you repeat yourself. Naturally, try not to write the same thing more than once but, if it happens, let it happen.

1. Who am I? ______________________________

2. Who am I? ______________________________

3. Who am I? ______________________________

4. Who am I? ______________________________

5. Who am I? ______________________________

6. Who am I? ______________________________

7. Who am I? ______________________________

8. Who am I? ______________________________

9. Who am I? ______________________________

10. Who am I? ______________________________

From this exercise, you should be able to get your first set of insights into your self-inventory. Take something as simple as your name. If it is Stephen or Steven, did you write "Stevie"? If it is Anna, did you write "Annie"? Do you think there is any difference between the way Stephen and Stevie, Anna and Annie sound? Do the names Stevie and Annie give you the impression that they might belong to younger people? Why? Then, there is the question of how you indicated your sex. Did you say you were a "male or female," "boy or girl," or "man or woman"? Could the way you refer to yourself be a significant consideration in your self-inventory? Why?

Another item to check out in looking over your answers is whether you are locked into the past, present, or future. Pick out how many of your responses referred to things you have already done, are presently doing, or are going to do. Next, examine your answers for positive or negative qualities. If you said you were a student, did you say what kind of student (excellent, good, fair, poor)? Still another consideration is whether your answers suggest you are goal or process oriented. For instance, did you say you are a driving instructor or simply that you teach driving? Does saying that you are a driving instructor give a more accurate picture of what you are or who you are? Does saying that you are a driving instructor imply that you have reached a particular goal? If you had a tendency to decorate yourself with titles in your answers, such as graduating senior, head teller, editor-in-chief of school newspaper, captain of a particular school team or club, does that point toward a goal orientation? Finally, there is the question of whether you think of yourself as someone who belongs to others or someone to whom others belong. It would be the difference between saying, "I am the daughter or son of Bill and Alice Jones," or "My parents are the Joneses".

At this point, a normal and quite understandable question to be asking is, "Where are the correct answers?" If you are asking whether the answers you gave to the question, "Who are you?" are correct, you will not find them here. There are no right or wrong answers. Any one of your answers could be twisted and turned to mean anything and everything. The more important concern here should be whether a particular answer is appropriate for you in particular. Naturally, this begs the logical question, "What is appropriate?" For our purposes, let us define appropriateness as meaning *that harmonious mental and physical state in which individuals best serve not only their own interests but the interests of those around them as well.* Common sense dictates that an answer under one set of circumstances might be considered appropriate, whereas under other circumstances, totally inappropriate. Be satisfied to treat this exercise simply as an opportunity to gain additional insight into yourself.

We can get still another perspective on *who* and *what* people are by looking backward in time. Men used to be identified in four ways: (1) place of birth (Jesus of Nazareth), (2) trade (John the Fisherman). (3) father's name (Isaac, son of Abraham), and (4) certain personality traits (Alexander the Great). In each case, in addition to the name, you became immediately aware of other things about the person. This is no longer true today. Being introduced to someone named Eric, Danya, John, or Mary gives you little to go on. Unless one is very outgoing and direct and asks, "What do you do for a living?" or "What are you?" all that is left is inference. As you know, an inference is a statement about the unknown, based on the known. Therefore, an introduction that involves nothing more than a person's name is a perfect invitation for inference. In our society, we have come to associate certain personality traits, occupations, and life-styles with specific names. Here are a few. Next to each name write the inference you are inclined to make about the person, based on the name alone:

1. Lulu ________________________________

2. Peter ________________________________

3. Seymour ________________________________

4. Duke ________________________________

5. Mary Ann ________________________________

6. Winnie ________________________________

7. Hubert ________________________________

8. Patsy ________________________________

9. Bart ________________________________

10. Bernadette ______________________________

11. Penny ______________________________

12. Stephen ______________________________

13. Lolita ______________________________

At the risk of talking about people as things (warned against earlier), your name often serves the same function that the name of a product carries on the shelves of your local supermarket. And, as you fully realize, a name can turn you off or onto a particular product. This is why product management spends millions each year trying to find the "right" name for a product. How about you–do you like your name? Why? If you were to change it, what name would you prefer? Why? Are you familiar with people whose first names are completely inappropriate to the fields they are in? Would you go to a physician named Dr. Toby Creekwater? You might but, if the pain were great enough, you might not be so quick to choose such a name from the yellow pages over a group of other names. Or would you? After all, what's in a name? Perhaps more than you think.

In taking stock of your "self," your name (*who* you are) is very important. Although others may have your first name, the chances of others having your first and last names are extremely limited. Your name distinguishes you from other people. As a doctor, lawyer, bank president, secretary, or cocktail waitress (*what* you are), you are one of many. Communication, in practically all its forms, begins with the recognition of *who* you are–your name. It establishes you as a living, breathing, feeling human being. The conversation that begins without recognition of *who* you are suffers from ill health; it begins with you as a nonperson. Equally unhealthy is the conversation in which an executive of a firm refers to you as his or her assistant, foreman, or traffic manager. Without any personal identification, you are identified as a *what*–as a creature that performs a function–period.

Your Assets and Liabilities

What are your good points? What are your bad points? Is it possible that what you once considered one of your plusses you now consider a bad trait? Do you think you could get at least three of your friends to agree unanimously with you on your good and bad points? Just how did you arrive at these characteristics you call "good" and "bad"? If you are anything like the rest of us, it was through a process of trial and error. From childhood, people have been complimenting us on certain things and criticizing us on others. And, over the years, we have come up with what we call our assets and liabilities. It is through a blending or synthesis of these characteristics that our *self-image* develops. How the mind does this is not known. All we have to go on is what people say and what they do. It is from these two avenues of communication that we make guesses about what is going on inside a human being's mind. Without a mind-reading machine, most employers are forced to base their hiring practices on what a prospective employee claims to have done or professes to be able to do in the future. Beyond this, a prospective employer must rely on such things as intuition and instinct.

Throughout your future business and professional life, your self-image (a mixture of your assets and liabilities) will continually be challenged—if not by you, by those you come in contact with. For some people, keeping a self-image intact is not a difficult chore; for others, it presents an ongoing problem. Without being aware of it, for many of us our self-image is a starting point or base line from which we must adjust. To communicate at all, we must take stock of our "self" and, with the information we glean, weave an acceptable, or at least tolerable, self-image. According to Kenneth Gergen, how you see yourself plays a critical role in your private emotional life, as well as in your relationship with others. In support of this view, he found that "one's estimate of self strongly influences [one's] goals and [one's] behavior in reaching these goals."*

Basically, there are three ways of arriving at a concept of your self-image. First, there is the way others make appraisals of you through their compliments and criticisms. From infancy, your parents have bestowed you with a wide range of praises and put-downs, based on either your behavior or your appearance. Coming at you from another direction were the observations and judgments made by your brothers and sisters. To these were added the compliments and criticism of friends, teachers, and neighbors, as well as passersby on the street. Separately or in concert, these appraisals played an important role in the development of your concept of self.

Second, the process of social comparison molds your self-image. What young boy or girl has not been compared to some other child at school or in the neighborhood, as conveyed by the well-known "Why can't you be like . . . ?" Even worse was the poor child who repeatedly had to suffer comparison with a brother or sister.

Third, the practice of personally labeling one's own good and bad characteristics shapes the self-concept. It seems that, for a variety of psychological reasons (which we shall not go into here), people manipulate the information they receive from their environment and assign labels that have personal survival value and meaning. As a result, many of these self-concepts are not only illogical, but are frequently inconsistent.

*Kenneth Gergen, *The Concept of Self* (New York: Holt, Rinehart and Winston, 1971), pp. 90–91.

The time has now come for you to take stock of your assets and liabilities. Fill out the following form as openly and honestly as you can.

Self-Inventory

Instructions: This inventory of your self deals with the here and now—the present. Under headings of assets and liabilities, you will find four categories: *physical* attributes, *psychological* makeup, *credentials,* and *special qualities.* Although such things as bias and prejudice are ordinarily to be avoided, for the purposes of this self-inventory, you are encouraged to admit your personal biases and prejudices.

ASSETS	*LIABILITIES*
Physical Attributes	
1.____________________	1.____________________
2.____________________	2.____________________
3.____________________	3.____________________
4.____________________	4.____________________
5.____________________	5.____________________
Psychological Characteristics	
1.____________________	1.____________________
2.____________________	2.____________________
3.____________________	3.____________________
4.____________________	4.____________________
5.____________________	5.____________________
Credentials	
1.____________________	1.____________________
2.____________________	2.____________________

Special Qualities

1. ________________	1. ________________
2. ________________	2. ________________
3. ________________	3. ________________
4. ________________	4. ________________
5. ________________	5. ________________

Classroom testing with this method of self-inventory showed that students were divided. Some had very little difficulty verbalizing their assets and liabilities, whereas others just couldn't seem to get going. A number were particularly bothered by not knowing exactly what the teacher wanted them to do. They appeared preoccupied with "doing the right thing." In spite of being told that there were no right or wrong answers to the questionnaire, they continued to feel frustrated. The majority, however, comfortably reached inside themselves and came forth with some interesting information. Under physical assets, their responses included such items as well coordinated, not bad looking, clean cut, athletic, energetic, young, conservative dresser, pleasant voice, strong, honest face. Physical liabilities brought these responses: short, female, sloppy dresser, smoker, talk too fast, get sick a lot, oily skin, overweight (about 10 pounds), small bust, heavy legs, poor eyesight, bite nails, big nose, not mechanically inclined.

Psychological characteristics netted quite a different assortment of assets and liabilities. Here are some examples. Under assets, there were: confident, intelligent, sensitive, optimistic, dependent, logical, friendly, trustworthy, genial most of the time, open-minded, good sense of humor, neat, can tolerage stress situations, can accept criticism, sympathetic, empathetic, follow things through to completion, get along well with people, like to organize, polite, eager to learn, common sense. Psychological liabilities brought these entries: say "yes" when I really mean "no," oversensitive with people I care about, cry when I'm angry or upset, shy with people until I get to know them, too modest, overly cautious, hot-tempered, act childish at times, suspicious, stubborn, can't take criticism, joke too much, moody, have difficulty making up my mind, too naive, easily persuaded by women, talk too much, get bored easily, get depressed when things don't go right.

In this inventory, credentials presented the least difficulty. As an asset, students recorded college degree, notary public, insurance broker's license, company clerk in U.S. Army, graduate of stenotyping school, Dean's List, American Red Cross Instructor's Certificate. As a liability, most of the responses settled on a growing phenomenon of overqualification. Other negative aspects of credentials included: having a degree in an area that has very few good jobs, having theoretical, as opposed to practical knowledge, being too specialized, having a degree from a school with a bad reputation.

Being asked, "What's so special about you?" is not an easy question for most people. The majority of those brought up in this country have been taught that it isn't nice to "blow your own horn." Self-praise is considered wrong–"bragging". Student reactions to the question of what's special about them bear out this unwritten law. Among the special qualities that were volunteered were: go out of my way for friends, good looks and brains, perseverance, the ability to stay cool when others around me are up-tight, can adjust easily to a changing environment, have a "take life one-day-at-a time attitude, know my limitations. Special qualities admitted to be liabilities were few and consisted of: tire of people quickly, always think about sex, fanatic sports fan, lazy, have an absolutely insane way of laughing, constantly need reassurance.

People in every business and profession expect things from one another. Generally speaking, these expectations are based on a belief that others possess both the ability and willingness to deliver them. A failure on either side to do what was expected provides ideal ground for a breakdown in communication. This very attitude leads directly to what you have just done –take your self-inventory. If performed in seriousness, you should have gathered before you a profile of your assets and liabilities. It is from these building blocks that you can achieve personal growth. Without such insights, many people remain locked into frozen self-images and self-concepts for the major part of their lives. Change requires a starting point, and the starting point here is a more courageous look at yourself.

What Taking Stock of Yourself Means

The exclusive subject of this chapter is *you.* The purpose is to hold a mirror up to yourself from as many angles as possible. People go to psychoanalysts and spend a great deal of money to talk about themselves. Every interview you ever have during your working years will be about *you.* How many times have people said, "Tell me about yourself"? Doesn't it stand to reason that if other people will want to know more about you, in important matters, some preparation is in order? This, in a nutshell, is what taking stock of yourself means.

Have you ever heard the expression, "Chance favors the prepared mind"? Do you remember that great feeling you had when, on an important job interview, you anticipated every question the interviewer asked? Perhaps you recall the good fortune to have studied exactly what a professor asked on a final examination. Regardless of the situation, whether it be a lawyer who has a particular case reference at his or her fingertips, a physician who happens to know the symptom picture of a rare tropical disease, a salesperson

armed with the precise argument that will close a very big business deal, or a government official whose experience makes it possible for a city to avert a dangerous labor strike, chance favors the prepared mind.

Those who fail to take stock of their natural resources risk walking around with an unprepared mind. You may think you know yourself, but chances are there is much more to learn. Darting off in a slightly different direction, try this exercise designed to provide you with glimpses of yourself from three different points of view.

Name of Exercise: Yourself at Three Stages of Life

Procedure:

Step 1. Paying absolutely no attention whatever to the fact that you may not be able to draw a straight line, draw a picture of yourself at 6 years of age.

Step 2. Now, draw yourself as you are today.

Step 3. Finally, draw yourself at 50 years of age.

You at age six.

You at your present age.

You at age 50.

After you have drawn yourself at the three stages of life, compare your analysis with a classmate who has done the same thing. Examine each other's work and discuss your impressions informally. The result will be some added dimensions of you.

Your Self-esteem and Assertiveness

Earlier, we spoke of your good and bad points. Now, taking several steps backward, let's discuss how you feel about yourself as a whole. Such an attitude is called self-esteem or self-worth. Perhaps more than any single factor responsible for successful communication, your self-esteem is the most important. Very few thoughts and actions can't ultimately be traced back to how you feel about yourself. In fact, one of the major variables in the development of a self-concept is the development of high esteem. The point is very simple and direct: To make sound decisions, logically and rationally interpret issues, and humanistically relate to others, you must be aware of yourself and have faith in your own abilities. To get some idea of what condition your own self-esteem is in right now, take the following modified version of Barksdale's test for self-esteem.*

SELF-EXAMINATION QUIZ

To determine your score, judge each of the following statements as follows: 0 if not true, 1 if somewhat true, 2 if largely true, and 3 if true.

________ 1. I feel other people are better than I am.

________ 2. I feel content and pleased with myself.

________ 3. I feel unable to cope with new situations.

________ 4. I feel friendly toward everyone I meet.

________ 5. I usually blame myself when things go wrong.

________ 6. I never feel any shame, blame, built, or remorse.

________ 7. I have a compulsive need to show off how good I am.

________ 8. I get a kick out of life.

________ 9. I am concerned about my reputation.

________ 10. When others are wrong, I don't feel a need to correct them.

________ 11. I have a strong need to have people say nice things about me.

There appears to be a strong connection between how you feel about yourself—your self-esteem—and how assertive you are. The word *assertiveness* should trigger in your mind such human traits as: energetic, self-starter, go-getter, motivated, outgoing, aggressive, and gregarious. As a rule, people who suffer from low self-esteem are rarely associated with these terms. If you are curious to discover just how assertive you are, fill out this inventory of assertiveness in taking stock of yourself.

*Liburn S. Barksdale, *Building Self-Esteem* (Los Angeles: The Barksdale Foundation for Furtherance of Human Understanding, 1972), pp. 6–7.

How Assertive Are You?

Instruction:

Place the number 1, 2, 3, or 4 in front of each of the following items, depending on whether your answer is *always, often, sometimes*, or *never.*

________ 1. Do you buy things you don't really want because it is difficult to say "no" to the sales clerk?

________ 2. Do you hesitate to return sales items to a store even when there is a good reason to do so?

________ 3. Do you hesitate to ask someone who talks aloud during a movie, play, or concert, to be quiet?

________ 4. Can you begin a conversation with a stranger?

________ 5. Do you have trouble maintaining conversations in social situations?

________ 6. Do people act as if they find you boring?

________ 7. Are you satisfied with your social life?

________ 8. When a friend makes an unreasonable request, are you able to refuse?

________ 9. Are you able to ask favors or make requests of your friends?

________ 10. Can you criticize a friend?

________ 11. Can you praise a friend?

________ 12. When someone compliments you, do you know what to say?

________ 13. Is there someone you can share your intimate feelings with?

________ 14. Would you rather bottle up your feelings than make a scene?

________ 15. Are you satisfied with your work habits?

________ 16. Do people tend to exploit you or push you around?

________ 17. Can you be open and frank in expressing both friendly and feelings to men?

________ 18. Can you be open and frank in expressing both friendly and angry feelings to women?

________ 19. Do you find it difficult to make or accept dates?

________ 20. Do you find it difficult to upbraid a subordinate?

Source: Modified from Herbert Fensterheim and Jean Baer, *Don't Say Yes When You Want to Say No.* (New York: David McKay, 1975), pp. 36–37.

Although you may be completely satisfied that the answers you gave in this quiz on assertiveness are accurate and truly correspond with the way you really are, it would be interesting to see whether your best friend agrees with you. To find out, cover up your answers with a sheet of paper and have your friend answer each question concerning your assertiveness. Then compare both sets of responses and discuss the basis for each response.

Your Orientation to Life

Everyone you know probably approaches living in a slightly different way. In spite of these differences, they all basically subscribe to one of three basic categories: (1) a single-valued orientation, (2) a two-valued orientation, or (3) multi-valued orientation. Single-valued people have tunnel vision. No matter what you discuss with them, they consistently hold tight to a single, immovable opinion or explanation. They are closed-minded to any view that has the nerve to differ from their own. In plain language, they are "one way" in all things.

The two-valued orientation to life is characterized by an "either/or" philosophy. For those who adhere to it, there is no middle ground. In conversation, they can be heard to make such statements as, "Look, you are either an American or a Communist." "Either you believe in God or you don't." Under no circumstances will two-valued people admit that anything exists between the extremes. For them, the word is neatly divided into thousands of little packages of twos. All that is left, from their point of view, is to make choices.

Although the two-valued orientation would appear to be considerably less frustrating to deal with in business and professional circles than the single-valued point of view, it too gets in the way of effective communication.

Take the attorney who gives a client the following option: "Either you pay the fine or you go to jail." How about the labor union leader who confronts his membership with the choice between a strike and being laid off? Or the politician who confronts her constituency with the attitude, "If I don't win the forthcoming election, I will drop out of political life." Each of these instances, offers absolutely no middle ground–no alternatives except the extremes are given to the people involved. All are strictly either/or situations.

The least common and, of course, the most desirable from the standpoint of more effective communication is the multi-valued orientation. People with this philosophy enjoy the reputation of being open-minded and flexible. A case in point would be the executive or national sales manager who is confronted with the problem of failing company morale. Rather than employ the one-way (single-valued) or the either/or (two-valued) approach to the problem, he or she would attack it on many fronts, that is, from many different angles (multi-valued approach). What if someone asked you the best way to become a millionaire? How would you answer? While you may not know the answer, there are those who might say such things as: (1) go into business for yourself, (2) play the stock market, (3) invest in mutual funds, or (4) marry someone very rich. Obviously, there is no one sure way to become a millionaire. Yet there are people with a surplus of opinions who are quick to share them with anyone who will listen. Among them are the single-valued, two-valued, and multi-valued types. Whereas a good lawyer could probably defend each with equal effectiveness, a common-sensical approach would dictate that in most business and professional settings, the multi-valued orientation promises the greatest amount of flexibility, soundness, and purpose in judgment.

Besides being single-valued, two-valued, or multi-valued, you can pick up another important clue to your inner self by finding out what you think people think. In reality, what you say about others tells more about *you* than it does about the people you are talking about. Have you ever noticed how certain employees of one organization talk about their competitors? Most of us tend to become suspicious of those who knock their competitors or their product. On a personal level, there are people who have the widespread reputation of bad-mouthing others. If fault can be found, these people manage to find it. If fault cannot be found, they invent it. In short, whether such behavior is personal or public, it can supply the alert observer with another source of what might be termed "instant insight" into the way a person communicates with others.

Here is another opportunity for you to be an alert observer of yourself. Go through the following list of statements which deal with the basic characteristics of human nature. Remember, your responses are not to be based on how *you* feel about these statements, but rather how you feel *society* views human nature.

Basic Characteristics of Human Nature

1 = Strongly disagree 2 = Disagree 3 = Agree 4 = Strongly Agree

________ 1. *Rather mechanistic:* Do things by habit rather than by choice.

________ 2. *Passive responders:* Must be motivated by external stimuli.

________ 3. *Apathetic:* Don't want to get involved with other people.

________ 4. *Assertive:* Do what they really want to do in most situations.

________ 5. *Actively* pursue their own goals.

________ 6. *Internally controlled:* Feel they can be and do what they really want.

________ 7. *Externally controlled:* Feel society dictates what they must do in each situation.

________ 8. *Conditioned:* Don't think for themselves.

________ 9. *Autonomous:* Look to themselves for reasons for doing things.

________ 10. *Cognitive beings:* Make choices on the basis of reason rather than emotion.

________ 11. *Aware of themselves:* Know what their choices are in most situations.

________ 12. *Self-motivated:* Don't need external motivation.

________ 13. *Irrational:* Subject to unconscious sexual and aggressive forces.

________ 14. *Products of their environment:* Have no means of counteracting this.

________ 15. *Pleasure seekers:* Cannot be altruistic.

________ 16. *Programmed:* Are happiest when they fulfill the norms of society.

________ 17. *Rational:* Make choices that are expressions of themselves.

________ 18. *Predictable:* Adhere to the norms of society.

________ 19. *Not responsible* for their behavior.

________ 20. *Motivated* by unconscious sexual and aggressive forces.

________ 21. *Unpredictable:* Free to choose their behavior.

________ 22. *Rational* because they make choices that are in line with society.

________ 23. Able to *adapt creatively* to any situation.

________ 24. *Aware* of their responsibilities to society and *committed* to helping others.

________ 25. *Responsible* for their own behavior.

________ 26. Capable of *meaningful relationships* through involvement with others.

________ 27. Open, honest communicators.

________ 28. Above using other people for their own gain.

________ 29. *In control* of their own destiny.

________ 30. *Dependent on others* for support in making their own decisions.

Source: George A. Borden and John D. Stone, *Human Communication* (Menlo Park, Calif.: Cummings, 1976).

Now that you've gone on record with regard to how you think people in the business and the professions think people are, go back and, using a different-colored pen, indicate how *you* think people are; I for example, think people are . . . . Note those statements you agreed with and those you disagreed with. Compare your responses with those of a classmate and the possible reasons behind your answers.

Your Thoughts and Feelings

The majority opinion in the field of psychology is that you come into this world with a "head full of nothing." A more fanciful term to describe this phenomenon is *tabula rasa*, from the Latin, which means a blank slate. Naturally, this does not apply to your brain, but rather to any thoughts and feelings you might have about the world in which we live. Whereas some researchers feel that a child is born into this world with certain information beyond those physical and psycholgoical traits associated with genetics and instinct, the question is far from being settled by modern science.

You probably have an opinion on practically everything you know. Those opinions are stored in your memory bank under the broad headings of *beliefs* and *disbeliefs*. If you weren't born with this information, where did it come from? Fundamentally, there are two sources: One consists of your senses (the ability to see, hear, taste, touch, and feel), and the other is the use of symbols that stand for things (words, signs, and gestures). Information from these two sources reaches your brain where it is processed into units of thought and is stored for possible future reference. Lumped together, this is the raw material from which your thoughts and feelings are eventually formed.

Unless you happen to be a mind reader, you haven't the slightest notion of what is going on inside another person's mind. To a large extent, because you know what is going on inside your own head, you reason that similar things are going on inside the heads of other people. Speculations about what is going on in other people's minds often masquerades as presumption, assumption, inference, intuition, and stereotyping. Sane and insane, logical and illogical, rational and irrational thoughts and feelings all travel these familiar highways of communication. Accountant, shipping clerk, ferry boat captain, brain surgeon, or fur trapper all share a common humanity; hence they share more than they realize in terms of interpersonal communications.

Two of the most frequently used methods of arriving at an opinion are through making assumptions and stereotyping. Let us consider assumptions first. An *assumption* is a point of view, guess or theory, the truth of which remains to be determined. Whether it is true or false can be determined only after a sufficient amount of evidence can be brought to bear upon it. You would not believe how much mental luggage you carry around in your head and guts that is based on assumption. To unlock some of the thoughts and feelings you have stored in your memory banks that are on assumption, try this exercise on assumptions.

Let's Assume

Instruction: Complete the following statements as candidly as you can.

1. When a position is said to pay top salary, I assume ________________

   ____.

2. When I see a physician driving a car that is 20 years old, I assume ______

   ____.

3. If I work on a job for a week and find it unpleasant, I assume ________

   ____.

4. When I call about a position three times and each time the secretary tells me the boss is not in, I assume ________________________

   ____.

5. If, after an interview, I am told to call back in about a week, I assume

   ____

   ____.

6. When I see a sign reading, No Refunds, I assume__________________

   ____.

7. When I hear about a business that grossed $10 million last year, I assume

   ____

   ____.

8. If a firm is in business for more than 50 years, I assume ____________

   ____.

9. When I hear of a department store chain that will honor its own credit cards, I assume ________________________________

   ____.

10. If someone works for the same company for 20 years, I assume _______

    ____.

11. If a doctor, lawyer, or accountant is licensed, I assume ______________

____.

12. If a person is said to be successful, I assume ______________________

____.

Do you notice anything special about the way you answered these questions? Did they seem to follow a pattern? Were many of them negative? Take questions 3, 4, and 5: Were all your answers pessimistic? How about 11 and 12: Were your answers optimistic? The way people assume things often gives us an idea of what is going on inside their heads. For instance, you must know people who always assume that something is wrong whenever they see a crowd. Then, there are those who, upon seeing a glass half-filled with water, will insist that it is half empty. Finally, there are those who automatically assume that any man who is home for lunch is unemployed or has been layed off from his job. Of all the ways we have for gathering information, assumptions without proper foundations lead the pack.

The next troublemaker in opinion-gathering is called *stereotyping.* It consists of singling out one characteristic (usually a bad one) of a class of people or things and attributing that characteristic to them all. In the vernacular, "Seen one, seen 'em all" says it best. Not only is the practice of stereotyping grossly unfair to the individual, it can also be very dangerous in the business and professional world. A classic illustration of this is the stereotype, if it breaks five minutes after you bought it, it was probably made in ______. Whatever you thought should go into the blank space, the word, Japan, filled the bill for a long time. However, as world trade changed its pattern, such places as Hong Kong, Korea, Singapore, and Taiwan began to displace it as the brunt of this stereotype. Like making assumptions, it is hard to conceive of just how much we stereotype. And, to firm up the charge that we all stereotype more than we would care to admit, complete the following sentences as frankly and spontaneously as you can.

Let's Stereotype

1. Show me an Irishman, and I'll show you a ______________________.
2. Anyone on an expense account ______________________________.
3. The boss who hires sexy looking secretaries ______________________

____.

4. Male secretaries are usually ______________________________.

5. Most politicians are ______________________________.

6. Nurses are usually ______________________________.

7. If he's Chinese, he probably owns a ______________________________.

8. If he's a doctor, he probably drives a ______________________________.

9. If something was stolen, it was probably taken by ______________________________

______________________________.

10. Good salesmen are usually good ______________________________.

11. Women who insist that their husbands be heavily insured ______________

______________________________.

12. Show me a partnership and I'll show you ______________________________

______________________________.

13. People in the restaurant business ______________________________

______________________________.

14. Anyone who has more than three drinks with an evening meal ______________

______________________________.

15. A college degree ______________________________.

Again, compare your answers with those of your classmates and inquire into their reasoning. It should also be mentioned that stereotyping changes with time, trends, and geographic locations. But most people do stereotype, and it does contribute, in part, to the development of our opinions on a variety of subjects. Consciously and unconsciously, these opinions give shape and form to our thoughts and feelings. Therefore, being aware of your personal stereotyping habits will provide not only an insight into how your head works, but will also give you an opportunity to do something about it, if necessary. The heart of the problem appears related to the fact that a shocking number of people practice stereotyping without even realizing it. Are you one of them? Switch on your psychological search lights and write down a few of the things you admit you stereotype in the spaces provided below:

1. ______________________________

2. ______________________________

3. ______________________________

4. ______________________________

5. ______________________________

Your Sense of Humor

Have you ever met anyone who denied having a sense of humor? Most people sincerely believe that if there is something funny out there, they will detect it. The truth of the matter is that this isn't so. Just as there are people who lack the ability to carry a tune, differentiate colors, or perform simple mathematics, there are those who have no sense of humor.

For some reason, the reputation of humor is not as good as it should be. Do you recall your public school principal's response to what was going on in a classroom from which laughing could be heard? That's correct—that the students were fooling around and not learning. Laughing and learning were never taken to be too compatible. Only recently has humor begun to be taken seriously—that is, being funny is no laughing matter.

On the strength of the expression, "You can best judge someone's character by noting well what that person finds laughable," several business organizations have begun to include in their screening of applicants a test of their sense of humor. I was once told by an administrator of an organization for retarded children that she would definitely be partial in her hiring practices to applicants with a sense of humor. There are probably many other businesses and professions in which a good sense of humor is not only helpful but indispensible. By the same token, there are a few other businesses and professions in which a sense of humor might be considered a liability. One that immediately comes to mind is the undertaking profession, more properly referred to as mortuary science. The last thing any funeral director needs in his or her employ is an employee with a ready grin and a quick wit.

Have you ever been in a movie theatre and found yourself the only one laughing at a particular scene? Or, the other way around, everyone was laughing but you. The things people laugh at cover a wide range of human experience: Surprise, ridicule, absurdity, exaggeration, distortion, exploitation. For a time, there were "sick jokes" going around, and the people who told them and laughed at them were looked upon by many as sick themselves. In many ways, jokes reflect the climate of the times. Take a minute to think of the funniest joke you ever heard, the funniest movie you ever saw, or the funniest book you ever read. Ask yourself why it was so funny. Insist that you answer yourself in very specific terms–exactly why was it so funny? You may discover that beneath what you deemed so laughable was some pretty serious human condition that, under other circumstances, could have been considered significantly less than funny. The point is this: Your sense of humor could conceivably play a vital part in deciding your future.

A great many people who are habitual joke tellers take themselves very seriously. When they tell a joke and you don't laugh at it, they frequently interpret it as personal rejection, that is, you are not rejecting the joke but the person telling it. Two things seem to offend people heavily: an attack on the way they speak and their sense of humor. It is therefore important for you to find out, if you don't already know, what kind of sense of humor you have. Read the following jokes, and fill in the reasons you do/don't find them funny:

Joke 1.

A man and woman had been married for 25 years. One morning, the woman got up and said to her husband, "John, I've had it with that stupid brother of yours. Either he leaves this house or I do." To which her husband answered, "*My* brother! I thought he was *your* brother."

Reasons: ______________________________

____

____

____

Joke 2.

A woman walked into a psychiatrist's office. The doctor asked, "What seems to be the trouble?" She answered, "I have amnesia." The doctor then said, "Tell me about it." She replied, "About what?"

Reasons: ______________________________

____

____

____

Joke 3.

A young man with one leg got on a bus and sat down next to a little old lady. Curious as to how he lost his leg, and not wanting to be obvious, she said, "Excuse me. You were in the war?" The young man looked at her for a moment and answered, "No." Not satisfied, the little old lady asked, "You had some kind of disease, maybe?" Again, he answered, "No." Finally, tired of her being nosey, the young man said, "Listen, lady, if I let you ask me one more question, will you be satisfied?" She then asked him, without any holds barred, "How did you lose your leg?" To which he answered as he hopped off the bus on his crutches, "It was bit off!"

Reasons: ____

____

____

____

There is no definite formula for humor. This is well illustrated in Sonny Fox's *Jokes and How to Tell Them.* He presents a series of jokes and permits the reader to choose the best punch line. Here is one of them:

Moe: What's today's date?
Joe: I don't know. Why don't you look at the newspaper in your pocket?

Three possible punch lines are (1) That won't help. It's a Chinese newspaper. (2) That's not a newspaper, it's a raisin bread sandwich. (3) That won't do any good, it's yesterday's newspaper. Fox gives punch line 3 as the correct answer because it shows that Moe is incapable of logic. Which did you choose? Why?

For a more expanded awareness of how to rate your own sense of humor, try the following classroom exercise.

Classroom Exercise: The Funniest Joke I Know

Procedure:

Step 1. Members of the class are invited to volunteer to tell the funniest joke they know (in front of the room).

Step 2. After each joke is told, a brief, open discussion should take place concerning whether or not it was funny–and why?

Step 3. After at least 8 to 10 students have told jokes, each member of the class should attempt to construct a sound definition of the word "humorous."

Step 4. Again, 8 to 10 students should be asked to read their definitions to the class and each, followed by a brief discussion.

Humor is a social phenomenon, an interaction among people. It reduces tension and permits people to see one another as they really are, brings them together in a very special way, and establishes the springboard from which a healthy line of communication may begin. Without question, sense of humor is one of the greatest aspects of communication.

Your Motivation

Your physical environment, family, religion, and culture, as well as the economic structure of the society in which you live are all social origins of motives—your motives. Social pressures teach you to expect certain things. The differences between what you expect and what you get result in either positive or negative effects. Ronald Levy captures these extremes in these two statements*:

> I think I have never felt so *completely* worthless, so broken, so apart in my life! Yet this feeling is *mine*! What do I do with it? How do I relate to it? It is here with ne now! [*Negatively* motivated.]

> I think I have never felt so valuable and together in my whole life! And this feeling is *mine*! What will I do with it? How do I keep it? It is here with me *now*! [*Positively motivated.*]

Each of these exclamations communicates a deep-seated feeling, a state of inner being. From it you get some idea of how the person who wrote it will behave. That is what *motivation* is all about—the reasons why people act the way they do. In a rather high-sounding sense, motivation refers to these forces, innate or acquired, internal or environmental, conscious or unconscious, that serve to stimulate, sustain, and direct human behavior. But in a lower key, motivation refers to behavior brought on by needs and directed toward goals. A motive is not something you can see, hear, feel, touch, or smell. It is an abstraction and, as such, can only be inferred from observing a person's behavior. Synonyms for motive include want, wish, need, desire, and drive.

What may seem like a simple matter is for many people terribly unclear: They don't know whether or not they are motivated. Have you ever been called a go-getter, dynamo, fireball, hustler, mover, or hot shot? These labels

*Ronald Levy, *I Can Only Touch You Now* (Englewood Cliffs, N.J.: Prentice-Hall, 1973)

are commonly assigned to those who show a high degree of motivation in a particular direction. Signs of such energetic behavior, frequently detected at an early age, prompt parents, teachers, and relatives to say such things as "My, with drive like that, you ought to become a ______." Whether or not you will be happy doing it seemed to be completely irrelevant to them. Their logic was plain: If you're highly motivated to do something, you'll be happy doing it. Unfortunately, it isn't that straightforward. For example, there are people who have a burning desire to become actors and actresses but who simply lack the talent. It is ironic how many people we meet who either have a definite talent for a particular field and lack the motivation, or who have the drive but not the talent.

There doesn't seem to be any short cut to finding what motivates a person. Many of us play-act at being happy and not motivated by what we are doing when we are really bored. In a recent study, subjects were asked, "What type of work would you try to get into if you could start all over again?" Seventy-six per cent of the blue-collar workers said they would not voluntarily choose the same work they are doing, and 57 per cent of the white-collar workers said they would not make the same choice again.*

> *Take a poll of your immediate circle of friends and see how many are (1) doing what they like, and, (2) would choose the same field again, if given another chance.*

What are some of the motivating factors in your life? Money, status, power, security? Psychologist Abraham Maslow suggests that your basic needs fall into five categories or levels†.

1. *Physiological*: Survival, hunger, thirst, sex.
2. *Safety*: Clothing, shelter, protection from physical harm, security.
3. *Social*: Friendship, belonging, love, affection, acceptance.
4. *Self-esteem*: Respecting oneself and getting respect from others.
5. *Self-actualization*: To become, to grow from within, to fulfill one's potential at an optimal level.

Although it is probably unnecessary to mention, it would probably be helpful to underline the fact that a need seldom exists by itself. Our needs emerge as mixtures, one in concert with another. Consequently, any effort to trace one specific need back to its source will frequently reveal an intimate relationship with other needs. Maslow contends that our needs are arranged in a hierarchy; that is, our most basic needs must be fulfilled before we can concentrate on fulfilling higher needs. Common sense certainly assigns a

**Work in America*, Report of a Special Task Force to the Secretary of Health, Education and Welfare (Cambridge, Mass.: MIT Press, 1972), p. 16.

†Abraham Maslow, *Motivation and Personality* (New York: Harper & Row, 1954).

higher priority to the need to fill an empty belly than to social acceptance by other members of a local ball team or garden club. Nevertheless, it is quite common for a synthesis to take place between physical and psychological needs. Consider a man faced with the need to feed his hungry family. Such a pressing need could easily motivate him to steal. Yet, he might be prevented from doing so because of an even greater need to maintain his self-respect or self-esteem. As a result, different needs may conflict, each bidding for recognition.

Most of the things you feel positive about also motivate you. Perhaps you have had people say to you, "Aw, all you ever think about is ______." It should be taken as an indicator of what makes you tick. With some additional introspection, you will discover other clues to your behavior. In the process, you will also learn that many of the things that motivate you privately will also motivate you in whichever occupation or profession you choose to pursue.

Be especially careful not to fall prey to one particular motivational myth that gives its unsuspecting victims the impression that good things will happen to them through the action of some mysterious force "out there." Masquerading as a lucky break, lady luck, good fortune, my big chance, or my ship coming in, such myths mislead people into placing the entire responsibility for their fate in the hands of something outside themselves. Thus, they leave their future in a precarious state. To an attitude like this, motivational researcher Frederick Herzberg would probably say, "There must be a 'generator' within a person before that person can be motivated, and that such a person will need no outside stimulation."

Management is constantly in search of ways to motivate people. The list of methods tried by management is impressive. Here are but a few: salary incentives, attractive working conditions, job security, fringe benefits (profit sharing, stock options, bonus plans, health benefits), promotions and good working hours, and vacations. Yet, in spite of these efforts, management reports continuing occurrences of low morale, frequent shutdowns, low productivity, excessive errors, absenteeism, inefficiency, and general lack of interest. The continued existence of these problems in business and industry strongly suggests that the question of motivating people still remains open for serious discussion and research Your contribution toward this end is to investigate what motivates you and thus become more sensitive to what might motivate others.

A most interesting anecdote that illustrates how people are motivated differently involves a newscast warning of a tidal wave that would completely cover New York within 24 hours. Absolutely no escape was possible. Various people who were interviewed volunteered how they would spend those remaining hours. A religious man said he would spend them in prayer; a woman with a husband and three children said she would spend them with her family, a bachelor said he would round up several of his friends with a similiar life-style and spend the time drinking and having a ball, a scientist indicated that she would get several of her colleagues together and discuss possible methods of deflecting the giant mountain of water. The answer given by a 10-year-old boy differed from them all. He said, "I am going to try and figure out how to live underwater." Along a similiar line, here is an exercise designed to reveal the direction you would take in a variety of situations.

Name of Exercise: If It Were Me, I Would . . . .

Procedure:

Step 1. Members of the class should be arranged in pairs.

Step 2. After reading the following situations, each student should enter a response in the appropriate spaces. When finished, papers should be exchanged, and a general discussion should take place concerning the possible motives behind each answer.

Situations:

1. John saw an ad in the newspaper advertising a particular typewriter he had been looking for at a very low sales price. Later that day, the store manager said they were all sold out! If it were me, I would ______________________

   ____

   ____

   ____

2. John had a very successful conversation with a potential employer on the telephone. She suggested that he come down for a personal interview and gave her address as Room 511 on the 42nd floor of the Empire State Building. On arriving, John found a sign reading: Elevators Out of Order.

   If it were me, I would ___________________________

   ____

   ____

   ____

3. Frank had just been discharged from the Army and, on his way back to his home town, he was robbed and left in a strange city without a penny in his pocket. If it were me,

I would ______________________________

____

____

____

4. Donald was taking his first course in statistics. Afraid that he might not pass, he made sure to study hard and see that all his assignments were in on time. On receiving his final grade, he almost collapsed when he read the word Incomplete. Being absolutely positive that he had handed in all his assignments, he spoke to his professor. He was told that his last paper was never received and that the Incomplete had to stand. If it were me, I would ____________

____

____

____

5. Joey had a pain in his chest for two weeks and, after some prodding from his family, went to the doctor. He was given some medication and sent home. A week passed and he felt no better. He went to another doctor, was given another prescription and, again, sent home. Another week went by and he still felt the pain in his chest. If it were me, I would ______________________________

____

____

____

6. Helene and Larry were invited to the home of a well-known artist whom they both greatly admired. He was now old, in poor health, and living on his social security checks. During the meal, Larry noticed that the soup he had been served had a fly in it. If it were me, I would ____________

____

____

____

SELF-EXAMINATION QUIZ

Having read this chapter, my answers to the following questions reflect my understanding of its contents.

1. Why is it important to make a distinction between people and things?

2. How can becoming aware of your assets and liabilities help you achieve personal growth and make a decision on your career?

3. In what way does having a prepared mind increase your chances of success?

4. How can a self-inventory influence your life in the right direction?

5. Why is a person's self-esteem so important?

6. What are the differences in a single-valued, two-valued, and multi-valued approach to living?

7. What is the basis for your thoughts and feelings?

8. Why is a sense of humor so important to effective communication in business?

9. How do motives shape a person's behavior?

10. How can altering items in your self-inventory influence your future?

Suggested Readings

Boulding, Kenneth, *The Image* (Ann Arbor: University of Michigan Press, 1956).

Burke, H. L., and Bennis, W. G. "Changes in perception of self and others during human relations training, "*Human Relations,* 14, 165–182 (1962).

Eisenberg, Abné M., *Living Communication* (Englewood Cliffs, N.J. Prentice-Hall, 1975) Chapter 2: Dimensions of the Self.

Frank, Joseph, *You* (New York: Harcourt Brace Jovanovich, 1972).

Gergen, Kenneth J., *The Concept of Self* (New York: Holt, Rinehart, and Winston, 1971).

Jourard, S. M., *Disclosing Man to Himself* (New York: Van Nostrand-Reinhold, 1968).

May, Rollo, *Man's Search for Himself* (New York: Norton, 1953).

Moustakas, C., ed. *The Self* (New York: Harper & Row, 1956).

Ostrovsky, Everett, *Self Discovery and Social Awareness* (New York: Wiley, 1974), pp. 267–274, 281.

Travaglio, R. F., "Response differences among employment applicants," *Personnel,* 49, 593–597 (1970).

WORK AREA FOR CHAPTER 1

Chapter 2

Interpersonal Self-Inventory

The more you make me like me, the more I will tend to like you.

MEMO

TO: Reader

FROM: Author

After reading this chapter, you should have a better understanding of:

1. Why actions speak louder than words.
2. How we have been conditioned to picture various people in the business and professional world differently.
3. What stereotyping practices exist among employers.
4. How eye contact can turn people off and on.
5. How to distinguish purposeful and purposeless gestures.
6. How your "smile" affects others.
7. How your handshake may be a clue to your mental and physical condition.
8. What role "touching" or "not touching" plays in your life.
9. How people stand in relation to one another.
10. What it means to be a "lark" or an "owl" in relation to the use and abuse of time.
11. What it means to have a high P.O.R. (personal odor risk).
12. How the way you dress advertises who or what you are.
13. What your own speaking style says about you.
14. How your vocabulary affects your ability to communicate.
15. How your pronunciation affects others.
16. What your vocal qualities are.

Chapter 2

The Silent Self

How much do you reveal about yourself without saying a word? Does your posture, manner of gesturing, stance in relation to others, or manner of dress advertise information about your silent self? These things probably say more about you than you think. Although you can, to a large extent, deceive people with words, it is surprisingly difficult to do so with nonverbal behavior. People who have a great deal of experience dealing with the public corroborate that the way a person behaves is often a much more reliable barometer of the inner self than what a person says. Exceptions to this generalization would probably be competent actors, actresses, and con artists. A persuasive illustration of how difficult it is to convince people not to believe what they see happens whenever you aren't feeling well: A friend stops you on the street and asks you how you are feeling. Not wanting to get into a discussion about what hurts you, you answer, "Fine. I feel great." Most people quickly see through your attempt to deceive, because there are certain visible signs that belie your words. The reverse is also true. If you say you feel terrible but look great, most people will be more apt to believe the way you look, rather than what you say.

The psychologist Albert Mehrabian conducted an interesting study along these lines. He wanted to find out about the various degrees of impact of communication. His study revealed that 7 per cent of the impact resulted from *what was said,* 38 per cent from *how it was said,* and 55 per cent from *how a person looked while saying it.** Bear in mind that Mehrabian's research did not apply to scientific discussions or similar kinds of technical exchanges of information. It was restricted to the more informal type of human communication. How accurate would you say his figures are? In most of your own private conversations, does the way you look when you say things generally have a greater impact on others than what you say or how you say it?

Originally, nonverbal communication, popularly called "body language," focused almost exclusively on body movements, gestures, and facial expressions. Today, because of increased public interest, researchers in the field of nonverbal communication have extended the subject to include a wider variety of human activity. Although this new discipline is far from having the status our society confers upon mathematics, physics, or biology, kinesics has attracted sufficient attention for you to give it some serious consideration.

Take a moment to think of yourself as a film star of the old silent movies. What might audiences seeing you on the screen learn about you solely on the basis of your actions? Let's turn this into an exercise in which you try to describe yourself without the use of words. Concentrate on such things as how you walk, sit, stand, eat, sleep, drive a car or bicycle, dance, shake hands, kiss, smile, or carry your books. Add to those expressions of body

*Albert Mehrabian "Communication Without Words," *Psychology Today* (September, 1968), 53.

language any others you think you possess. When you have finished, show your list to a close friend or member of your family. Ask them to agree or disagree with your impressions of your silent self. It is amazing how many of us are completely unaware of some of the things we do. Have you ever had someone imitate the way you walk? "You're kidding. I don't really walk like that, do I." Or perhaps you've been accused of having a certain look on your face, to which you answered, "What look?" The point is that, in addition to your being in command of your verbal language, it is equally important—if not more important—for you to be in command of your body language as well. In the spaces provided below, add a description of your silent self to your personal inventory.

Your Nonverbal Profile

____

____

____

____

____

____

____

____

____

____

The controversy between words and actions is a long-standing one. People seem to arrange themselves in two camps—those who feel that what you say is less important than what you do (actions speak louder than words), and those who feel that what you do is less important than what you say. Although those who know anything about human nature will agree that these are both extreme positions, they would be inclined to caution us that most people fall somewhere in between, and that most word/action choices are strongly influenced by the specific circumstances at the time. In either case, however, if you are willing to take the time and effort to examine what people say or do, you will usually find that it leads back to that "inner self" they are trying so hard to conceal from view. If, by some chance, that someone happens to be you, here are some areas of your silent self you might consider worthwhile looking into.

Perception

Have you ever tried to guess someone's occupation or profession by how he or she looked? It is interesting to speculate whether certain people go into a particular occupation or profession because they look like they belong in it, or whether they begin to look a certain way once they are in it. Obviously, we have been conditioned to picture various people in a given way because of how they have been portrayed in television and movies. The typical truck driver is big and well muscled. The physician wears a suit and tie and glasses and has graying hair at the temples. The librarian, simply dressed with hair pulled back in a bun is invariably bespectacled. And, of course, the opera singer, fat, with very good posture, is conservatively dressed. Each of us seems to have a mental picture of how we think various people in different businesses and professions should look. And, when we meet someone who drifts too far from this image, we are prompted to say, "Funny, you don't look like a ______ ."

Subscribing to a stereotyped image of how people in various fields should look has some very definite drawbacks. One of the most striking drawbacks is that someone planning to enter a particular field is discouraged from going into it because people hooked on the stereotype say, "You say you are going to be a college professor. Funny, you don't look like a college professor." The truth of the matter is that fewer people conform to the traditional stereotyped image than you think. Whereas it has served the purpose of directors and producers in film, theater, and television to maintain a bigger-than-life image of certain characters in the public mind, it has also served to mislead.

In recent years, business and professional stereotypes have undergone some rather noticeable changes. A dramatic example of such a change was seen in the film some years ago entitled, "Guess Who's Coming to Dinner?" In it, the daughter of Spencer Tracy and Katherine Hepburn brought her new boyfriend home to dinner. Her parents were not only shocked by the fact that he was black, but were completely bowled over when they learned that he had a doctorate in physics. As you know, for at least the first quarter of a century of film-making, black men were usually cast either as servants or entertainers. The general public had been conditioned to accept them only in these limited roles. Well, you can imagine how surprised white audiences were across the country upon seeing a black man cast in the role of a physicist. Soon, the mold was broken and black men and women began to be accepted in a wider variety of roles. But what about orientals? They, too, were victimized by certain stereotyping practices. Chinese and Japanese people were also locked into roles either as servants or owners of restaurants and laundries. The American Indian, too, incurred the wrath of stereotyping. With few exceptions, they were characterized as savages, enemies of the white man, and not to be trusted. The list of stereotyping on the basis of ethnic differences is by no means short. Any given week of television fare will provide you with countless examples of ethnic stereotyping in pre-1950 films.

Little by little, from that time forward, you will be able to see the ethnic stereotype undergo changes for the better. Although still a long way from being completely fair, the ethnic image seems to be moving in the right direction.

As though stereotyping on ethnic grounds were not enough, people have also been classified on the basis of their body type. Confidentially, would you describe yourself as fat, muscular, or skinny? If the words fat and skinny are too harsh for you, try chubby and wiry, slender and plump. But regardless of which labels you find most comfortable, the hard fact remains that others respond to what they see rather than what you think they see. Of course, this should not be taken to mean that how you see yourself is unimportant. It is only that out there where you make your living, how others perceive you often takes precedence over how you see yourself.

Have you noticed that, among a great many employers, there is a tendency to single out a particular personality trait or psychological characteristic they appear to be preoccupied with? Experience has shown that employers concentrate on such things as cleanliness, politeness, proper dress, promptness, respect, thoroughness. To this list we add the quality of physical appearance. Aren't there certain restaurant chains whose waitresses are all of the same general physical type? Obviously, someone in personnel has set a standard for applicants and their body types. In certain companies you will see no fat people. Why? Probably for the same reason. Airline hostesses are perfect examples of selection on the basis of body type, along with the other requirements set forth by company policy. Fortunately, employment based on body types represents only a small segment of the marketplace. In the majority of instances, hiring practices are usually geared toward competency and potential.

No claim is being made here to persuade you that unless you look a certain way or possess a specific body type you will not be able to get into a given business or profession. Suffice it to say that being aware of such discrimination practices may, in some instances, prove helpful. Stereotyping in the business and professional community is much less frequent than you might imagine. Make it a point to observe the following people you encounter for an entire week; (1) college professors, (2) librarians, (3) salespeople, (4) policeofficers, (5) barbers and beauticians, and (6) bus drivers. Carefully notice the silent self of each one and see whether you can detect any nonverbal traits they have in common. All things being equal, you should discover that in each of these fields, there are far more differences than you had imagined. Furthermore, whatever similarities you did observe may have been conditioned by the society in which you were born and reared. In short, the expression, "Funny, you don't look like a ______." should be responded to with a great deal of caution. Susceptible people tend to place barriers in their paths rather than bridges.

Eye Contact

Throughout history, few parts of the human anatomy have received more attention than our eyes. Consider the number of different messages the eyes can communicate. There are mean, jealous, suspicious, angry, seductive, dishonest, sleepy, dirty, wise-guy, evil, contented, hypnotic, intelligent, dull, apathetic, and shifty looks. More than any single form of human interaction, the eyes seem to be able to establish the most immediate basis for a relationship. Whether it be a party, board meeting, interview, or convention, the first thing people do is "eye each other." Instantly, surpassing the speed of our most modern computers, the mind seems to set the psychological stage for any relationship solely on the look in a person's eyes. Allowing for the occasional error in judgment, the eyes appear to be an extremely reliable source of information about the persons behind them—so much so, that in certain primitive societies the "guilty look" in a man's eyes might be enough to condemn him.

Eye contact has attracted a great deal of attention in the field of human communication. For example, Argyle and Dean found that when two people like each other, they establish eye contact more often, and for a longer duration, than when there is tension in their relationship.* What salesperson could not make good use of a bit of information like this? What applicant for a position could not benefit from it during an interview?

Here are a few other findings that have come out of eye contact research. Think of a situation in which each example could be applied in a business or professional situation:

1 People of a higher status, communicating with persons of lower status, tend to maintain greater eye contact.

____

____

____

2. Speakers rate someone who looks at them as being more instrumental to their goals and tend to value them more than they do someone who looks at them less.

____

____

____

3. Speakers feel more powerful when they receive more eye contact from people they are addressing.

____

____

____

4. People tend to use more eye contact with people from whom they seek recognition or approval.

____

____

____

*Michael Argyle and Janet Dean, "Eye contact, distance, and affiliation," *Sociometry,* 28, 289–304, (1965).

5. The less eye contact there is between two people, the closer they can come to one another; the closer they come to one another, the less eye contact there will tend to be.

____

____

____

6. Women seem to look at each other significantly more than men do when they talk with one another.

____

____

____

7. In a group situation, those who spend the most time looking at their fellow discussants (looking and listening while the person is speaking) see themselves as having more influence than those who spend less time looking at the speakers.

____

____

____

How would you rate your own eye contact? Do you look at people when you talk to them? Granting that it will often depend on the person you are speaking with and the way you feel at the time, there does seem to be a tendency for most people either to maintain or not maintain eye contact in the majority of their interpersonal transactions. Prying even further, how do you feel having a conversation with someone whose eye contact is poor? Do you get the feeling that he isn't really listening to you, has something else on his mind, has little respect for you, or has some kind of psychological hang-up about face-to-face communication with others? To understand your own eye contact better, answer the following questions. Do you establish eye contact when:

1. Talking to one of your professors:

   Good ___ Fair ___ Poor ___ Bad ___

2. Talking with a steady boyfriend or girlfriend:

   Good ___ Fair ___ Poor ___ Bad ___

3. Ordering a meal from a waiter in a restaurant:

   Good ___ Fair ___ Poor ___ Bad ___

4. Talking with someone of whom you are afraid:

   Good ___ Fair ___ Poor ___ Bad ___

5. Speaking with someone whom you outrank in an organization:

   Good ___ Fiar ___ Poor ___ Bad ___

The importance of eye contact cannot be stressed enough. If, your responses to these questions tell you that your eye contact is not as good as you would like it to be, it would be an excellent idea for you to give it some special attention. Not only will it make a noticeable improvement in the general quality of your communication with others, it will make people listen to you more attentively and tend to lend more credibility to what you have to say. Those who have superior eye contact usually have the conversational advantage. Jean-Paul Sartre has suggested that when it comes to eye contact, to look at another encroaches upon a person's autonomy, and when two glances meet, a wordless struggle ensues until one or the other succeeds in establishing dominance. Eyeball encounters like this make up a substantial part of practically all human communication and, therefore, should not be overlooked.

Gesture

Thus far, we have been talking about nonverbal communication in its broad sense. We shall now take a closer look at gesturing. Any gesture you make could be classified either as *purposeful* or *purposeless.* Pretend you are being interviewed for a position and that while the interviewer is talking, you unconsciously pick at your fingernails or the arm of the chair. These gestures would be purposeless, since they detract from, rather than contribute to, your chances of getting the position. On the other hand, if you were to smile and nod appropriately when the interviewer seemed to be making an important point, such gestures could be taken to be purposeful From the other side of the desk, an interviewer who shuffles papers frequently, looks out the window, or drums a pencil on the desk during your interview is displaying purposeless gestures. On the more positive side, an occasional approving smile or the enthusiastic shaking of your hand at the close of the interview would be considered purposeful. Whether a particular gesture is purposeless or purposeful is always open to argument. There are some people who delight in reading all kinds of meaning into the raising of an eyebrow or the straightening of a tie. The objective of this section is to do little more than make you aware of the gestural side of your silent self. As a spot check, go down the following list and respond as honestly as you can as to whether you:

1. Fool with your keys.	Yes _____	No _____
2. Play with the change in your pockets.	Yes _____	No _____
3. Repeatedly touch your hair.	Yes _____	No _____
4. Tear paper into tiny pieces.	Yes _____	No _____
5. Continuously move your foot or knee while sitting.	Yes _____	No _____
6. Bite your nails or cuticles.	Yes _____	No _____
7. Crack your knuckles.	Yes _____	No _____
8. Suck air through your teeth.	Yes _____	No _____
9. Repeatedly adjust an article of clothing you are wearing.	Yes _____	No _____
10. Frequently check your wristwatch to see what time it is.	Yes _____	No _____
11. Peel off fingernail polish.	Yes _____	No _____
12. Chain smoke.	Yes _____	No _____
13. Put such things as pencils, pens, paper clips, into your mouth.	Yes _____	No _____
14. Rub or scratch various parts of your body (nose, arm, thigh, buttocks, neck, eyes, scalp)	Yes _____	No _____
15. Crack or pop chewing bum.	Yes _____	No _____

Where and how often you perform these essentially purposeless gestures appears somewhat less important than the fact that you *do* perform them. The reason for this is that only after you become conscious of the fact that you do them can you begin to rehabilitate these negative aspects of your silent self. Wouldn't it be sad if, in five years from now, you were an executive in a big corporation and, behind your back, people said, "What a bright, talented person. The only thing I can't stand is the way s(he) repeatedly looks at his/her watch and taps his/her pencil during a meeting."

List some of the purposeless gestures you have observed in public, at school, or on the job.

Smile

One of your most valuable gestures in the business and professional world will be your smile. Conservatively speaking, millions of dollars could probably be traced back to someone who smiled at the right place, at the right time, and to the right person. A smile on a physician's face can even speed a patient's recovery, and the lack of one can inhibit it. It has been found, that people, for example, do not smile the same way in all parts of the United States. This may be due to variations in the muscle contractions people display around their mouths. Whatever the reasons for these differences, reading a smile is not always as simple as it appears.

Work in the field of body language suggests that fundamental expressions are the same in all cultures. If someone is happy or wants you to think he is happy, he'll show you a smile. But, in terms of that basic response, there are variants. Whereas most smiles are fairly reliable indicators of a person's mood or temperament, there are exceptions. Most frustrating among these is the smile on the face of a police officer issuing you a speeding ticket, a judge conferring sentence, a teacher telling you that you will have to repeat a course, and an employer informing you that your services will no longer be required. Some justification for such frustration may derive from the belief that a smile in one society may portray friendlieness, in another embarrassment, and, in still another, warn that hostility and attack are imminent.

Whereas Southerners seem to think they're friendlier because they smile, New Englanders think they're more reserved because they don't. As you were cautioned earlier, it would be unwise to accept either of these impressions as final. It is important for you to realize that although a smile has the ability to play an extremely important role in communication, it can be very misleading. Take the case of people who smile and don't know that they are smiling. If you ask, "What are you smiling at? They will answer, "Who's smiling?" Then there are people who, because of an unusual development of the muscles around their mouths, think they're smiling when actually, they're not. Counterfeit smiles sometimes masquerade as leers, smirks, and sneers. Because smiling is such an important tool of communication, it would behoove you to take stock of your own smiling habits.

> *Keep a 24-hour Smiling Log. At selected times of the day, make it a point to smile a great deal. Naturally, avoid smiling for no reason at all. Smile when you meet people on the street, at school, on the job, at home. Jot down in your log other peoples' reactions to your smiles along with your own reactions. Compare your findings with those of your classmates.*

Handshake

The handshake qualifies as an important gesture. We shake each other's hands in this country on arrivals and departures, at social functions, to seal a deal, and as an expression of congratulations. How would you describe your own handshake? Most people haven't given it much thought. Basically, aside from classifying handshakes as strong, medium, and weak, they can also be grouped according to whether they are self-determined or other-determined. Self-determined handshakes include those which are significantly influenced by a person's physical and mental health. Someone whose vital energies are down or who is suffering from an inferiority complex will reflect this state in his or her handshake. Then, again, when someone is really feeling great and clearly shows signs of superiority complex, the handshake will reflect it. In many ways, our handshake gives others a clue to who and what we are.

Other-determined handshakes are influenced by the person whose hand we are shaking. For example, dashing young men have been known to shake the hand of a beautiful young lady differently from the way they shake the hand of another dashing young man.

The most interesting aspect of handshaking is the style. You probably encountered all styles of handshakes. There are the Pumpers who, once they have your hand in theirs, begin to move your arm up and down as if they were pumping water or churning butter. Then there are the Crushers, who look you straight in the eye and summarily try to break every bone in your hand. Another handshaking style is the Massager, who holds your hand and gently gives it either a medical or romantic massage, depending on your age and sex. The Trapper, having taken your hand, immediately takes it prisoner by placing another hand on top of it so that it cannot escape. Least appealing are the Limpies whose hand remains motionless in yours, like a dead fish, until you release it. Finally, a most distinctive handshake is delivered by the Shocker who, without warning, gives your hand and arm one violent shake that goes up into the base of your brain like a bolt of lightening and leaves you temporarily paralyzed. Needless to say, each of these handshake styles leaves a rather definite impression of the shaker.

Fortunately for us, however, most people we meet do not display these extremes and offer instead a mild and reasonable mixture we label normal handshake.

> *As a personal nonverbal experiment in handshaking, spend tomorrow using different forms of handshakes on the people you meet and note their reactions along with your own. Again, compare your impressions with those of your classmates.*

Touch

A final consideration under the heading of gesturing involves the act of touching. Let us begin by singling out people who cannot communicate unless they touch the person they are talking to. Facetiously, they might be referred to as *touchophiliacs.* Their tactile tactics include finger-poking, back-patting, arm-grabbing, and thigh-smacking (while seated) Curiously, many of these touching habits have been so deeply integrated into the life-style of the touchophiliac that it is flatly denied when called to his attention.

In contrast to the touchophiliac is the *untouchable*, characterized by a pronounced aversion to being touched while communicating with others. Picture a scene in which fate happens to bring together a touchophiliac and an untouchable. The outcome is not too difficult to predict. Does your silent self lean in either of these directions? The reason it is so important for you to be "in touch" with whether your gesturing habits include or exclude certain tactile tendencies is because they will seldom be brought to your attention by others.

Perhaps out of a sense of politeness or courtesy, most people would rather avoid than expose the touchophiliac or untouchable. What would you do if you went to a dinner party and were seated next to a touchophiliac who, for the entire evening, punctuated practically every remark with some form of physical contact? Would you say to the person, "Would you mind not talking with your hands?" or, "Would you please keep your hands to yourself?" The alternative open to you if you preferred not to say anything is to ask the host or hostess not to seat you next to that person in the future. What would you do if, at the same dinner party, you chanced to sit beside an untouchable whose reaction bordered on the hysterical whenever you happened, even momentarily, to make the slightest physical contact? In all likelihood, your response would not be significantly different, that is, it would take the form of avoidance rather than exposure.

> *List as many businesses or professions in which touching while talking would be considered an acceptable practice. Then name those in which it would be considered unacceptable. For each, give the reasons you feel this way.*

Posture and Place

"Every individual has a characteristic basic posture to which he returns whenever he has deviated from it."* Although such things as how you feel mentally and physically, where you are at the time, and the people you are with may all influence how you stand, there is a basic "postural you" that

*F. Deutsch, "Analysis of posture behavior." *Psychoanalytic Quarterly,* 16, 195–213 (1947).

your friends and family can usually recognize on sight. Do you have a clear picture in your mind of your posture? What do you think it tells others? Does it convey self-confidence, arrogance, egotism, humility, shyness, courage, hostility inferiority, or friendliness? On the basis of a series of experiments in which he photographed a variously arranged human mannequin, William James concluded that, "postures do give clues to attitude, and that placement of the trunk and head contribute most to interpretations of postures."*

Although you may not think it important now, your basic posture could one day become a significant factor in whatever field you ultimately enter. To illustrate this possibility, imagine yourself in 5 or 7 years as a trial lawyer arguing an important case before a jury. Without ever having given it any thought, your basic posture happens to exhibit a considerable amount of flexion—head bent forward, arms generally folded across chest, and with feet closely approximated. It is generally agreed upon by several researchers that the closed posture generates a negative attitude, whereas the open posture depicts a more positive attitude. Quite possibly, your posture could work against your best interests. Obviously, your postural disposition goes well beyond the courtroom. The way a prize fighter carries himself down the aisle to the ring influences the crowd, just as the way an executive walks through the halls of an organization often has an impact on other employees, and the posture of a ball player stepping up to bat with the bases loaded seldom fails to have a psychological effect on the pitcher and the crowd (for example, Willie Stargel's powerful gestures). In short, it seems that posture communicates much more about a person than most people realize.

In addition to how you stand, it is also important for you to become aware of how you stand in relation to others. According to Professor Jeffrey Fisher and Don Byrne, "getting on someone's 'good side' " is more than a figure of speech. In two different studies, researchers found that women feel more comfortable when approached face to face by strangers. Men prefer strangers to approach them from the side. With friends, however, women like them to come from the side, and men prefer a frontal approach. When the researchers were asked to explain these preferences in angles of approach, they suggested it might have something to do with the fact that competitive situations generally show people in face-to-face relationships, whereas cooperative ones show them side by side.†

If you would care to do some experimenting of your own, approach a few strangers and friends from both a side and front angle. Notice whether the way you approach them makes any difference in their reaction. If they do not display any

*William James, "A study of the expression of bodily posture," *Journal of General Psychology*, 7, 405–436 (1932)

†Jeffrey D. Fisher and Donn Byrne, "Re: Apt angles of approach," *Long Island Press*, Feb. 16, 1976, p. 11.

noticeable difference, ask them directly, "Did the way I approached you make any difference in how you felt?"

An experiment such as this one might be especially interesting if you happen to have a job in which you meet the general public. Approaching men and women from different angles and noting their reactions could represent a ready-made source of valuable information.

Each of us is surrounded by an invisible bubble of space—a personal bubble. Not only does it vary in size from person to person, but also from situation to situation. Have you ever noticed that when a stranger walks up to you and gets too close, you begin to feel uncomfortable and draw back? Your personal space was invaded without your permission. It seems as though the word "unapproachable" has physical as well as psychological meaning. By the way, do you know how big your personal bubble is? It is very simple to find out. Here's what you do.

In class, have 6 to 8 students line up on one side of the room standing approximately 18 inches apart. On the opposite side of the room, have the same number of students do likewise. There should be a distance of 12 feet between the two groups. At a signal from the teacher, all the members of one group should begin to slowly inch forward toward a corresponding member of the opposite group. When a member of the advancing group reaches a point where the stationary member begins to feel uncomfortable, that person should call out the word,

STOP! By measuring the nose-to-nose distance between them, the stationary person's bubble size can be determined. The procedure should then be reversed in favor of the other side.

An anthropologist named Edward Hall has studied the distances people stand from one another. Calling it informal space, he has proposed the following breakdown:*

1. *Intimate zone*: A distance from contact to 18 inches in which secrets whispering, touching, love-making, wrestling, or comforting occur.
2. *Personal zone*: A distance of 1½ feet to 4 feet at which normal personal interaction occurs.
3. *Social zone*: A distance of 4 to 12 feet that most people maintain during a social gathering or business transactions.
4. *Public zone*: A distance from 12 feet to the outer limits of normal hearing, as experienced by the public speaker in relation to an audience.

Operating on the assumption that most people are not excessively outgoing, flamboyant, or demonstrative, invading one's personal bubble could be a rather threatening experience. Consequently, becoming sensitive to how others feel about the personal space they inhabit is an excellent form of communicative insurance. Begin by becoming sensitive to your own personal space.

Time

Everything you do involves time. How you handle it or how it handles you communicates a great deal. For example, are you a "lark" or an "owl?" Putting it another way, are you a day person or a night person? Day people go to sleep at a reasonable hour and get up early; night people do just the opposite. Have you ever had a job that required you to be at work at a very early hour? How did you like it? Were you able to rise and shine, feel bright-eyed and bushy tailed, and dash off to work whistling a merry tune? Or was getting your eyes to open a major operation, getting yourself dressed even more difficult, and setting out for work an almost impossible task? If you identify with the former, you are probably a lark; if you identify with the latter, you are probably an owl. The way a person structures time is at its worst when an owl employee chances to work for an lark employer (although the advent of flexitime work schedules in the future should obviate this problem).

What about your reputation for arriving at meetings, classes, social functions, and various modes of transportation (buses, trains, and planes)? Are

*Edward T. Hall, *The Silent Language* (Garden City, N.Y.: Doubleday, 1959).

you generally early, late, or on time? Do you finish eating before everyone else, or do they have to wait for you to finish? Are you inclined to be a patient or impatient person? Answer these questions honestly and then ask six people who know you rather well whether they agree or disagree with your self-evaluation. It may help steer you toward or away from a business or profession in which a particular time orientation is necessary.

> *List as many businesses or professions in which special attitudes and management of time are necessary. For example, teaching handicapped children demands a great deal of patience; or, the ability to cope with jet lag to which international airline personnel are constantly exposed. Discuss your list with other classmates.*

Smell

Two days before he was scheduled to arrive home, Napoleon is rumored to have sent his mistress a note reading, "Don't wash. I'm on my way home." Maybe it's true, maybe not. But it raises a question, perhaps an embarrassing one to some: How much do you smell?

"Man survived because nature endowed him with an unpleasant taste and unpleasant smell." This is the opinion of Dr. Louis Leaky, the famous anthropologist who discovered the earliest bones of *Homo sapiens* estimated to be 400 million years old in Africa. Leaky further suggests that because human flesh is not palatable and smells unpleasant, cannibals only partake of it as part of a ritual. What greater insurance of survival is there than tasting and smelling bad?

How concerned are you with how you smell? Do you bathe every day, every other day, once a week, or are you too embarrassed to say? Would it surprise you to learn that Queen Isabella of Castile bragged that she only had two baths in her life? That when Queen Victoria ascended to the throne there wasn't a single bathtub in Buckingham Palace? Except for brief periods in history, the use of soap or even water for washing was considered unnecessary or undesirable. Because the Puritans of early America regarded bathing as injurious both to health and morals, they went around unwashed and unperfumed. Laws banning bathing entirely, or limiting the number of baths a person was permitted each year, were passed in such states as Virginia, Pennsylvania, and Ohio.

Dr. Mary T. Hunsicker, a dermatologist, calls this business of "smelling clean" a twentieth century phenonomenon. In fact, big business thinks enough about how you smell that it spends well over a billion dollars a year reminding you of it.* Why? Because it feels confident that your best friends won't tell you. How many friends have you informed lately that they offend —yes, smell bad? Probably very few. Your hope is that someone else will do

*Phyllis Battelle, "Took time, but mankind came clean," *Long Island Press,* Dec. 11, 1974, p. 15.

it for you. Unfortunately, because so many others also shirk this unpleasant duty, those with bad breath, body odor, or malordorous feet may go on for years without being told that they offend. This is particularly sad when it happens to a dentist who has recently opened a new office. Would you go back to a dentist who had bad breath? For some strange reason, the offending party is often the last to find out about it.

As luck would have it, the majority of offending odors that emanate from people are correctable. To find out about them and, in the process, your own odor risk, take the following quiz.

Personal Odor Risk (P.O.R.)

Instructions: Place a circle around the number you feel most appropriately represents the extent to which the following items apply to you.

Cigarette smoking	+1	+2	+3	+4	+5
Cigar smoking	+1	+2	+3	+4	+5
Garlic eating	+1	+2	+3	+4	+5
Use of deodorants	+1	+2	+3	+4	+5
Use of colognes or perfumes	+1	+2	+3	+4	+5
Taking baths or showers	+1	+2	+3	+4	+5
Wearing freshly laundred clothes	+1	+2	+3	+4	+5
Drinking alcoholic beverages	+1	+2	+3	+4	+5

To arrive at your P.O.R. score, add up the numbers you have circled. If the sum falls between 0 and 10, your P.O.R. is low; if it falls between 20 and 29, your P.O.R. is moderate; if it falls between 30 and 40, your P.O.R. is high.

Clothes

If your clothes could talk, what do you think they would say about you? One researcher interested in the relationship between clothes and personality discovered that among those tested, people who scored high on "decoration in dress" were conscientious, conventional, stereotyped, conforming, nonintellectual, sympathetic, sociable, and submissive. Those who scored high on "Economy in dress" were responsible, conscientious, alert, efficient, precise, and controlled.*

Have you ever tried to guess a person's occupation or profession by their manner of dress? There is a story about a senator who was traveling around his home state trying to drum up some votes to ensure his reelection. Having found in a prior election year that dressing comfortably in khaki pants, a short-sleeved shirt and hiking boots caused his constituents to talk to him

*L. Aiken, "Relationships of dress to selected measures of personality in undergraduate women," *Journal of Social Psychology*, **59**, 119–128 (1963).

more freely, he decided to dress the same way again. Accompanied by his campaign chairman, a tall, personable, smartly dressed young man in a smart suit and tie, the senator happened to visit the office of a lawyer friend. In his absence, they chatted with the lawyer's staff. On his return, the lawyer asked his secretary what she thought of the senator. "Oh, he's very nice, very handsome, and I'll certainly vote for him," she said. "But who was the guy in the boots and khakis?" *

A revolution seems to be going on concerning dress between people over and under the age of 30. Are you involved in it? What determines the way you dress these days? Is it based on the way you feel, where you are going, with whom you are going, the people you want to impress, the extent of your wardrobe, the weather outside, or don't you care one way or the other? The bottom line is: Do you dress for yourself or for others? If you dress for for yourself exclusively, you might run into some difficulty when you go out into the job market. This will be particularly true if your preferences in clothes are dramatically at odds with what is commonly referred to as the "conventional look."

Drs. Jane Anton and Michael Russell conducted a study that appears to support this view. They sampled more than 100 personnel recruiters from 17 different industry groups, recruiters who hired more than 75 per cent of college graduates for their firms since 1972. Among the many other things they discovered, they found that: (1) it is best for a job applicant to dress neatly, (2) a young man may create a mildly positive impression if he wears a sport coat, shirt, tie, and slacks, but makes a stronger impression if he wears a suit, and (3) the wearing of jeans, shorts, sandals, or lack of bras in the case of women applicants, creates the impression from "mildly" to "strong negative."†

A moment ago you were asked what your clothes would say about you if they could talk. Because they cannot talk, let's go to the next best thing and find out what some of your classmates think your clothes say about you.

Classroom Exercise: Your Clothes Tell Me . . . .

Procedure:

Step 1. Prepared with a blank sheet of paper and pen, pair off with one of your classmates.

Step 2. Proceed to list your impressions of your partner, based on howhe or she is dressed.

Step 3. Exchange papers and discuss the basis for the impressions each of you have compiled.

Step 5. Repeat this process with another classmate.

*"Humor on the campaign trail." *Readers Digest*, Aug. 1976, pp. 35–36.

+Pamela Swift, "Keeping up . . . with youth," *Parade*, Nov. 9, 1975, p. 14.

An excellent topic for classroom discussion for airing different views on the role of clothing in society is Uniforms in Institutional and Organizational Life. Pros and cons should be raised concerning the wearing of uniforms in the armed forces, prisons, orphanages, parochial schools, hospitals.

Any discussion about clothes should include color. Look at what you are wearing right now. Do your clothes say anything about your mood or personality? Historically, colors have been associated with various character traits and values. For example, red is often coupled with passion, courage, cruelty, justice, and health. Because green is the color of nature, it has been considered the easiest color to live with. Blue, the color of the sky and seas, has been said to have a calming effect. The reasons behind our responses to colors are still, for the most part, unknown. However, in spite of any scientifically convincing evidence, our language seems to abound with color-linked references: green with envy, scarlet woman, red-hot news, once in a blue moon, yell blue murder, yellow belly, blue-blood, rose-colored glasses, black is beautiful.

Color is the most pervasive factor in the world. You see form here and there but everything has color. An illustration of its relevance to increasing the incidence of air travel can be seen among airline passengers who fear flying more than they admit. They find green too cold and blue too much like a continuation of the sky outside. Earth colors, especially browns, are more reassuring and airlines would be wise to concentrate on them in plane decor.

Conduct a personal survey and find out what colors you favor most. Try keeping a Color Log for 2 weeks in which you note what you wear each day and the mood associated with it. After doing this, try wearing colors contrary to how you feel and see whether they affect your mood.

The Speaking Self

Earlier, you were asked whether the way you looked provided others with cues to your personality. Here the same question is asked with regard to the way you speak. Is there anything distinctive about your speech? Do people know it is you the moment you utter two or three words on the telephone? Do you speak the same way to children, police officers, clergymen, and people holding very high positions? Do you have a clear picture of how you sound in your own head? A great many people, upon hearing themselves played back on a tape recorder say, "Is that me? Is that really me? I can't believe the way I sound."

Style

Putting aside for a moment the way *you* think you sound, how do you think you sound to others? It is extremely difficult, if not impossible, to separate you from your style of speaking; i.e., your style is *you*. According to Paul Valéry, "Style signifies the manner in which a man expresses himself, regardless of what he expresses, and is held to reveal his nature, quite apart from his actual thought—for thought has no style."*

The style you assume when you speak often affects not only the person to whom you are speaking, but you as well. It is like wearing jeans and a sweater during the week and, on the weekend, putting on a nice suit or a dress. Not only does dressing up make others behave differently toward you, it frequently causes you to behave differently toward yourself. As Lord Chesterfield described it, "Style is the dress of thoughts." See if you can pick out from the following five styles of speaking, the one that most closely resembles your own:†

"Those individuals do not posses any ________." [*Literary-poetical-supererudite style*]

"Those men haven't any ________." [*Literary-prose-cultured style*]

"Those men haven't got any ________." [*Spoken standard style*]

"Those guys haven't/ain't got any ________." [*Colloquial lower class style*]

"Dem guys ain't git none ________." [*Vulgar and slang style*]

Wilson and Arnold propose that humanity's expression of inner self probably emerges more clearly in style than in any other aspect of human communication. Try to imagine what kinds of people would use each of the following styles of speech:‡

1. The posterior portion of the mansion embraced a rude pergola under which a saucy damsel attired in a bathing costume retired.
2. The rear of the house supported a rickety arbor beneath which sat a beautiful girl in a bathing suit.
3. The back of the club propped a saggy shade below which a hot-bikinied babe laid.

*Paul Valéry, "Style" in *The Problem of Style*, edited by J. V. Sunningham, translated by Eugenia Haufmann and Gertrude Vakar (Greenwich, Conn.: Fawcett, 1966), pp. 18–19.

†From Mario Pei, *Language For Everyone* Copyright (c) 1956 by The Devin-Adair Co., Old Greenwich, Conn., p. 65.

‡John F. Wilson and Carroll C. Arnold, *Public Speaking as a Liberal Art* (Boston, Mass.: Allyn and Bacon, 1974), pp. 212–213.

Does the remark, "My, does she sound intelligent" ring a bell? What exactly could there be about someone's manner of speaking that suggests intelligence? Although research dealing with judging personality on the basis of voice has produced some conflicting results, it has attracted considerable attention and interest–particularly among those engaged in screening, hiring, and admitting applicants for various reasons. To give you some idea of the conclusions certain studies have disclosed, let us turn to one that concentrated on the differences between male and female voices. It suggested such things as: (1) males and females with flat voices were perceived as withdrawn, sluggish, cold and masculine, (2) males and females with nasal voices were taken to possess a wide array of socially undesirable characteristics, and (3) males with throaty voices to be older; more realistic, mature; sophisticated; and well adjusted. Females with throaty voices were perceived as being less intelligent, more masculine, lazy, dull, sickly, unemotional, naive, neurotic and uninteresting.*

Other research can be found zeroing in on identifying age, sex, height, and weight, status, body type, occupation, education, regional dialect, and emotional states (for example, anger, sadness, jealousy, sympathy). One study in particular had a very practical application with regard to witnesses and jurors in a courtroom. It seems that the subtle differences in the way lawyers and witnesses speak can have a profound effect on the outcome of a criminal trial according to William O'Barr, professor of anthropology at Duke University. He discovered that witnesses tend to be more believable to juries if they use a narrative style of speaking. Also, the speech characteristics of women tend to make heard testimony less believable to jurors.†

Here is an exercise that will give you and your classmates firsthand experience with the extent to which a person's manner of speech can conjure up certain stereotypes.

Name of Exercise: Acoustic Stereotyping

Procedure:

Step 1. Several members of the class who either own or have access to a tape recorder shoudl tape two voices completely unfamiliar to the class. This should be done a day or two prior to the date the exercise is to be performed. (Each voice sample should run 1 minute.)

Step 2. One after the other, the tapes should be played to the class. As each is heard, all students are to write on a sheet of paper their impressions of the speaker. Their notations should include both *physical* (anything about their appearance) and *psychological* (anything about their personality, attitudes, values, and beliefs).

*See Mark L. Knapp, *Nonverbal Communications in Human Interaction* (New York: Hold, Rinehart and Winston, 1972), pp. 151–155.

†"Verdicts linked to speech style," *New York Times*, Dec. 14, 1975.

Step 3. After all the tapes have been heard, an open discussion should follow a replaying of each tape. During the replays members of the class are invited to compare their reactions to the taped voices. Serious attempts at explaining these reactions should likewise be made.

Your speaking self consists of several characteristics. Most obvious is your vocabulary. Unfortunately, you have a reading and speaking vocabulary and, although you may recognize and understand the meaning of a great many words, you may not use them all when you speak. This phenomenon may have become apparent while watching and listening to some well-known author being interviewed on television. Having read and admired an author's work and then hearing that person grope and fumble for words can be a dramatic source of disenchantment. The reverse may also be true; a person may speak extraordinarily well and write poorly. In certain businesses or professions, one's spoken vocabulary may be found to be more important than its written form. Physicians, teachers, politicians, attorneys, and salespeople all lean heavily on their ability to speak. Inversely, authors, script writers, ad writers, and editors rely on their ability to write. At which of these two forms of expression are you more proficient—speaking or writing? How you answer could represent a guideline for selecting a career.

Pronunciation

Are you careful not to mispronounce words. It might be more important than you think. There is a story that illustrates the role correct pronunciation could play in a professional's life. It seems that at a large Eastern university, a V.I.P. from the world of library science was invited to address its library staff. After the usual introduction, this V.I.P. began to speak. Ten minutes into his speech, he happen to mention library science in a rather atypical way. He pronounced the word library as though it were "liberry." As the word left his mouth and struck the ears of his audience, a dead silence fell over the room. The thought loomed in the mind of practically every member of the audience: "L-i-b-e-r-r-y science!" They couldn't understand how on earth someone with his background and status could mispronounce such a word. How much faith would you have in a doctor who said you had "g-o-l-d stones" or a voice teacher who told you to drop your "l-a-r-n-i-x?" Although you may personally feel that being able to understand a word is all that counts, be forewarned that there are people who would dismiss everything else you said on the strength of your having mispronounced one word they felt you should have known how to pronounce correctly.

But, this attitude is, by no means, new. It was held in classic times by Cicero who said, "Nobody ever admired an orator for correct grammar, they only laugh at him if his grammar is bad, and not only think him no orator but not even a human being; no one ever sang the praises of a speaker whose style succeeded in making his meaning intelligible to his audience, but only despised one deficient in capacity to do so."*

Before leaving the subject of pronunciation, here is a moderately amusing anecdote that seems fitting. A woman with an accent was having trouble becoming pregnant. On the insistence of her husband, she went to a doctor. That evening, upon returning home, her husband asked, "Well, dear, what did the doctor say?" She answered, "He said I have a fish in my canal and that if I have a baby, it will be a mackerel." Thoroughly confused by her report, the husband decided to call the doctor himself. After repeating what his wife told him, the doctor said, "No, what I told your wife is that *she had a deficiency in her canal* and that if she did have a baby, *it would be a miracle*"—an obvious case of mispronunciation.

> *In a brief essay, recall any experiences you had had in which the pronunciation of a word played an important role.*

Voice

There are several factors responsible for the way your voice sounds. First, there is your **range of pitch**. It may be wide or extremely narrow, resulting in what is commonly referred to as a monotone. Ordinarily, standard speech consists of raising and lowering the voice. Austin gives several excellent examples of how pitch is varied. He indicates a raised pitch with the sign of an arrow pointing upward placed over the word | ↑ | and a lower pitch pointing down | ↓ |.†

1. Women will use a higher pitch than normal to indicate innocence and feminity.

   ↑ ↑
You mean this is for me?

2. Males will similarly use a lower pitch to signal masculinity.

   ↓ ↓
Come on, baby.

3. American Negro speech is characterized by intermittant use of high pitch.

   ↑ ↑ ↑ ↑
Man, you can't do nuttin' 'bout dat.

**De Oratore*, translated by H. A. Rackham (Cambridge, Mass.: Harvard University Press, 1948), Book 111, Chapter 14, pp. 41–42.

†William Austin, "Nonverbal communication," in *Culture, Class, and Language*, edited by A. L. Davis (Urbana, Ill.: National Council of Teachers, 1972), pp. 160–161.

Intensity A second consideration is intensity—that is, the loudness or softness of your voice. Few things are more disturbing to a soft-spoken person than someone who is loud. Likewise, loud people are driven up a wall by those who speak softly. While one pleads, "Please, would you mind keeping your voice down," the other pleads, "What's that you're saying? Speak up! Don't mumble."

Vocal intensity varies not only from person to person, but from family to family, organization to organization. Surely, you have been in homes where everyone seems to be shouting at everyone else, as well as those in which everyone speaks so softly you can hear a pin drop. The same extremes frequently apply to department stores. Visit the most expensive and the most elegant department store in any fair-sized city and notice the level at which its salespeople speak. Then, go to the most inexpensive and inelegant store and notice the level at which its salespeople speak. For some curious reason, there appears to be an inverse relationship between price and vocal intensity, that is, the higher-priced the establishment, the softer the people who frequent it speak; the lower-priced the establishment, the louder they speak. Restaurants are often classic examples of this intensity ratio.

An attempt at establishing whether a person speaks loudly or softly occasionally runs into difficulty. It seems that the way one hears one's own voice is different from the way others hear it. Loud-spoken people have the reputation of denying their loudness when so accused; the same goes for the soft-spoken ones. "What? Me, loud? Who's shouting?" or "I thought I was speaking loud enough to be heard. You mean you can't hear me?" How would you rate your own vocal intensity? Now, ask a random dozen people you know to tell you how they perceive your voice volume and see if it compares favorably with your own opinion.

Tempo A third quality of your voice is its *tempo.* Are you a fast, slow, or medium talker? The same phenomenon exists here as it did with voice volume; people who speak rapidly have difficulty coping with those who speak slowly, and vice versa. With the average speech speed ranging from 125–150 words per minute (wpm) and the average thought speed from 500-600 wpm, tempo difference can present an occasional problem. For instance, picture a salesperson with a speech speed of 115 wpm visiting a new account. The customer, while politely listening to the sales pitch, does so against the background of a 550-wpm thought speed. Because of this tremendous differential in speeds, the customer has ample time for mini-thoughts which may have little or nothing to do with the product or service being offered. The result: much distraction, poor attention, and probably no sale.

Vocal Coloration Laughing, crying, sobbing, sighing, moaning, groaning, whining, snoring, throat clearing, and noisy forms of breathing all are forms of vocal coloration. Although any one of them can occur by itself without any relationship to spoken language, they frequently occur in speech-related situations. Take laughing. Would you go so far as to judge an individual on the basis of how he or she laughs? Have you known people whose laughs are completely inappropriate to their speaking voices? Any one of these vocal colorations could create a breakdown in communication. Or, if not an actual breakdown, a climate for one. A classic example of this happened to a very beautiful fashion model while she was making her rounds of the agencies. During an interview, with everything else going well, she chanced to let go with a laugh that curled the interviewer's toes. It was such a shocking departure from her lovely speaking voice that one would think a ventriloquist was in the other room. Although she got the job, it certainly gave the interviewer cause to reflect rather carefully before hiring her.

The tendency to sigh a great deal without knowing it can also create some difficulty in any field where there is the need for face-to-face relationships. The usual response to repeated sighing is that the person is: (1) bored, (2) not feeling well, (3) impatient, or (4) annoyed. Any of these responses can be very frustrating when the sighing person subjectively feels none of them. Throat-clearing may also be misunderstood. It may be judged to mean: (1) a bid for attention, (2) nervousness, (3) a signal to "watch out," or (4) a sore throat.

Thus, whether in public or private, vocal colorations—as with words—may give someone an erroneous impression. They should, therefore, be carefully monitored for ambiguity along with the spoken word.

Vocal Crutches Similar to, but not identical with, vocal colorations are vocal crutches. They embrace such utterances as *uh, uh-huh, um, mmmmm*, and *er*. They seem to be identical with actual linguistic sounds in the language but do not appear in the kinds of sequences that can be called words. As is the case with vocal coloration, most of the people who employ vocal crutches are rarely aware of the extent to which they do use them. Perhaps you have a professor or an employer who is a notorious user of one of them. If you have, make it a point to count the number of times it is used in any given period of time. If it is mentioned to the speaker, nine out of ten times it will either be denied or questioned closely. Should you be interested in discovering the extent to which you lean on one or more of these vocal crutches, a tape recorder is strongly recommended. Speak into it without reading from a book, magazine, or script. Your remarks should be completely "off the top of your head." On listening to a playback of the tape, the first time, jot down which crutches you employ. Then, on the second hearing, record the number of times you utter each one A final test will be to make another recording successfully reducing or eliminating your vocal crutches.

Emphasis How many different ways could you say, "What do you mean? Would the word(s) you emphasized make any change in its overall meaning? Try it. Read each of the following and stress the word that is underlined:

What do you mean?
What *do* you mean?
What do *you* mean?
What do you *mean*?

Now try:

I deserve a big raise.
I *deserve* a big raise.
I deserve *a big* raise.
I deserve a big *raise.*

In a class on the Rhetoric of Women in The Twentieth Century, a teacher wanted her students to appreciate the difference emphasis through punctuation can make on a thought. She wrote this sentence on the blackboard: "Woman without her man is nothing." The teacher then asked members of this coed class to punctuate the sentence. The women in the class wrote it this way: "Woman! Without her, man is nothing." The males wrote: "Woman, without her man, is nothing." Obviously, through punctuation, the emphasis was shifted and with it went its meaning. The art of knowing what, when, and where to emphasize a particular word or thought can make all the difference in a communication.

Vocabulary

Without words, we are immediately thrown back to the grunting and groaning stage of the cave dweller. Without words, today's technology would be impossible. Without words, life is empty. Words strung together give us language which, in turn, enable us to examine our inner and outer worlds. Words act as stepping stones on which we can move nearer or further apart from each other. Words can act as either walls or bridges.

The collection of words you carry around in your head do not all, necessarily, come out of your mouth. Most of us have two vocabularies. We employ one while speaking and the other while reading or writing. It is quite possible that you may recognize and understand the meaning of a written word and never use it orally. Perhaps you know someone who is able to comfortably read a pornographic novel and becomes positively hysterical at having to speak certain words aloud. Making a distinction between your spoken and written vocabularies could be important if you are faced with a decision as to whether you should call, write, or meet someone you wished to impress. Whatever your decision, the words you use could represent an invaluable form of public relations.

At best, your vocabulary should grow as you grow. Unfortunately, this is seldom the case. The majority of people you will encounter have been using the same worn out words they have been using for the greater part of their lives. New words have a way of frightening them. What is even worse, when they do learn a new word, they are often reluctant to use it for fear that others will not know its meaning or, they will be accused of showing off. Such an attitude toward words can easily stifle the growth of any language and, in the process, dampen any attempt at creating a state of healthy interpersonal communication.

Aside from a body of words known as "commercial speech," which is lean, utilitarian, and deals with objects rather than people, there is also a body of words that serves to unite all human beings (for example, love, security, dignity, consideration, prestige, kindness, loyalty, courtesy, faith, trust, helpfulness, happiness, sympathy, appreciation, patience, respect, devotion, and honor. Each, in a variety of combinations, provides the glue necessary for humanity to endure, for groups to "stick together." The sad commentary on these survival terms is that they are rapidly disappearing from commerical and professional rhetoric. They are being pushed aside by legions of computers whose language bears absolutely no resemblance to ours. The prophecy of H. G. Wells has come to pass: We make humans behave like machines and machines behave like humans. All that remains is for a distinction to be preserved between man and machine. Thus, the words we use to convey how we think and feel toward one another could well be a giant step in that direction.

The vocabulary you acquired while growing up was not specialized, that is, it was not designed to meet a specific technological demand. Like millions of other boys and girls, it was probably dominated by words related to play and study. Only when your thoughts began to turn in the direction of a career did it begin to take on certain field-related terminology. If your interests pointed you toward becoming a clinical psychologist, words such as awareness, ego, id, consciousness, libido, and motivation surely began to creep into your vocabulary. If your goal was a career in merchandising, discounts, production costs, job lots, and commissions became additions to your vocabulary. Each field has its own vocabulary which differentiates it from other fields. Many of them are commonly referred to as *buzz words.* Spend a half-hour talking with anyone in a particular business or profession and you are bound to be exposed to some words you will not understand. To illustrate this, here are some buzz words. See whether you can define them and identify the field in which they are used:

	Definition	*Field*
1. Run-through		
2. Adoption		
3. Point		
4. Swatch		

5. Heads

6. Tricks

7. Simmer

8. Station

9. Pot

10. Fare

11. Cattle call

12. Postponement

13. Rigg

14. Cream puff

15. Pilot

Going down the list of buzz words, you must have noticed that several of the terms could apply to more than one business or profession. This is less significant than the fact that their meaning is expected to be known to any responsible member of the field in which it is used. Not knowing it immediately arouses suspicion. For example, if you were applying for a position as a typesetter and were asked whether you prefer to work with "hot or cold type," you would be expected to be familiar with these terms. Although you may have answered other questions satisfactorily, being unfamiliar with such basic vocabulary of the printing field would probably disqualify you.

It seems near impossible for some people to separate the word from the thing, the person from his or her vocabulary To them, you are what you say. The person who uses "dirty words" is also considered a dirty person. Hence, to these people–and there are a great many of them out there–you and your vocabulary are one and the same. If your speaking self is cluttered with negative language, (difficult, problems, unimportant, waste of time, pointless, unnecessary), there is a good chance that you will be considered a "negative person" rather than merely someone who happens to use negative language. Naturally, the opposite also applies to the person who uses "positive language." Once you open your mouth and allow words to escape, you are painting a picture of yourself in other peoples' minds. Unfortunately, how they use your words to paint these pictures will depend largely on the meaning they assign them.

Words are as human-made as plastics, automobiles, rowboats, and beach unbrellas. There is no such thing as the "real" word for something. Take the simple buzzing sound made by a bee. In this country, we say *buzz*; in Arabic, they say *taneen*, in French, *ronronne*; in Spanish, *zurrier*; and in Turkish, *wuzultu.* Which of these words is the real word for the sound a bee makes. Obviously, they all mean the same thing, and it would be foolish to regard one as the "real" word and the others as false. The study of *semantics* deals with this sort of thing, namely, the meaning of words. Above all else, meanings are in people, not in words.

Words are symbols, that is, they stand for things. The objects for which they stand are known as **referents**. The process by which people connect a symbol (a word) with a referent (an object) is called a **reference**. As you have just seen, the symbol for the sound made by a bee is different in many languages. In the case of a word like buzz, there is actually something out there in the material world to which the word or symbol refers. This is not true, however, with such words as love, motivation, success, happiness, prestige, power, or self-respect. They are all abstractions and, as such, lack referents. There is nothing in the physical world that you can see, feel, smell, taste, or hear called *love.* As a result, it is highly unlikely that people will have exactly the same definition for it. Test this phenomenon for yourself by defining the following words:

1. Love ______________________________
2. Motivation ______________________________
3. Success ______________________________
4. Happiness ______________________________
5. Prestige ______________________________
6. Power ______________________________
7. Self-respect ______________________________

If you compare the definitions you have supplied with those given by others, you will detect similarities, but no list will contain perfectly matched meanings. Abstract words like these are probably responsible for the greatest number of misunderstandings among business and professional personnel. To illustrate, if you were involved in a legal dispute and your lawyer said, "Don't worry," how would you interpret the word *worry*? It could easily mean one thing to your lawyer and quite another to you. Your vocabulary is filled with words that you attribute identical meanings to those of a great many people you know. When it comes to abstract words, such a belief is a luxury few of us can afford.

The fewer abstract words you use in your vocabulary, the more effective your communication will tend to be; i.e., abstract words often confuse meaning, concrete words clarify it. One reason for such clarification is that concrete words have referents. People using them are usually able to point to objects in their environment as material evidence of their existence. This cannot be done with abstract words.

Second, concrete words spark mental images. When the word *money* is used in a conversation, immediately a mental picture of either bills or coins is generated by the brain. In contrast, an abstract word like *motivation* generates no image at all. Don't be misled. There is nothing wrong with abstract words. Without them, our language would be lifeless and uninteresting. The only thing to remember is that when you use abstract words, greater care and consideration should be exerted. Why? Because the risk you run of being misunderstood is substantially greater. Meanings conveyed by concrete words in most instances are more explicit than those conveyed by abstract ones.

Another aspect of your vocabulary is that it consists of words that are new, old, taboo, and inappropriate. Words, like people, are born, die, change, become popular and unpopular, and sustain abuse. But above all, they have the distinct ability to seriously alter people's lives. The size and character of your vocabulary can seriously affect *your* life. The most brilliant people will probably suffer needless underachievement in their work if they lack the vocabulary to express themselves adequately. An enriched vocabulary should be viewed as "success insurance." *To repeat*: Your vocabulary should grow as you grow. And, the best way to facilitate this growth is through the old and established method of learning one new word each day.

An excellent and enjoyable method of determining how rich or poor your vocabulary is to play ping pong with words. Fire words back and forth with a friend or classmate and try to stump each other. Start with moderately easy words, and slowly work up to more difficult words.

SELF-EXAMINATION QUIZ

Having read this chapter, my answers to the following questions reflect my understanding of its content.

1. How do actions speak louder than words?

2. In what ways have we been conditioned to conjure up mental pictures of how people in different businesses and professions look?

3. Explain how certain employers stereotype their employees.

4. Describe the manner in which the average person uses eye contact.

5. Explain the difference between purposeful and purposeless gestures.

6. Explain how a smile communicates.

7. What are some of the ways a handshake can disclose a person's mental or physical state?

8. As a mode of nonverbal communication, what is the role touching plays in the average person's life?

9. What is the significance of how people stand in relationship to one another?

10. Differentiate "larks" and "owls" in terms of communication.

11. How does odor influence interpersonal behavior?

12. What do your clothes communicate about you?

13. Describe your own speaking style.

14. How can your vocabulary affect your interpersonal communication.

15. Tell how a person's pronunciation of words can influence other people's reaction to them.

16. Describe your own vocal qualities.

Suggested Readings

Cole, Jim, Helpers: *A View of Our Helpfulness* (Ft. Collins, Colo.: Shields, 1973)

Goffman, Erving, *The Presentation of Self in Everday Life* (Garden City, N.Y.: Doubleday, 1959).

Johnson, David W., *Reaching Out* (Englewood Cliffs, N.J.: Prentice-Hall, 1972).

Jones, E., "What it's like to be a black manager," *Harvard Business Review,* **51**, 108–116 (1973).

Laing, R. D., *The Divided Self* (London: Tavistock, 1960).

Maslow, Abraham H., *Toward a Psychology of Being* (New York: Van Nostrand-Reinhold, 1962).

Powell, John, *Why Am I Afraid to Tell You Who I Am?* Niles, Ill.: Argus Communications, 1969).

Rokeach, Milton, *The Open and Closed Mind* (New York: Basic Books, 1960).

Wheelis, Allen, *The Quest for Identity* (New York: Norton, 1958).

WORK AREA FOR CHAPTER 2

Chapter 3

Investigating a Career

There is no such thing as being in the wrong business or profession; they are only side roads and detours leading to the right one.

MEMO

TO: Reader

FROM: Author

After reading this chapter, you should have a better understanding of:

1. What motivates people toward certain careers and not others.

2. How and why people blindly drift into fields which do not interest them.

3. Which ingredients make a positive career philosophy possible.

4. How to go about investigating the career in which you are interested.

5. What things you should be sure to know before making up your mind about a career.

6. What resumes are all about and how to draw up your own.

7. How you can more effectively communicate on the telephone.

8. How your hopes, fears and frustrations about a career are not unique — that countless others share them with you.

Chapter 3

Deciding what to do with your life is probably the single most important decision you will ever have to make. Someone in close touch with the human condition once said, "Intelligence is not a matter of noting what people do when they know what to do, it is more a matter of what they do when they don't know what to do." This is particularly ture when trying to decide upon a career. If you know what you want to do–that is, become a doctor, lawyer, accountant, musician, engineer or business person–your task will be substantially easier.* For instance, if your mind is set on a career in nursing, there are many booklets, services, and agencies standing ready to assist you. The same guidance and counseling is also readily available in practically every other established field. All that is required of you is that *you know what you want to do.* Obviously, this is easier said than done. Where does one start? If you have read the first two chapters of this text, the answer is elementary. The place ot start is with YOU!

Career Needs

People decide on different careers for different reasons. Each person, in some way, fulfills a real or imagined need. How clear are you on the subject of your own needs? Will the career you choose fulfill them? Here are some of the more commonly expressed career needs a majority of people seem to harbor. Compare and contrast them with your own.

Financial

Have you ever had a job about which you've said, "I don't particularly like the job, but the money is good." Perhaps you know people who feel this way about what they are doing for a living. It is important that you clearly establish in your mind how you feel about money before deciding upon a career. Why, because should financial gain be your highest priority, you must make certain that the career you select is one capable of delivering what you want most–*money.* It is also worthwhile mentioning that if this is your primary goal, you must be prepared to make compromises in other areas, should they arise.

Power

How necessary is it for you to exert influence over others? Does your psychological disposition require that you be in an authoritarian position? Do you feel uncomfortable taking orders? If so, you must ask yourself this question: "What careers will allow me the opportunity to exert power over others? Politics, medicine, education, theater, journalism, and advertising are but a few fields in which one can exert a dramatic influence upon the lives of others.

*To avoid being misunderstood, I might add that knowing what you want to become or do with your life is by no means a guarantee that you will succeed. You may want to be an opera singer, for example, and have little vocal talent for it.

Status

Perhaps your need is to become someone of importance, of distinction, someone who will be looked up to and treated with respect. If it is, you had best consider a career in which you can grow and develop and not be frozen into a position from which you cannot escape. Once you are willing to admit that status is important to you, and that without it your chances of being happy are poor, you are in a position to screen out those careers that are least capable of affording you the opportunity of acquiring it.

Security

Today, more than ever before, there is a growing preoccupation with security in the job market. Increasing numbers of young men and women are opting for careers in civil and federal service because they offer more security than the private sector offers. Large corporations, recognizing this felt need for security, are now offering it as one of their major means of attracting new blood into their ranks. Hence, if you cannot cope with uncertainty—the thought of having one job in May and another in June—it is crucial that you seek out a career that does not expose you to such a risk.

Creativity

There is no such thing as a creative job or profession. Creativity exists in people who bring it with them to whatever they happen to be doing. A truly creative person can take the most boring and meaningless job and make it come alive. If you honestly are a creative type, be sure to select a career in which your creativity will flourish and not be stifled. Be advised, however, that there are careers that, on the surface, nurture the creative spirit whereas, in reality, they are dreadfully bland and traditional in their ways.

Benefits

Unlike the first half of this century, job benefits have become big business. Security alone does not seem to be enough for a large segment of the working population. In an age of soaring costs of living, the work force in this country has become educated to need something more than job security. Thoughts now run in the direction of regular salary increments, guaranteed paid vacations, profit sharing, extended medical coverage, shorter work week, stock options, bonuses, and so forth. Should you tend to think in these terms, selecting a career may be easier simply because you can immediately rule out those failing to offer such benefits.

Location

Would being away from home six months out of the year bother you? Does the thought of having to travel more than 50,000 miles a year sound out of the question? If your answer is an unequivocal "yes," then you must approach certain careers with caution. For instance, the probability of having to be away from home a great deal and traveling extensively is appreciably higher in such fields as film-making, acting, national and international sales, certain branches of government service, engineering, advertising, and journalism. It is not uncommon to find people whose careers make such demands on them needing more than one residence. A number of movie stars have a home or apartment on the East Coast as well as the West Coast; some also have a home abroad.

If your temperament requires that you be with your family all year round, that you have roots, steer clear of a career in which you are obliged to work in different locations. There may be other attractive compensations, but if this is one of your primary career needs, respect it and direct your energies toward a business or profession that is location-stable.

Independence

No matter what career you decide to pursue, it will involve working as a team member or on your own. To some people, the element of personal freedom and on-the-job independence is "a must." Their personalities simply will not tolerate the concept of group effort, team spirit, or committee life. They work best alone. Have you noticed how some physicians prefer working on a hospital staff while others elect to go into private practice on their own. This choice exists in practically every field, that is, working by yourself or with others. Therefore, if you know you are a "loner," be guided by that fact. Investigate those job opportunities that feature independence, self-reliance, self-motivation, and personal judgment. Remain aware, however, that although many careers permit considerable independence, few, if any, are completely detached. Sooner or later, the author, painter, and inventor must communicate and work with publishers, agents, dealers, and corporation representatives if their labors are to bear fruit. Most of their time, however, is spent working by themselves, and this, to them, is essential.

Acceptance

Acceptance by one's peers is frequently an emotional, rather than an intellectual, phenomenon—more illogical than logical. As such, the act of acceptance or nonacceptance could be viewed as the way people feel about one another. Defining acceptance in this manner, quite naturally, precludes those situations in which credentials, experience, reputation, and special knowledge are used as yardsticks of evaluating people.

Few things are as frustrating and depressing as working with people who do not accept you. Rejection by a group goes beyond race, color, and creed. It could be based on a person's sense of humor (or lack of it), speech pattern, political viewpoint, willingness to work, punctuality, politeness, mode of dress, table manners, or trustworthiness. Any one of a number of behavioral characteristics could result in not being accepted by one's fellow workers. With this as the reality, what can be done to prevent it from happening to you? No matter how you reason the question of group acceptance, the bottom line will alyways be: *You can't please everyone.* What you can do, if you wish, is to think defensively when contemplating a career. To illustrate, imagine that you want to enter the field of fashion as a buyer; further, imagine that your taste in clothes leaves a great deal to be desired. Being as clothes conscious as most buyers are and not displaying a similiar consciousness by the way you dress, you may be jeopardizing your chances of being accepted by them.

Being accepted by one's peers brings to mind a story about a colleague of mine. Hard-pressed for extra money, she decided to take a summer job in a law office. Realizing that she could not tell the interviewers in the employment office that she was a college professor, she reshaped the truth a little by saying she had one year of college education. The first day on the job, she met and went to lunch with "the girls." The conversation, as one would expect, was centered at a level considerably lower than the type to which she was accustomed on campus, but, she adjusted her remarks to the situations appropriately (she thought). At the office, she was assigned several filing jobs, which she performed competently (she thought). When asked questions by various attorneys, she answered correctly (she thought). After three days on the job, she sensed "the girls" had become a little distant—less willing to include her in their office activities. She no longer felt accepted by them. On the fifth day, the head of the firm called her in and asked, "What do you really do for a living, Mary? You obviously don't belong here." Not only did her employer notice that her work and knowledge far exceeded the level of other members of his clerical staff, they also sensed that she "didn't belong." The point serves to illustrate how, in every field, its members are bound to each other by a number of visible and invisible traits they hold in common. And, should someone enter their ranks who does not manifest them, their acceptance will apt to be guarded. Although the lack of one of these traits should by no means deter you from pursuing a career, you should be aware that such a trait exists and that its absence could be of some relevance. For your own edification along this line, ask several people in the same field if there are any traits common to most of them. Compare these traits with your own and ask, "How well would I fit into this field?"

Physical

With the exception of those who have a clearly defined handicap, most of us have the uncanny ability not to see our own physical shortcomings. This is a character trait that should not be indulged when contemplating a career choice. Such physical qualities as size, strength, appearance, manual dexterity, endurance, speed of movement, ability to go without sleep, eyesight, hearing—along with general health—should be carefully considered in relation to the demands expected to be made by a particular career.

Take the case of a young woman who wanted, more than anything, to become a registered nurse. She was a top-rate student, and got into the nursing program of a top-rate school. Pulling straight A's in all her clinical subjects, she was riding high until some practicum courses came along—courses requiring manual dexterity. No matter how hard she tried, she was all thumbs. As a result, she was almost dropped from the program. Fortunately, a friend who was not as good in her clinical subjects but who made great beds, offered to exchange tutoring skills. They both succeeded in getting their RN degrees. The moral of this story is not that she shouldn't have gone into nursing without being sure that her manual dexterity was up to par, but, rather, that she should have known about it in advance and done something in anticipation of such an eventuality.

To some extent, the majority of businesses and professions make physical demands on the people in them During the tax season, accountants work hard long hours—often pushing their endurance beyond what they are accustomed to during the rest of the year; salesmen selling on the road must have good digestive systems because of the need to eat in different restaurants all the time; surgeons, whose specialities require that they perform long and tedious operations, must often possess above-average physical strength and stamina. Such examples are plentiful. Below is a list of businesses and professions. Next to each, insert the physical needs you think would probably be required.

Airline pilot ______________________________

Sculptor ______________________________

Television repairman ______________________________

Restauranteur ______________________________

Newcaster on radio and T.V.______________________________

Farmer ______________________________

Concert pianist ______________________________

Beautician______________________________

Night club performer ______________________________

Diamond cutter ______________________________

Automobile mechanic ______________________________

Author ______________________________

Photographer ______________________________

Archeologist ______________________________

Chemical engineer ______________________________

Having read these brief descriptions of the various needs people possess, and their possible relationship to selecting a career, rank them according to your own preferences. A 1 should appear next to your strongest need and a number 2 next to your weakest. The other should be ranked accordingly.

Financial	________	Benefits	________
Power	________	Location	________
Status	________	Independence	________
Security	________	Acceptance	________
Creativity	________	Physical	________

Environmental Factors

You were not born with any of the ideas you may have about what to do with your life. You got them from family, friends, and society while you were growing up. As an adult, you must now sort them out and make a choice. There is absolutely no guarantee that you will make the right choice. If the statistics mentioned earlier are reliable, the majority of people currently in the job market made the wrong choice; that is to say, they admit that if they had it all to do over again, they would not choose the same business or profession they are in. Without reading more into a poll like this than we should, simply use it as a warning against being too casual in making career decisions that could last the rest of your life.

Family

You have already been apprised of the reduction in tendency for young men to follow in their father's footsteps when it comes to a career. Many a father, these days, must turn to a stranger because his son refuses to take over his business or profession. With the advent of women's liberation, many young women are now finding the prospect of keeping house and raising children less rewarding than their grandmothers did. Fewer and fewer careers are being offered as "strictly for men" or "strictly for women." There was a time when the career of nursing attracted only women; today, many young men are enrolled in nursing programs. As a result, parents have had to revise their thinking in counseling their children about a career. The concept of what is man's work and what is woman's work seems to be rapidly fading from view.

In spite of changing times (many) parents still exert a strong influence on their children with regard to their future. Using bed and board as a tool of persuasion, they insist that they pursue a particular course of study or enter a particular line of work until they are out on their own. Too often, such parents are self-serving. Although in many of these cases, they are convinced they are doing what is best, it may not be in their son's or daughter's best interest. Right or wrong, their offspring often claim that their feelings are being compromised—that what they think, feel and want is being ignored or treated as immature.

The opposite is also true. There are parents who take their children's futures very seriously and, so to speak, do their homework. With patience and understanding, many fathers and mothers listen to what their children say, try to read between the lines, and on the basis of what they discover, make every effort to help them gather information on the subject. They willingly and enthusiastically share with them the lessons they have learned from their own experience. To them, selecting a career is serious business and no child should be deprived of the benefit a concerned and intelligent parent can supply.

> *Write a brief essay describing the manner in which your family has influenced your thinking about a career. If appropriate, include the influence of any of your relatives.*

Friends

Superimposed on the influence exerted by your immediate family unit was that of your friends. Invariably, as you brought little boys and girls into your home, comparisons were made. Parents were occasionally heard to say, "Why can't you be like ______?" Whether they meant it or not isn't the issue. The point is, you were being compared with one of your friends and the comparing usually continued throughout your school years. One would think that such a practice would stop when you became an adult—but did it? Human nature often prompts interest in what our friends are going to do with their lives. Some elect to continue their education by taking an advanced college degree or attending a trade school; others are willing to forego a formal education in preference of gathering practical experience out in the field, while others—lacking any specific direction, take a more fatalistic approach by going "out there" to try to find themselves.

The degree to which your thoughts about a career are influenced by friends will depend on several factors: (1) how independent a person you are, (2) the persuasiveness of your friend(s), (3) whether you have already made up your mind about a career, and (4) the extent to which you are committed to what your parents want you to do. Peers can, in certain situations, generate an enormous amount of influence upon a person. At times, they can easily overpower a family's influence. Because of this, career decisions based entirely upon the recommendations or activities of friends must be weighed carefully. Although friends might imagine themselves as having the same attitudes, values, and beliefs, they are usually separate and distinct people who must be treated separately and distinctly when it comes to deciding on a career. Often times, the hidden danger is that friendship tends to create an illusion of "oneness and sameness." While this form of human relationship is surely a desirable and worthwhile pursuit, it must not be allowed to erase the personal needs of an individual.

Society

None of us lives in a vacuum. In addition to the influence our environment has on us in the form of family, friends, co-workers and fellow students, there is an even broader influence–society, as a whole. Founded on mixtures of race, color, and creed, this melting pot we call "America" touches each of us through the magic of the mass media. Books, radio, magazines, television, films, and newspapers constantly sketch life in the United States in terms of how it was, is, and will be in the future. Against such a background of information, careers are formulated and forged.

Escaping one's heritage is no easy task. Bits and pieces of the past appear to be locked into our language. For example, certain members of our society cling to the notion that you should go into business for yourself, that working for someone else is not the road to success. Others, subscribing to an opposite viewpoint, advise against self-employment, arguing that it creates needless worries and headaches. Each culture brought with it the norms upon which this country was founded–sets of mores that continue to thrive in many minds and hearts. The result is that many young adults of foreign-born parents become caught up in a contest of values between the old and the new. To show you just how much of an influence such an admixture of opinion may have had on your ideas about people and the fields they should go into, complete the following sentences:

1. Most Jewish young men become doctors, lawyers, accountants
2. Most Italian young men become ____________________
3. Most Puerto Rican young men become ____________________
4. Most Mexican young men become ____________________
5. Most Greek young men become ____________________
6. Most Polish young men become ____________________
7. Most French young men become ____________________
8. Most Swedish young men become ____________________

9. Most Japanese young men become ______________________

10. Most Irish young men become ______________________

11. Most German young men become ______________________

12. Most Chinese young men become ______________________

13. Most Blacks become ______________________

14. Most American Indian young men become ______________________

15. Most Arabic young men become ______________________

Add to these examples any other culturally different types of young men and speculate as to what they would become in this country. Also prepare a similar list for young women.

The city, state, and federal government publish lists of occupations as guides to a career. This is but one way society furnishes its citizenry with information. A specific example is the *Occupational Outlook Handbook* developed by the U.S. Bureau of Labor Statistics in Washington, D.C. It gives a picture of employment opportunities from now until 1985. As an indication of how it may shape one's thinking about a career, it lists as providing good to very good opportunities in such fields as accounting, engineering, banking, science, dentistry, architecture, and other health-related professions. It lists as providing poor opportunities in such professions as law, teaching, and journalism. Unfortunately, information like this will not come to you—you must go to it. What is more, you will have to develop a positive career philosophy.

Positive Career Philosophy

Many employers making hiring choices on a skill-irrelevant basis. Put another way, employers often hire people, not skills. It should go without saying that such a point of view must not be taken to mean that skills are unimportant. It simply means that the emphasis should be placed on the skillful person, rather than the skill—the potter, rather than the clay; the thinker, rather than the thought.

A philosophy is a way of looking at something. Here, we are looking at a way of investigating a career. Toward this end, you must work at perceiving yourself as a gatherer, sifter, synthesizer, and interpreter of information. Your success may depend on your ability to do this. Thinking negatively increases your chances of negative results. Thinking positively increases your chances of promoting positive results. A reasonable question you might ask at this juncture is, "How can I think positively about a career I haven't decided on yet?" True, but the difference is that you should be thinking positively about the *process* of investigating a career until such time as you do decide. Negative phrases such as, "That field is already overcrowded," or "I don't want to start at the bottom," immediately place you at a disadvantage. Success-minded people have been observed to have blind spots in their thinking processes. Whereas, people who are not success-minded tend to see all kinds of obstacles, barriers, and roadblocks in their paths, success-minded ones do not. Although they may be aware of their existence, they are seldom disturbed or discouraged by them.

Time

Developing a positive career philosophy also requries a special attitude toward time. As touched on in the previous chapter, time must be viewed as a friend, not an enemy. If you are given 24 hours to complete a job and half of that time has already elapsed, think in terms of there being 12 hours more, rather than the fact that you have lost 12 hours. Concentrate your energies on the present and use the past and future as guidelines. Tactfully avoid the company of those whose thoughts dwell heavily on what used to be, or how things will be in the future. Their advice and counsel too often will lack the benefit of a realistic overview; i.e., an inability to make a sober and comprehensive analysis of how things are under existing circumstances.

Competion

Competition is the *sine qua non* of any business or profession. Without it, growth of any kind is almost impossible. "The road without obstacles doesn't go anywhere" is a saying which captures the role played by competition. On whatever level people compete with each other, there will be those who thrive on it and others who abhor it. Nevertheless, it is out there and must be confronted in proportion to an individual's ability to cope with it. The positive approach should never allow a person to be dissuaded from entering a particular field because of the existing competition. If anything, it should constitute a challenge.

Courage

The man who never made a mistake never made anything! Certain members of the older generation are forever implanting the element of failure in the minds of the younger generation. Most young men and women, naturally, have an ample supply of personal courage—the courage to *be*. If left to their own devices, they would make a whole raft of mistakes. It is that older generations, who compulsively endeavor to spare them the pain and suffering of such mistakes, give them advice on how to avoid them. Among the elders, fortunately, there are some voices which encourage them to try, experiment, experience things for themselves, make mistakes, and have the courage to say, pick up a phone and make that call, write that letter, or get on a bus, plane, or train anytime your career is at stake. But, "What if I call and the position is filled—what if I write and they don't answer—what if I get there and someone else was hired?" So, the position was filled, they didn't answer your letter, and someone else was hired. So what? Your total loss included a coin for the telephone, a postage stamp, and bus, train, or plane fare—not a very large investment when it comes to your future and the rest of your life. Anytime you are able to transform your thoughts about a career into action, it takes courage and involves risk. A positive career philosophy must possess such courage and take such risks.

Flexibility

Although many young people enter a career with a positive philosophy, they often become terribly disappointed when it fails to materialize. After all, a career choice is, at best, a well-thought out guess. A healthy career philosophy must always stand ready to have its course interrupted, altered, or terminated by fate or circumstances. A surprisingly large number of people have had their careers disturbed because of ill health or financial embarrassment and, to their own amazement, reestablished themselves in completely new careers with considerable success. None of this would have been possible had they lacked the ability to adapt to change. In short, psychological flexibility was their saving grace.

Self-Worth

With all due respect to such universal values as honesty, humility, and sincerity, *never give any information about yourself that can be construed negatively.* Your chances of establishing and maintaining a viable career will be significantly greater if you refrain from giving others ammunition that can be used against you. Somehow, people seem to have a keener eye for what is wrong than for what is right—the negative rather than the positive. Too often, our nonverbal behaviors are dead give-aways. It is one thing to look bored, anxious, or annoyed, but quite another to confirm in verbally. Having learned this lesson, many successful people have developed the ability to substitute unnecessary negative remarks about themselves with periods of positive silence or affirmative eye contact. Make it a point the next time you hear yourself on the verge of saying something negative about yourself to *stop*, rethink the thought, and either say something positive or lapse into a few seconds of that positive silence behind some affirmative eye contact.

Self-pity

The temptation to think you are the only one having a difficult time trying to decide upon a career can be a serious drawback. Often all it takes to straighten you out is a few candid discussions with other members of your peer group. You will very quickly discover that what you are going through is not unique. To varying degrees, they are going through the same thing.

Just finding out that the way you have been feeling is perfectly normal can spare your nerves considerable unrest and aggravation. A positive approach is frequently a shared one, taking its strength and nourishment from the exchange of information through interpersonal communication.

Interaction

Indispensible to a positive career philosophy is an open system of interacting with others. People aren't mind-readers. If you do not communicate what you think and feel to them, they are forced to rely on other less dependable means; such as, assumption, presumption, inference, implication, and even intuition. Placing people in this position, making them relate to you in these terms carries a high degree of risk. Figuratively speaking, noninteraction in the business and professional world is tantamount to nonexistence. Who you are, what you are, and what you promise to become may well depend on the extent to which you interact with others. Keeping your lines of communication open is a luxury you cannot afford to ignore, and your willingness to do it will become apparent in the next section of this chapter.

Devising a Plan of Action

Until now, we have been talking about the investigation of a career from a strictly theoretical standpoint. You have been asked to reflect on your personal needs and how they were arrived at through the influence of family, friends, and society. Some characteristics of a positive career philosophy were advanced, and you should now be ready to consider the more practical aspect of deciding on a career, that is, exactly how to go about making such and important decision.

Where to Look

There is no better place to find information about career offerings than a good library. Although students generally find what they are looking for, it is usually representative of only a small part of the information that actually exists there. The reason many of them are short changed in this way is because they do not know how to take full advantage of a library system. Entering the library with either a subject topic, book title, or author's name, the majority of students head for the catalogue files. If successful, they proceed to the check out section. If not, they leave the library, deluding themselves that they have made a thorough search of the literature; others seek out a librarian for help. To say the least, libraries have much more to give than most students realize. This certainly applies to the subject of careers. Many have a separate and distinct section or desk devoted exclusively to career opportunities. For example, you are aware that your school library probably contains:

1. Cross-reference directories (business and industry by geographic area, intrastate)
2. Dun and Bradstreet directories
   a. Million Dollar Directory
   b. Middle Market Directory
   c. Metalworking Directory
   d. Principal International Business Directory
3. State industrial directories (alphabetical, geographic by county and town, by product or service.
4. *Literary Market Place* (lists publishers for artists, writers, editorial workers).
5. City directories (have yellow, classified pages, as does the phonebook).

To help you further is *The Occupational Outlook Handbook*, put out by the Bureau of Labor Statistics. It contains enlarged descriptions of about 700 careers, the nature of the work, places of employment, qualifications and advancement, employment outlook, earnings, and working conditions. This handbook can be purchased from the Superintendent of Documents, Washington, D.C. 20402.

Many professions, trades, and vocations have compiled their own career information. If you are interested, you may write them directly.

Accounting

American Institute of Certified Public Accountants
666 Fifth Avenue
New York, N.Y. 10019

Advertising

American Association of Advertising Agencies
200 Park Avenue
New York, N.Y. 10017

Airline Stewards and Stewardesses

Airline Pilot Association
1329 E. Street, N.W.
Washington, D.C. 20036

Journalism

Sigma Delta Chi
Professional Journalistic Society
35 East Wacker Drive
Chicago, Ill. 60601

Business Schools

United Business Schools Association
1730 M Street, N.W.
Washington, D.C. 20036

Teaching

National Commission on Teacher Education
and Professional Standards, NEA
1021 16th Street, N.W.
Washington, D.C. 20036

Medicine

American Medical Association
535 North Dearborn Street
Chicago, Ill. 60610

Dentistry

Division of Career Guidance
Council on Dental Education
American Dental Association
211 East Chicago Avenue
Chicago, Ill. 60601

Law

Information Service
American Bar Association
115 East 60th Street
Chicago, Ill. 60637

The next place you might care to look is in some of your local newspapers. Each, generally, has an employment or classified section where you will find a wide variety of jobs listed—especially in the Sunday editions. Perusing them will give you some idea of the kinds of jobs that are available, the types of people being sought to fill them, and the salaries they are paying. In most cities, there is also a newspaper which is exclusively devoted to civil service positions. It lists the tests which applicants can take and when they are being given.

Having made a serious survey of the information available to you in your school or local public libraries, as well as having scanned your local newspaper's want ads for several weeks, you should have gotten some idea of the kinds of work a great many people are doing for a living. Whether any of them would interest you may still need to be decided. In any case, you have taken the first step in investigating a career—you have looked.

People You Should Communicate With

There are four kinds of people associated with any business or profession: (1) vocational or guidance counselors, (2) people currently working in the field, (3) people retired from the field, and (4) people in the business of getting other people jobs. Employment agencies provide you with a different perspective of the particular career in which you are interested.

Vocational or guidance counselors have information about the career you may have in mind. But unless a person has actually worked in a field, the possession of any information regarding it must be considered as "knowledge about," or second-hand knowledge. Personal experience derived from having been in a business or profession is "knowledge of acquaintance," or, first-hand knowledge. Thus, the majority of vocational and guidance counselors can be said to have "knowledge about." If one of them should suggest nursing as a career, chances are they have never assisted at a surgical operation, attended to the medical needs of a terminal patient, or given someone an injection of Vitamin B-12. The information about nursing they are familiar with was probably gleaned from various source materials at their disposal. Consequently, any emotional insight they might have concerning the career is through inference. By definition, *inference* is a statement about the unknown based upon the known. As you must be aware, vocational and guidance personnel have at their disposal an enormous amount of career data (booklets, manuals, encyclopedias, directories). Although the services of such professional assistance can be of inestimatable help, you must be conscious of the fact that their help is predominantly of an objective nature. They cannot tell you what it *feels like* to be a doctor, lawyer, accountant, police officer, or watchmaker. But telling you what it feels like to be an architect may not be what they are there for. They more than adequately fulfill their professional responsibility to you by apprising you of the field-related information at their disposal. But how important is it for you to know about the *experiential* side—the *emotional* side of a career? Perhaps greater than you think.

Face-to-face communication with someone currently in the field often provides that emotional supplement found missing from many vocational and guidance sessions. A visit with a neighborhood dentist in an active and ongoing dental office will provide you with another kind of career insight. The feedback you will get may include the odors and sounds dentists are exposed to all day, the physical activities involved in the particular branch of dentistry you find interesting, the types of people who frequent dental offices, the hours they keep, and (perhaps) the things they complain about. Granting that you could read about these characteristics of a career in dentistry on a printed page somewhere, it is not the same as being on the spot, experiencing through your own senses. Contrary to what you might think, a great many dental practitioners will take time out of their practices to advise a young man or woman planning to enter the field. While there are certainly those who will refuse to see you, there are a good number of dentists whose humanitarianism far outweighs their desire to make money.

In whatever career you think you might be interested, make it a point to personally communicate with someone in it. If they will allow you, tape the conversation so that you can listen to it several times under less distracting circumstances and digest its possible value. Be very observant during the interview. Notice how the person is dressed, whether they have a happy or sad look on their face, watch how they interact with others in person or on the telephone, determine whether the surroundings appear stressful or calm. In short, absorb all the information you can verbally, nonverbally, and vocally. Most important of all is that you come to the interview prepared with a list of questions. Sit down the night before and patiently think through any of the things about the career you do not understand or about which you are confused. Don't be afraid that you will ask a stupid question. The only stupid question is often the one that *isn't* asked! The question you ask, while it might seem stupid to you, could be extremely relevant in the eyes of the experienced individual. Don't limit your interviewing to just one or two people. The more, the better. After communicating with several members of a particular field, you will find yourself in a position to draw a few tentative conclusions both about the field and the people in it. Whether your conclusions are accurate or not will have to wait until you have the benefit of your own experience on which to base them.

Retired people have a special advantage—they don't have to worry about being fired or reprimanded for what they say. Consequently, they are inclined to be refreshingly candid about the field they are retired from. For this very reason, it is imperative that anyone interested in a career speak with some of its elder statesmen.

One of the most unforgivable crimes any society can commit is to waste the wisdom and experience of its retired citizens. Some may no longer be able to run and catch the 8:15 bus or train to the office, work a full 8-hour day without resting, or quickly express their thoughts, but they often possess the "gift of wisdom." Because they are no longer caught up in the little things, they are able to put their finger on what is important and what is not important.

Those retired from business and professional life seem to enjoy giving advice to those who will take the time to listen. This characteristic could work heavily in your favor. If you could arrange several interviews with retired people having specialized backgrounds in your field of interest, do it. Their names and addresses can usually be gotten from the professional organizations or unions to which they once belonged. You will find most of them extraordinarily warm and receptive to your request for a personal interview. Again, go prepared with questions written up beforehand. Bear in mind, when formulating your questions, that people who are retired are no longer struggling up the ladder of success. They now have that distinctive benefit which comes from hindsight. Their past might well make up bits and pieces of your future. During the interview, be patient and let the person you are interviewing talk. Remind yourself that the reason you are there is to learn from *their* experience, and not primarily to voice your own experience.

Finally, the people with whom you might consider communicating are those whose business it is to find and place you in a suitable position. It is important for you to remember whenever dealing with a private employment agency that it is a profit-making business. In some cases, you will be required to sign a legal contract before they send you out on a job or interview. Read every word before you sign, ask questions freely about anything you don't understand and, if need be, indicate that you would like to take the document home and read it over carefully. If they object, you might have just cause to wonder why. In short, before signing, make perfectly sure that your interpretation of what the contract says agrees with their interpretation.

To make sure an employment agency is reliable, ask if it is licensed and bonded, a member of the National Employment Association, and adheres to a code of ethics with copies available to clients. Also find out who pays the fee (if there is one), you or the employer, and the terms of paying it. Although state employment offices may not be as useful as you would like, they are free. However, whether you should communicate with people in private or state employment agencies, be as careful as you can to insure that your understanding of the job or position they are talking about is the same as theirs. Terms such as sales trainee, field representative, or assistant managers may involve duties quite different from what you might expect. Phrases like "rapid advancement, adjustable hours, liberal benefits, and interesting work" could take on an entirely different meaning from an employer's point of view. Make it apparent to whomever you speak that communicating clearly is one of your main concerns. This will usually set a positive tone for the communication to follow.

Getting Tested

There is divided opinion as to the value of testing when it comes to evaluating an individual's suitability for a career. Some rely heavily on test scores, whereas others come close to regarding them as a waste of time. Between these extremes, however, moderately oriented advisors and counselors use testing as but one of several methods of measuring characteristics or abilities.

Intelligence Tests

Intelligence tests have, for some time, been the object of very heated and lively debates among educators and members of Parent-Teacher Associations. One faction consisted of those wanting Intelligence Tests to be done away with entirely, the other wanting them preserved but the scores disclosed only to those parents or guardians wanting to know them. Persuasive arguments exist on both sides of the issue. Traditionally, the IQ Test is designed to measure how well you can read, write, work with numbers, and solve problems. It also measures what you can learn by determining how well you can do what you have learned, so far. Only by some far-reaching inference does it measure such human qualities as loyalty, sincerity, honor, respect, consideration for others, courage, or humility. Again, the question of what makes an individual happy and content in a career must be raised. Does competence alone guarantee these typically human goals? Perhaps it is what intelligence testing "doesn't test" that makes the difference between success and failure. The controversy is far from being settled and, until it is, those redeeming qualities inherent in it should be taken advantage of. Treat your I.Q. as but another indicator of your potential.

Personality Testing

Personality testing is another method of getting a picture of how you relate to others and how you behave when faced with problems. Because careers could be grouped into three classes—those in which you work with people, those in which you work with ideas, and those in which you work with things, the group you prefer is partially determined by the kind of person you are—your personality. As with IQ testing, personality testing is not a pure science. All it provides the subjects being tested is a series of generalizations or clues as to how they would think or act in a variety of situations. Coming away from such testing with labels like introvert, extrovert, or ambivert—inner or other directed—could, at times, be misleading in susceptible people. Let's assume that someone was given a battery of personality tests and told that he or she was an introvert. If such a person were to accept the label of introvert as fact, it could, conceivably, establish a misleading psychological base line from which subsequent behavior would follow. This is not to say, however, that personality testing is valueless. It could be extremely valuable as long as the person being tested does not expect from the procedure that which it cannot deliver, that is, a scientifically precise and infallible analysis of his or her personality. Thus, entering into this or any other kind of testing situation must be accompanied by a realistic assessment of its worth and a reasonable expectation of what it can do for you. Armed with such a perspective, you might want to know about still another testing procedure.

Interest Inventory Test

The Interest Inventory Test is designed to help you discover your line of interest. This type of test gives you an opportunity to see what you like as you go about comparing many activities and selecting the one that appeals to you most. Once you discover your area of interest, your ability can be checked more specifically and be related to the career for which it is most suited.

It is quite possible that you have already had several different jobs which might suggest a hidden interest. List on a sheet of paper every job you ever had, whether or not you were paid to do it. Rank them according to how much pleasure or satisfaction you derived from each one. Here is an example of a graduate student's responses based upon an uninterrupted progression upward from grade school through a graduate program of study.

___5___ Sold popcorn and peanuts at carnivals and fairs.

___4___ Worked as a clerk in a country general store.

___6___ Photographer's assistant.

___10___ Secretary in a claims department for an insurance company.

___8___ Checker in a supermarket.

___7___ Secretary of Dean of Students in college.

___3___ Secretary of head of graduate department.

___9___ Secretary of a vice-president in an import–export firm.

___2___ Choral conductor in church.

___1___ Church soloist.

On being questioned as to what characteristics numbers 1–2–3 had in common, she said, "They all dealt with esthetic man on a personal level" and had music as a common denominator. Numbers 8–9–10 she found impersonal in nature and dealt with "corporate man."

Here, in marked contrast, are the responses of an adult male who, at age 40, returned to complete his college education. Carefully read the jobs he has had and see whether you can decipher his core area of interest.

___12___ shoe shine boy

___18___ sold newspapers on a corner

___14___ worked as a clerk in several big department stores

___2___ counselor at camps for several summers

___20___ plumber's helper

___6___ drove delivery truck

___15___ artist's model

___5___ drove taxi cab

___9___ laborer in steel mill

___17___ short order cook

___3___ bartender

___13___ bouncer in bar and grill

___16___ assistant on the road to salesman of children's clothing

___10___ waiter in pizzeria

___1___ master of ceremonies

___11___ barber

___19___ door-to-door salesman of encyclopedias

___7___ laborer digging cesspools

___21___ worker in ski pants factory

___4___ masseur in health club

Let's look at numbers: 1 (master of ceremonies), 2 (camp counselor), and 3 (bartender). What do they have in common? All are characterized by a one-to-many situation, a situation in which the subject exerts complete control over both the job activity and the other people involved, a state of independence. Numbers 19 (door-to-door salesman), 20 (plumber's helper), and 21 (worker in a ski-pants factory) seem to possess a diametrically opposite common denominator. All are highly regimented and involve taking orders from an immediate superior.

Do you think having this many different jobs is unusual for someone who has never really found an area of interest? Question some of your friends and relatives about the different jobs they have had in their lives. See if those they enjoyed the most eventually led them to a business or profession possessing similar qualities. This brings to mind another consideration when discussing a person's area of interest–aptitude testing.

Aptitude Test

An aptitude test, sometimes called a prognostic test, measures your ability or capacity to learn, with training, certain skills or knowledge. Many groups, as well as schools, use standardized aptitude tests. These include tests for one's ability to acquire skill in art, clerical work, mathematics, music, reading, and speaking a foreign language. An aptitude test cannot predict success or failure in any subject. All it can do is show whether a person has the ability to succeed with training and desire.

> *Have you ever taken any of these tests? If you have, in a paragraph or two, describe your reaction to them. Then compare your responses with those of a classmate who also took the test.*

It should, at this point, be blatantly obvious that testing alone cannot and should not be used as the sole basis for anyone deciding upon a career. Returning for a moment to something that was said in the section dealing with your developing a positive career philosophy, you must perceive yourself as a gatherer, sifter, synthesizer, and interpreter of information. Although you should remain open to influences from several directions, in the final analysis, it is *you* who must make the decision. These tests are but one source of such influence.

Sensing a Career

Practically every business or profession is located somewhere–office buildings, industrial parks, professional centers, and so forth. It is in such places as these that members of any given field can be observed working independently or in concert. It is one thing to read about a career in a book, booklet, or pamphlet—a career requiring that you spend the next 25 or 30 years of your life in a hospital, research laboratory, or a plant in which they manufacture nuts and bolts—but quite another to conduct an on-the-spot visit, to *sense* it. Anyone entertaining thoughts about a career in medicine, journalism, plastics, architecture, publishing, oceanography, or farming should make it a point to visit several places where people engaged in such careers ply their trade, craft, or art.

Words, at best, are poor substitutes for the information brought to you by your senses. Take the characteristic smell found in most hospitals, lumber yards, factories where they manufacture automobiles, plastics, or leather goods. No verbal description in a career booklet can compare with actually being there. Then there are the visual, auditory, and tactile experiences associated with each career. It is not wise to casually assume you will be able to handle such sense experiences without checking them out beforehand. If you are wondering how to do it, don't. All it usually takes is a telephone call or a letter indicating your interest in the field and your desire to visit the premises. Properly worded requests are infrequently denied serious young men and women. Bear in mind, however, that granting such invitations by business and professional establishments must be at *their* convenience, not yours.

In the event an internal on-the-spot "sensing" is not possible, be prepared to accept an alternative; that is, sensing its external environment. You will be surprised how much can be learned about what is going on inside an organization by observing it from the outside. Such things as its architecture, size, number, and kinds of people going in and out, and location are all nonverbal clues to the quality of life in that particular career. Naturally, in those cases where a firm had nothing whatever to do with the external appearance of the building they occupy, its architecture should not be used as an indicator—unless, of course, they chose it initially for its appearance.

Have you ever been invited to a party at an address that was completely unfamiliar? After wandering around for awhile in a strange neighborhood, you finally find the correct building number. From the outside, you get the immediate impression that the inside will be weird and the people giving the party even weirder. Why? Just because the doorman looked like Herr Doctor Frankenstein's servant, Igor, the lawns and hedges surrounding the building were completely disheveled, the walk leading up to the entrance was broken in several places, and the area was poorly lighted? Yes, it is quite possible that a set of external indicators like these could easily prejudice you against the inside. Although it is perfectly reasonable to expect the apartment of the people giving the party to be immaculate and the people themselves charming hosts, the fact that they would chose to live in such a building does say something about them. Here, it is necessary to say that the external appearance of anything should never be used as an exclusive indicator of its internal character. It should, however, be some sort of an indicator.

Sensing any career in which you find yourself interested is a "must." You dare not be guided exclusively by what you read or what others tell you.

Make it your business to visit places where the career can be observed in progress, where people are engaged doing what you may one day find yourself doing.

Decision-making Checklist

Thus far, this chapter has helped you investigate your career needs, the environmental factors exerted upon you by family, friends, and society, the elements of a positive career philosophy, as well as devise a plan of action. Taken together, the information and insights you have gleaned should enable you to answer the following questions:

1. What is the specific job title you are interested in?
2. If there is a job or career description, have I read it?
3. Does a job in this career project growth and lead to greater specialization?
4. What kind of training is offered?
5. What kind of hours will I have to put in?
6. What are the fringe benefits (vacations, holidays, sick days, health insurance, pension, savings, and life insurance programs)?
7. After the initial training period, what learning opportunities are available? (in-service, workshops, tuition plan)
8. How are promotion and advancement determined?
9. Are the criteria for evaluation clearly stated in writing?
10. Who does the evaluating and how often?
11. Will the evaluations be discussed with me?
12. How stable is the field?
13. Is the field expanding or shrinking—and how fast?

These are but a few of the more important questions to which you should know the answers before you proceed to the next stage—preparing and sending in a résumé. And, to test just how well you have investigated a potential career, consider performing this classroom exercise.

Name of Exercise: Career Probe

Purpose: To discover how well a student has researched a particular career.

Procedure:

Step 1. Each member of the class is to either be assigned or to choose a career to be researched. The objective will be to become sufficiently informed about a specific career that practically any reasonable question pertaining to it will be answerable.

Step 2. After a period of time has been allotted in which to gather the necessary information, students will alphabetically be called upon to make their presentations to the class. The time limit for each career should be from 8 to 12 minutes.

Step 3. As each speaker's presentation concludes, all members of the class should feel free to fire questions about that career at the speaker. In a way, the point of this exercise is to try to "stump the speaker."

Step 4. After every student has made a presentation, a group discussion should take place in which the value of the exercise should be discussed in relation to the investigation of a career.

Building a Résumé

The word résumé comes from the French and means "summary." In more colloquial terms, a résumé is your personal advertisement, a collection of words arranged in a special way which, when read by a prospective employer, conjures up a reasonable facimile of you. You have two options when it comes to a résumé: You can build your own, or have one prepared for you. Because most people have an emotional investment in the preparation of a résumé, they have difficulty doing it. As a result, a number of firms have recently sprung up who will build you a résumé for a fee. All they require from anyone who wants a résumé built is *information*. They will do the rest. Without ever seeing you, hearing the sound of your voice, or shaking your hand, one of these résumé-writing firms will give birth to an individual solely on the basis of the information they are given. Whereas many of these services make genuine and often successful attempts to be creative and to capture distinctive qualities of the person being described, there is a tendency for a number of them to take on an assembly-line quality.

If it is at all possible, you should try to build your own résumé. Why? Because you, better than anyone else, know the message you want to convey—not just the more obvious message concerning names, dates, and places, but the deeper one tied in with how you think and feel. One of the major stumbling blocks toward achieving this end is finding the right words. Although a number of books are readily available to provide you with a suitable résumé outline, what they generally are weak in providing is that personal touch that makes the résumé distinctively yours. To illustrate one of the major reasons for this tendency, here is a list of positive action words commonly used in the commercial preparation of résumés:

Capacity	Competence	Successful
Maturity	Ability	Capable
Effectiveness	Capability	Competent

Qualified	Performance	Trained
Experienced	Expanding	Organized
Well-educated	Developing	Implemented
Stable	Enlarging	Coordinated
Productive	Specialist	Leadership
Proficient	Demonstrated	Proven
Knowledgeable	Vigorous	Demonstrated
Significant	Profitable	Creative
Responsible	Thorough	Iniated
Potential	Pertinent	Established

Another characteristic of commercially prepared résumés is that they have been charged by certain members of management as being *too* professional and lacking style—they tend to stick out like sore thumbs in a pile of résumés. Some personnel departments have been known to give less credence to professionally prepared résumés because they suggest that the person was too lazy to prepare his own. Care should be taken here not to interpret these criticisms as a basis for avoiding having your résumé prepared commercially. They should simply alert you to the fact that such weakness in a résumé is to be guarded against if possible. Those who prepare professional résumés are usually very flexible and quite willing to do whatever you want. All they require is that you know what *you* want.

Building your own résumé requires that you become aware of certain factors. To illustrate this, imagine that you are the director of personnel in a large corporation. Your main function is to see that its work force needs are met. Every morning, your desk greets you with a stack of résumés from young men and women who feel they are qualified to become part of your organization. It is your job to screen them and decide which ones warrant a personal interview. In all probability, you will quickly reject those résumés that are not clear, readable, and informative. As a busy executive of a large corporation, you cannot afford to spend too much time figuring out what an applicant is trying to say. On the average, any résumé you pick up has about one minute to make a positive impression. If it fails to do this, you pass it by.

Most résumés consist largely of names, dates, and places that reflect your past and present activities arranged in chronological order. It takes considerable effort and creativity to present such information in an interesting and distinctive manner. However, there are aspects of a résumé that allow the writer to emerge with greater force. One such place is where the question, "Tell me about yourself" is asked. Here are a few examples of how students from one eastern university handled it.

Example 1:

In describing myself, the first thing that comes to mind is my independence. I am a very independent person—very capable of functioning on my own. I am a responsible person—once I know what my goals are and what my objective is. I work toward it diligently. Once I become involved in something, I give my all to it. I am a hard worker. Sensitive is also a good word to describe me. I'm open to other people and appreciate when they are open with me. I like to be with people and relate to them.

Example 2.

I find myself to be very witty and imaginative. I have a creative mind, which I would like to use in your agency. I am very agreeable and flexible. I am very open and easy to get along with. While no one is perfect, I do have my faults. I do catch on quite fast when a new task approaches me. I am always willing to try something once. I enjoy challenges and always invite them. In my opinion, I feel I have a very good sense of humor. I feel that I learn something new everyday which helps heighten my knowledge and awareness.

Example 3.

I am what I value. I value intelligence and common sense, open mindedness and determination, love, and sensitivity or logic. If I'm to assume that I am anything, it's that I'm diverse. I value change and uncertainty so that I'm both as uncertain of who I am as of what I might be.

Example 4.

I am a very independent person who does not like to be told what to do. I am sort of a mixture of introvert and extrovert. Around people I do not know well, I am rather introverted and keep to myself; but among close friends, I am extremely extroverted and a leader at times. Also, I find that when competing in sports, I am very extroverted. Maybe this is why I enjoy sports so much. I am a responsible person and am dependable. I have a penchant for neatness. I enjoy working with children. I am an animal lover. Physical work appeals more to me than sitting behind a desk. I enjoy traveling and visiting places I've never been to before.

Example 5.

Considering myself a realist, I thrive on creativity and critical thinking. I'm a believer in a modern attitude (although some people of the past centuries held it) that man can shape the future, and make things come true by exercising control over events. I'm a moody individual who manages to get along fairly well with others. Basically, I'm serious and independent. I'm usually well organized in my study and work habits and am generally neat and accurate when working; moreover, my persistence and dedication to complete whatever job I am assigned has, in the past, benefited both my employer and myself.

Having experienced working under pressure, I've been constantly complimented on my resourcefulness, patience, and uninhibitedness (free from the usual social and psychological restraints) In conclusion, my foremost features are self-assertiveness and ingenuity.

Write several paragraphs of your own in response to the question: TELL ME ABOUT YOURSELF. Compare it with the samples just given. In what ways is it similiar/different?

Nonverbal Aspects

Aside from what a résumé actually tells a prospective employer in words, it also communicates without words. In fact, most résumés begin communicating before a word is read. Such immediately obvious things as: (1) the color and texture of the paper on which it is written, (2) whether it is handwritten, printed, xeroxed or typed, (3) the number of pages, (4) how the material is organized, and (5) its overall neatness could easily prejudice a reviewer from the outset. Be assured that any employer or personnel manager who has strong feelings about the importance of neatness will rarely, if ever, take the time to read the content of a résumé that is sloppy, unintelligibly written by hand covered with thumbprints. It is not uncommon to find, after awhile, those who review résumés develop certain idiosyncrasies—specific notions about what a résumé should or should not be like from a nonverbal aspect.

Contrary to the beliefs held by many young men and women, the impact of a résumé is not always based on an individual's ability to type 100 wpm, operate a giant computer, or drive a 12-mule team. Whereas any of these or a number of other skills could certainly be the sole basis for hiring someone, those nonverbal aspects of a résumé should never be underestimated or ignored. Why do you think so many firms require a photograph to accompany a résumé? Why should how you look have anything to do with your ability to perform the job for which you are applying? Of course, if the position is one in which appearance constitutes the larger part of the basis for hiring (actor, model, etc.), it makes better sense. But, what about those jobs in which *how a person* looks plays only a minor role? Is it possible that many employers, while they insist that an applicant possess certain skills, also harbor the psychological need to like them nonverbally? The desire to meet someone face-to-face before hiring them seems to suggest this. Would you hire someone with an outstanding résumé sight-unseen? Occasionally, a *pseudoaffective* state exists between applicants and their résumés. As *pseudo* means false and *affective* refers to the emotions, a pseudoaffective state is one in which the picture of an individual conjured up by a résumé differs markedly from how that person comes across in person. It is not unusual for a firm to get very excited about a résumé and then be terribly disappointed during a personal interview. The reverse can also happen; a lukewarm résumé is occasionally heavily outweighed by a dramatic and exciting personal interview. Thus, regardless of where your strengths lie, when building your résumé, make sure to take into consideration the potential impact of its nonverbal characteristics. It will give you an edge over competitive résumés.

Building Blocks

Résumés vary considerably with regard to their contents and layout. There doesn't seem to be a single "accepted format." From a practical standpoint, the résumé responsible for getting you the job is the acceptable one. Despite the fact that there are a number of job-specific rśeumés from which you can choose and several different approaches taken by them (e.g., chronological approach, functional approach, informal approach, imaginative approach), you will find that the building blocks–the elements or components from which they are constructed–differ only slightly from one another. Essentially, they embrace the following items variously arranged. You will observe that, in some cases, synonyms for these terms have been placed in brackets.*

General Data
Job objective
  (occupational objective, occupational goal, position objective)
Experience.
  (chronology, employment details, employment history, work experience, employment highlights, background, employment record)
Education
  (training, qualifications, credentials)
Personal data
Military service
  (military record)
Outside activities
  (hobbies, affiliations, sports, service, other accomplishments, extracurricular activities, personal interests
Licenses
  (certification, accreditation)
References
  (recommendations, affidavits)
Physical limitations
  (health record–past/present)
Knowledge of foreign language
Salary range
Availability
Travel and relocation

*For further information and examples of a variety of résumé formats, see: *Résumés That Get Jobs: How to Write Your Best Résumé* (New York: Arco, 1976), 2nd ed.

Literary accomplishments
(published works, honor awards)
Special skills
(technical knowledge)

No matter how carefully you prepare your résumé so its words will convey *your* meaning, there is the standing risk that whoever reads it will invest them with *their* own meanings. At best, what you must hope for is a close approximation of meanings. As if this were not enough, a word could be construed differently when combined with other words. Because of this, you must select your words discretely so that their meanings will be ensured, regardless of who reads them. Avoid words that place you in a negative light. During the construction of your résumé, ask yourself constantly, "How does what I am saying relate to the position for which I am applying?" Words, like the stepping stones across a stream must lead to the job you want. A well-built résumé should do just that. So that you may see what a resume looks like, here is a sample:

Personal Résumé

JOHN VINCENT AHEARN, Jr.

Home Address:
401 West 11 Street
New York City, N.Y. 10045

Telephone:
[212]664-3201

PERSONAL DATA

Appearance:
5 feet 8 inches
174 lbs.

Marital Status:
Single-free to travel

Date and Place of Birth:
January 18, 1949, New York City, N.Y.

Military Status:
Honorable Discharge from U.S.M.C.

EDUCATION

Bachelor of Arts, Rutgers University, New Brunswick, New Jersey 80465 To be granted in June, 1977. Major in Marketing (B+ average), Minor in Journalism (B+ average), Emphasis on courses in salesmanship, advertising, product management, and communication.

Résumé (cont.)

CAREER OBJECTIVES

Hope to obtain a position with direct customer contact leading to a more responsible position in sales management. Prefer working for an organization in which customer service is a high priority.

WORK EXPERIENCE

Salesman (Summer 1970)
Braxtile's Swim Pool Company, 8824-09 Booner Lane, Chicago, Ill. 12573
Sold swimming pools by soliciting customers in the field and by phone. Earned over 2500 dollars in commissions under supervision of sales manager.

Sales Clerk (Worked evenings after school during 1968–1969 and 1969–1970)
Campus Mod Shop, 557 Main Street, Chicago, Ill. 12574
Sold men's furnishings and sporting clothes under the supervision of the store manager.

REFERENCES

Dr. Robert John Myers
Professor of Marketing
Putgers University
New Brunswick, New Jersey
(512) 887-2126

Mr. Jonathan Brenner
Sales Manager
Braxtile's Swim Pool Company
8824–09 Booner Lane
Chicago, Ill. 12573

Cover Letter

A cover letter should accompany every résumé. Running interference for you, it may create the first impression of your ability to communicate and may determine whether you are considered for employment. It may look something like this:

Acme Pharmaceutical Corporation
30001 Cunningham Plaza
Chicago, Ill. 30907

Dear Sirs:

I understand from reading the trade journal that you have just opened a new territory in the Northwest. I have been successfully engaged in the sales of pharmaceuticals for the past 12 years and would very much like to represent your company.

I am well known in the field and have been instrumental in launching several sales campaigns which have met with enormous success. I am confident that, given the opportunity, I can do the same for you. I have a considerable number of faithful accounts which will follow me.

I plan to be in the Chicago area the last week in October and would certainly appreciate the opportunity to discuss how my employment could be an invaluable asset to the Acme Pharmaceutical Corporation. Enclosed you will find my résumé containing any background information you might wish to know.

I shall look forward to hearing from you and a most productive meeting of the minds when we talk in October.

Very truly yours

Warren L. Magoun, Jr.

Enc.: résumé

From such a cover letter, a potential employer can learn many things about you. Design your letter so that it keeps his needs and your ability in mind. Whereas all this may seem elementary, it is remarkable how many mistakes are made in such employment correspondence. As a safeguard against your making some of these mistakes here is another checklist:

1. Is the letter brief and clear?
2. Have you spelled the employer's name or the name of the firm correctly?
3. Is the person's title to whom you are writing written properly?
4. Is your opening remark not more than five lines?
5. Is it based on fact, rather than opinion?
6. Have you enlarged a little on one but not more than three phases of your experience?
7. Have you indicated that a résumé is attached or enclosed?
8. Have you stated one but not more than two abbreviated examples from your résumé?
9. In the abbreviations from the résumé have you retained the most significant facts?
10. Have you asked for the job and told the employer you wish to work for him/her?
11. Have you asked for an appointment?
12. Have you used simple, direct language and correct grammar and, of course, typed it neatly on standard-size white paper (8½ x 11)?

Telephone Follow-up

By now your cover letter and résumé have been mailed, hopefully delivered, and read by an employer or personnel manager. Two weeks have passed and you haven't heard a word; your anxiety is getting the best of you. Should you write again, call on the telephone, or tax your patience further? A discrete telephone call is the recommended course of action under these circumstances.

Although we spend countless hours on the telephone, many of us lack good telephone technique It is the exceptional student who can remember ever taking any course in public school, high school, college, or graduate school in which fundamental telephone techniques were taught. In the event you cannot include yourself among those few who were taught how to communicate over the telephone, the following advice should be very helpful.

Your voice is one of the most important aspects of any telephone conversation. Unlike a face-to-face conversation, which gives you the benefit of the other person's nonverbal behavior, it is completely absent in a telephone exchange. If, according to psychologist, Albert Mehrabian, how a person looks during a conversation constitutes approximately 55 per cent of its impact, you will have to make a substantial compensation for this loss through the use of your voice. You must remember that on the telephone, your voice is *you*. With a little effort and practice, you can develop what the telephone comapny calls a personal interest tone. The following words serve to describe the difference between a good telephone voice and a poor one.

The voice with a "personal interest tone" is:

Pleasant
Cordial
Cheerful
Interested
Helpful
Sincere
Warm

The voice that lacks a "personal interest tone" is:

Expressionless
Mechanical
Indifferent
Impatient
Inattentive
Repelling

One way to find out how your voice sounds to others is to listen to it played back on a tape recorder. Be aware, however, that if you use one of those very inexpensive models, it will probably give you a misleading impression of how your voice really sounds. Asking friends, "How do I sound on the telephone?" is not usually much help either. While they may describe your voice as normal, alright, pleasant, OK, or natural, it is seldom described in any detailed manner. Then there are such factors as time, place, and circumstances which may also affect their judgment of how you sound. Generally speaking, voice descriptions are predominantly influenced by the emotions—not the intellect. The exception to this is when a voice is being analyzed, evaluated, or diagnosed by a speech expert.

You can learn to control several of your vocal qualities and, by so doing, significantly improve your telephone voice. These include such elements as your speech-speed, volume, pitch, rhythm and articulation. There is a climate of opinion among many communicologists that *people tend to feel more comfortable communicating with those whose speech pattern and vocal qualities most closely approximate their own.* Have you noticed that fast talkers are inclined to be annoyed by slow talkers, loud talkers by those who whisper, smooth talkers by those whose speech is jerky, those with high-pitched voices by those with low-pitched ones, and articulate individuals by those who are inarticulate. Needless to say, any one or a combination of these vocal differences could easily sabotage a telephone conversation—especially with a prospective employer you are trying to impress.

For a fuller realization of how people react to a strange voice, try this exercise in class.

Name of Exercise: Acoustic Stereotyping

Purpose: To become aware of the wide variety of personality traits people so readily assign to others exclusively on the basis of their voices.

Procedure:

Step 1. Prior to the date on which this classroom exercise is to be performed, the teacher should prepare five taped voices of people completely unfamiliar to the class. Preferably, there should be either three males and two female voices or, three female and two male.

Step 2. On the day of the exercise, the tape recorder should be centrally placed in the classroom and each student prepared with a pencil and paper.

Step 3. On a sheet of paper, students should copy the following:

	Voice 1	Voice 2	Voice 3	Voice 4	Voice 5
Age					
Intelligence					
Temperament					
Education					

Step 4. After all five voices are played to the class and each responded to according to the outline presented in Step 3, an open discussion should follow in which comparisons are made of the responses to each voice. Speculation is to be encouraged as to why certain voices elicited different stereotyped reactions.

Step 5. All members of the class are invited to relate situations or experiences in which either their voices were completely misjudged or where they have grossly misjudged the voices of others.

Given this insight as to how much can be gleaned from the voice of a person making a simple telephone call, here are some final hints for you to bear in mind when you follow-up your résumé with a telephone call:

1. When making your call, get on with it.
2. Tell whomever answers the phone the name of the person to whom you wish to speak.
3. If you don't know the person's name or who might be in charge of the business you're calling about, generally state the nature of your call so that you can be transferred to the proper office.
4. To the next person who answers, give your name in the same breath as your request to speak to a specific person. If your name alone is not sufficient identification, add your affiliation: "This is Mr. Herbert Lowe of Makuwell Pharmaceutical Company. May I speak to Mr. Jacoby?"
5. If you have reached the party to whom you want to speak, plunge immediately into the purpose of your call. Repeat your name only if his or her greeting gives you the feeling that you have not been announced.
6. Avoid small talk and thereby show that you respect the other person's time.
7. Try for a personal interview. Do not give in to a telephone interview.
8. If a prospective employer does try to interview you on the phone, give only enough information so as not to offend. Suggest that you would like to see him or her personally. Suggest two dates that you will be in the area. Ask which would be more convenient. Do not overtalk. Keep throwing the ball back to the prospective employer.
9. At all times during the conversation, remember to speak directly into the receiver, use the other person's name occasionally, listen carefully, speak clearly, adjust your speech speed and volume to that of the other party, have a pad and pencil ready in case you have to jot something down, be polite by using "thank you, I beg your pardon, yes, and I would be delighted," instead of some of the more common slang expressions such as "yep, nope, gottcha, and right on."

10. Use a quick windup sentence about what you want the other person to do, or what you're going to do. Then hang up gently.

Experience

There is no such thing as not having *any* experience. To be alive is to have experience. It is, therefore, nearly impossible for you to come to any decision about a career without experience. Granted that there are different types of experience, some more relevant than others, they all count toward one's collective experience. You will recall that this text is founded on the premise that organizations and professions do not exist in any real or material sense—only as people communicating with people having common interests and goals. Consequently, any experience you have dealing with people will provide you with a basis for dealing with them in the future. Regardless of the career you should decide upon, communicating with people will be part of it.

You have just finished reading a chapter dealing with the investigation of a career through communication. In all probability, many of the things that were mentioned you have either thought about or experienced. It may also have confirmed or denied various notions you have had about yourself in relation to the pursuit of a particular career. A productive way of bringing the chapter to a close is to talk about it in the light of those experiences you have brought to it. Here is a classroom exercise that makes this possible.

Name of Exercise: Career Clinic

Purpose: To get each member of the class to volunteer his or her experiences and ideas as they relate to the various sections of the chapter.

Procedure:

Step 1. Members of the class should sit in a large circle.

Step 2. In sequence, an open discussion should engage each of the following concepts:

a. Personal career needs.
b. Personal factors that have influenced each member of the class in terms of a career.
c. Ingredients of success.
d. Personal method of checking out a career.
e. Personal attitude toward résumés.
f. Personal problems assoicated with talking on the telephone.

Step 3. Exercise should end by extending any student an opportunity to ask the entire class a personal question pertaining to deciding upon or investigating a career.

SELF-EXAMINATION QUIZ

Having read this chapter, my answers to the following questions will reflect my understanding of its contents.

1. What motivates certain people toward one career and not another?

2. How and why do people often drift into fields that do not interest them?

3. What are the ingredients of a "positive career philosophy"?

4. How does one go about investigating a career?

5. What things should an individual know before deciding on a career?

6. What is a résumé, and how should it be drawn up?

7. What are some of the requirements for effective telephone communication?

8. How can the realization that other people share your hopes, fears, and frustrations with regard to a career be helpful?

Suggested Readings

Burnes, Alan, ed. *Jobs and the Color Barrier* (West Haven, Conn.: Urban American Service, Pendulum Press, 1969).

Career Job Guide (New York: National Educational Advertising Service, Inc., 1974).

Dumphy, Philip W., ed. *Career Development for the College Student* (Cranston, Ill.: Carroll Press, 1976).

Figgins, Ross, *Techniques of Job Search* (San Francisco, Calif.: Canfield Press, 1976).

Fregly, Bert, *How to Get a Job* (Palm Springs, Calif.: ETC, 1974).

Grunberg, Michael, ed. *Job Satisfaction* (New York: Halsted Press, 1976).

Kirby, W. S., and Patrick, Reardon, *Job Hunting Secrets and Tactics* (Chicago, Ill.: Follett, 1977).

Lembeck, Ruth, *Job Ideas for Today's Woman* (Englewood Cliffs, N.J.: Prentice-Hall, 1974).

McClure, Larry, *Career Education Survival Manual: A Guide Book for Career Educators and their Friends* (Salt Lake City, Utah: Olympus, 1975).

Powell, Randall C., *Career Planning and Placement for the College Graduate of the '70's* (Dubuque, Iowa: Kendall/Hunt, 1974).

Professional Career Tests (New York: Arco, 1975, 3rd ed.).

Waking, Edward, *Jobs in Communication.* (West Caldwell, N.J.: Lothrop Lee and Shepard, Division of Wm. Morrow & co., 1974).

WORK AREA FOR CHAPTER 3

Chapter 4

Surviving an Interview

Successful interviewing should seek to reduce surprise to a minimum.

MEMO

TO: Reader

FROM: Author

After reading this chapter, you should have a better understanding of:

1. . . . What the role of interviewing is in the business and professional world.

2. . . . Why an interview is multidimensional.

3. . . . Why so many people are deathly afraid of an interview.

4. . . . How you can prepare for an interview.

5. . . . Why qualified people often fail to get the position for which they were interviewed.

6. . . . What the basis is for fearing an interview.

7. . . . Why questions are so important in an interview.

8. . . . What relationship exists between perspective and perception to an interview.

9. . . . How the interview is used within the organization.

10. . . . What various phases are involved in an interview.

11. . . . Why different types of interviews exist.

12. . . . Why the differences between interviewer and interviewee are so valuable.

Chapter 4

Interviews frighten most people. The reason is probably fear of the unknown. Like taking an examination, starting a new job, or being promoted to a more responsible position, not knowing the questions or what will be expected of you beforehand can be extremely unnerving in a susceptable individual. Whereas most interviews, jobs, and advanced positions have certain characteristics that can be anticipated, they nevertheless have the reputation of generating a fair amount of anxiety in the average person. Experience has shown, however, that the more one is prepared, the less anxiety and apprehension tends to develop.

In the public mind, an interview is customarily regarded as a situation in which two people ask and answer each other's questions. Although this is fundamentally true, it has been found to be an oversimplification of what actually happens. Both the process of interviewing and the people involved have recently attracted the attention of some serious research. Among the questions that have been raised are: (1) Does the best-qualified person necessarily get the job? (2) Is there a psychological realtionship between a person's self-image and successful interviewing? (3) Does what you say, how you say it, or how you look when you say it carry the greatest weight in an average interview? (4) Can a person prepare for an interview much like one prepares for a role in a play?

Take question 3, for example. "Does what you say, how you say it, or how you look when you say it carry the greatest weight during an interview?" In 1974, the Western College Placement Association asked 114 representatives of companies from 17 industries to rate the importance in an interview. Using terms like *strong positive, positive, neutral, negative,* and *irrelevant,* the survey indicated that blouses, high heels, and stockings were considered positive; rated negative for men and women were sandals, shorts, and jeans. Perfume and jewelry were neutral.

Dr. Arthur Witkin, chief psychologist for an organization that does psychological testing for industry, cautions women not to look too visually provocative. He claims that it makes it difficult for the interviewer, male or female, to visualize them as an asexual job applicant. Athena Constantine, Director of University Placement and Career Services at Columbia University, gives men and women this advice, "If you are going to make a mistake, make a mistake on the side of being conservative." IBM's manager of corporate college relations, Wayne Dickert, warns job applicants not to dress so that their attire will detract from the interview.* Experts, in general, seem to stress neatness, a leaning in the conservative direction and an appearance which seems to suggest a readiness to "go to work" immediately. Overall, there is a consensus of opinion among interviewers that an applicant's dress plays an important role in job procurement. In short, the question of appearance has, along with a variety of similiar questions, provided a challenging foundation for the research now going on in this area.

If you were to look through the current literature dealing with the dynamics of interviewing, you would discover that, to a large extent, it is approached from a managerial or administrative point of view. This is not difficult to understand if one realizes that the majority of such field-related material is sponsored by management. A large number of corporations offer training programs in which trainees are given booklets or manuals from which they are instructed in the art of interviewing. Only incidentally is the role of being interviewed touched upon. Of course, from management perspective, this emphasis on the interviewer makes perfect sense. Where, then, does one learn the art of becoming a successful interviewee? This felt need has recently been met by a wide variety of college courses, magazine articles, and paperbacks. The role of the interviewee has come of age and no longer must take a backseat in an interview. Young men and women can now be groomed to enter an interview with self-esteem, courage, assertiveness, and dignity—not with the negative "hat-in-hand" attitude.

This chapter takes a holistic approach to the subject of interviewing. It subscribes to the belief that a successful interview is a synthesis—an interactive blending of personalities in which there is a meaningful sharing of information and intent. Whereas it is quite possible for either an interviewer or an interviewee to come away from an interview with a feeling of personal

*Dee Wedemeyer, "Dressing to pass the job interview," *New York Times*, April 27, 1977, p. C11.

success—to have achieved some private purpose, the truly successful interview should yield such a feeling from both parties. Borrowing again from the position that organizations do not actually exist in any material sense, only people with common interests and goals working together, this same concept can now be applied to an interview, that is, it does not exist in any material sense—only people, giving, and getting information from one another through the dynamics of communication.

More important than asking the right question or giving the right answer, surviving an interview requires an understanding of the interviewing process from both sides of a desk. Just as a good lawyer must be able to argue both sides of a case, so must anyone engaged in an interview be aware of the other person's position. Thus, in the pages to follow, while the interviewing experience will be looked at from several angles, one object will be paramount—that you survive it with distinction.

Interview-a-Phobia

Just as *photophobia* denotes a fear of light, *hydrophobia* a fear of water, and *claustrophobia* a morbid fear of being closed in, *interview-a-phobia* refers to a fear of being interviewed. With the exception of those individuals who are very secure in their jobs or who have an extremely high degree of self-confidence, the majority of people are frightened of being interviewed. Listed below are some of the most commonly held fears. Read them and place a circle around the number which most accurately reflects the extent to which it represents your own level of fear or apprehension:

1. I will be asked questions I cannot answer.

   0 +1 +2 +3 +4 +5

2. The interviewer will embarrass or humiliate me.

   0 +1 +2 +3 +4 +5

3. I won't get the job.

   0 +1 +2 +3 +4 +5

4. The interviewer will not like my appearance.

   0 +1 +2 +3 +4 +5

5. I will be cross-examined by the interviewer.

0 +1 +2 +3 +4 +5

6. I will be made aware of my own shortcomings.

0 +1 +2 +3 +4 +5

7. I will feel and behave in an extremely nervous manner.

0 +1 +2 +3 +4 +5

8. I will be made to take some kind of test (typing, shorthand).

0 +1 +2 +3 +4 +5

9. I will be offered too little money.

0 +1 +2 +3 +4 +5

10. I will be asked very personal questions.

0 +1 +2 +3 +4 +5

11. I will not make an intelligent impression.

0 +1 +2 +3 +4 +5

12. I will have to be in competition with many other people for the position.

0 +1 +2 +3 +4 +5

13. I will be caught in a lie about my past experience.

0 +1 +2 +3 +4 +5

14. I will sound overconfident.

0 +1 +2 +3 +4 +5

15. I will be kept waiting for a long time before the interview.

0 +1 +2 +3 +4 +5

16. The interview will be held in a very unfamiliar or uncomfortable place.

0 +1 +2 +3 +4 +5

17. The position will not turn out to be the same as the one that was advertised.

    0 +1 +2 +3 +4 +5

18. I will not have a good rapport with the interviewer.

    0 +1 +2 +3 +4 +5

19. I will undersell myself.

    0 +1 +2 +3 +4 +5

20. I will forget what I had planned to say.

    0 +1 +2 +3 +4 +5

Scoring Yourself:

By adding up the numbers you have circled, you will have your Interview-a-Phobia Index, 80–100 = Terrified; 60–79 = Very frightened; 40–59 = Apprehensive; 30–39 = Casual; 0–19 = Unconcerned.

How you scored on this set of questions can be very useful if you are psychologically ready to "learn from yourself." Your response to each question is a clue to your thoughts and feelings toward being interviewed. You should be particularly interested if you scored Terrified or Unconcerned. Contrary to what you might think, being unconcerned about an interview is almost as bad as being terrified. A normal healthy reaction to the thought of being interviewed is one of concern, of reasonable preoccupation with what will happen. Being terrified and unconcerned have the tendency to alienate you from the reality of an interview situation and, in its place, substitute a distorted reality. Both seriously reduce or eliminate the extent to which any meaningful communication occurs between interviewer and interviewee.

Depending on individual personality traits, most people would be inclined to score as Very Frightened, Apprehensive, or Casual on this quiz. A great deal would then depend on how these psychological states are transcribed into verbal, vocal, and nonverbal lines of communication. There are, for example, people who feel very frightened, apprehensive, or casual on the inside, but who present a somewhat different impression from the outside. One of the survival objectives associated with the idea of being interviewed is to disguise or cover up certain negative characteristics with positive ones. This, however, is not easily done with a trained and experienced interviewer. What, then, is the value of trying to prepare for an interview? Simply to raise your awareness of yourself in relation to the interview experience to a higher level. This accomplishment alone will reduce the fear of the unknown and that can make all of the difference.

Questions: The Heartbeat of an Interview

Take "the question" out of the interview and you have no interview. Questions reflect the objectives, course, intent, and character of any interview. By carefully noting the questions being asked by both the interviewer and interviewee, one can learn a great deal about the direction from which each is coming. To my mind, the question generally far outweighs the answer in importance in any interview. Here, now, to further heighten your self-awareness with regard to the dynamics of interviewing, are a battery of the more difficult questions commonly asked by interviewers. Without preparation, answer them as best you can in the spaces provided.

1. Tell me about yourself.

2. Why should I hire you?

3. What motivates you to put forth your greatest effort?

4. What are your greatest strengths and weaknesses?

5. How do you plan to achieve your career goals?

6. What do you expect to be earning in five years?

7. How do you think a friend or professor who knows you well would describe you?

8. How do you determine or evaluate success?

9. What subjects did you like best at school? Why?

10. How do you think a person's worth should be judged? By whom?

11. If you were hired for this job, what three things would concern you most (in the order of importance)?

12. What major problem have you encountered in your life and how did you handle it?

13. What are your short- and long-range goals?

14. What makes you think you will be happy in this job or career?

15. If you were confronted with a choice between a raise in salary and having a title conferred on you (vice-president, assistant sales manager), which would you choose? Why?

16. What qualities do you think a successful administrator, manager, supervisor should possess? Why?

It would come as a delightful surprise to most readers if the "correct" or "right" answers were to accompany these questions. Unfortunately, there are no fixed correct or right answers to them. The answers will vary to the same extent as the people involved with them vary. Just as *meaning*, not words, has been indicated to exist in people, correctness and rightness, not answers, exist in people. For argument's sake, take question 10: *How do you think a person's worth should be judged?* The correct or right answer will depend on the bias or leaning of the individual interviewer. Some would regard an answer stressing *motivation* as correct or right, another would stress *financial gains,* and still another would stress *reputation among one's peers.* Each is correct or right on the basis of a different set of criteria.

Perhaps one of the best methods of preparing oneself for these types of interview questions is to do some calculated generalizing about the nature of the work involved in the particular field and the kind of people who do it. There has always been speculation as to whether people are drawn to certain jobs or careers because of particular traits or whether they develop certain traits because of a specific job or career.

Although the practice of stereotyping has already been warned against in an earlier chapter, some discrete generalizing is recommended here. Picture yourself in a hypothetical interview for a position with an accounting firm. As a recent graduate in accounting anxious to get started in your career, you want to answer the interviewer's questions satisfactorily. In the form of this discrete generalizing, you could say the following to yourself:

1. Accounting demands exactness when dealing with figures. Therefore, I will make it a point to include in my answers information that reflects my concern for exactitude.
2. Because organizations are usually run according to tight schedules and demanding timetables, I will also load my answers with information suggesting a firm awareness and willingness to conform to meeting deadlines.
3. Realizing that such qualities as honesty and ethics are essential to the field of accounting, I will be sure to communicate to my interviewer examples of those character traits in me. In short, whatever job or career you are being interviewed for, make it your business to find out as much as you can about the attitudes, values, and beliefs held by the people in it. This should prepare you for some discrete generalizing.

To get your "generalizing muscles" in shape, here are six professions. Make three discrete generalizations about each.

1. Practice of medicine: ______________________________

2. Law: ______________________________

3. Engineering? ______________________________

4. Teaching: ______________________________

5. Artist? ______________________________

Compare your responses with those of your classmates.

Psychology of an Interview

Interviewing has been likened to a matching of wits, a dueling contest, and psychological warfare across a desk. One might even go so far as to label participants of an interview as "corporate actors" programmed to mouth certain words according to some organizational script drafted by a giant computer. A more conventional definition of an interview is advanced as, "A form of communication involving two parties, at least one of whom has a preconceived and serious purpose, and both of whom speak and listen from time to time.* Essentially, this definition captures the traditional elements found in most definitions. Of special importance is the fact that it conspicuously neglects to mention those nonverbal and paralinguistic elements so often crucial to an interview. It does, however, pinpoint the existence of a preconceived purpose harbored by one or both parties to an interview. Let us take a moment to talk about the personal background each person brings to an interview.

No one ever walks into an interview as a "blank slate"—completely without any preconceived attitudes, values, and beliefs. The sum of this information stored inside a person's head generally acts as a base line or starting point from which most interviews proceed. In such a context, an interview is a sort of matching game in which bits of information are compared and contrasted in search of compatability.

Take a simple bit of information concerning punctuality residing in the head of an interviewer and the absence of such a bit in the head of an interviewee. What do you think might be the consequences once the interview got under way? Naturally, the interviewer will, at some point, raise the question of punctuality and concern about employees arriving at work on time. The interviewee, in turn, will be hard pressed to understand why something as unimportant as punctuality is being brought up, or why such a fuss is being made about getting to work a few minutes late. This is but one small example of the bias people bring to the interview table. A review of Chapters 1 and 2 will do much to refresh your memory as to the kinds of things that can affect any communicative interaction.

Interviewing is a real-life exercise that uses knowledge gleaned from such fields as human communication, applied psychology and sociology. Successful interviewing takes considerably more than an open mind, honesty, and the ability to tell the difference between right and wrong. Although these qualities are surely worthwhile pursuits, they need to be coupled with the ability to shift psychological gears quickly in relation to any situation. An indispensible prerequisite of such a talent is *perspective*—the ability to see things in a true relationship. A close kin of perspective is *perception*, "The raw material delivered to the brain by the sense organs . . . and interpreted by the individual in accordance with his past experience and in furtherance

*Robert S. Goyer *et al., Interviewing: Principles and Techniques* (Dubuque, Iowa: Kendall/Hunt, 1968), p. 6.

of whatever activities he may be engaged in at the moment.* That activity is the interview.

Selective Perception

Imagine six applicants for a position waiting to be interviewed. After each of them has been interviewed by the same interviewer, they are asked to describe the interviewer's verbal and nonverbal disposition. How close do you think their respective descriptions would be? Before answering, also imagine how six witnesses to an automobile accident would describe what happened. With only a limited amount of life experience, you must be willing to admit that, in both cases, variations would exist in their renditions of what they heard and saw. Why? Because the study of selective perception teaches not only that are we inclined to perceive what we know rather than what we see and hear, but also *only selected aspects* of what we see and hear. As proof, read the following sentences and count the number of F's in the box.

> *Interviewing is a fine art and the result of many years of faithful practice and concentration. It must, however, be approached with a sincere desire to succeed.*

Perceptual Probe A

If you counted *three* F's on your first try, you're wrong! Try again, except this time, count very slowly. If you counted *five* F's, not only are you correct, but you are probably scratching your head, wondering why you missed the other two F's the first time. It was because the F in the word (of) sounds like a V and seems to disappear when it is read.

If you need further proof that your perception of what's out there is selective, try this experiment. When looking in this box, describe what you see.

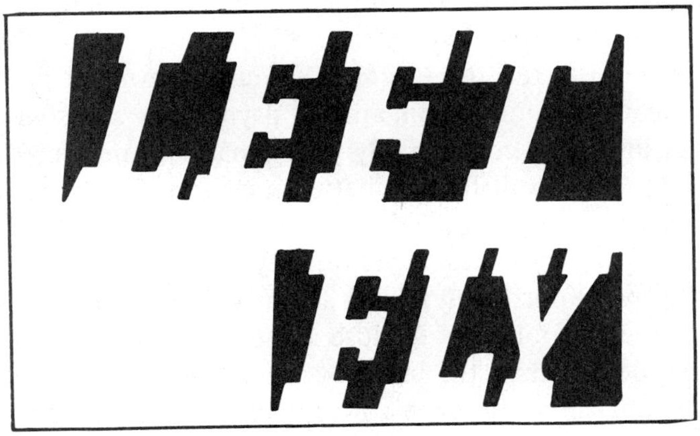

Perceptual Probe B

*D. M. Johnson, *Essentials of Psychology* (New York: McGraw-Hill, 1948).

Do you see anything familiar or identifiable? Most people first report seeing a series of strange black shapes meaning absolutely nothing. Get ready for a shock. Study Perceptual Probe 3 again, but this time, concentrate on the white shapes, not the black ones. Be patient and you should soon see words appear in white on a black background. Normally, when we read, the areas between the letters are white. Here, it is in reverse—white letters on a black background. So you see the words *left* and *fly*?

These are but two of many different kinds of probes involved in selective perception. They all drive the same message home—we experience patches of our environment and convince ourselves that we are experiencing all there is. An awareness of this phenomenon alone has the capacity to improve the effectiveness of your performance during an interview. By becoming sensitive to the idea that what you are perceiving is not necessarily what the other person is perceiving, you already have acquired what might be called a "communicative advantage, or edge." Just being aware that the information you received from your senses may be inaccurate or slightly distorted is enough to make a significant improvement in your perspective, as a whole.

Uses of an Interview

Basically, there are two reasons for any type of interview: (1) to get information, or (2) to give information. Furthermore, contrary to what some believe, the interview enjoys a much wider range of uses than simply an employer's tool for screening job applicants. The physician who inquires about the nature of a patient's pain or ache, the lawyer who cross-examines a witness on the stand, a detective who interrogates a suspect, a talk-show host who chats with a guest, a priest who hears confession, a casting director who holds auditions, the street corner inquirer who gathers data for a statistical study, and the guidance or marital counselor who is engaged in a problem-solving situation with a client are all practicing some form of interviewing. Incidentally, there is no such thing as a "real interview." Any situation in which people assemble for the expressed purpose of giving and getting information could be labeled an interview. Most frequently, people emerge in pairs, committees, panels, or small groups.

Interviews are also situation-specific; that is, designed to fit the need presented by a given situation. For example, under one set of circumstances, it might be necessary for an interview to be limited in time. Under other circumstances, it might be the questions, setting, location or format which require adjustment.

It is interesting to note the extent to which the course and purpose of an interview can be affected by altering any one of these factors. Because an interview is a dynamic rather than a static experience, it is very sensitive to subtle changes in its participants. As a result, business and professional administrators find it an excellent barometer of what is going on. For instance, in the average organization, those coming in and those going out usually do so through an initial selection interview and a final exit interview. These, if successfully performed, can provide management with some valuable information concerning morale among its personnel, grapevine patterns, rumors, and work attitudes. Without question, the interview in its various forms has the capacity to reflect any changes existing within an organization. To underestimate its worth is to rob any business or profession of an extremely practical and readily available tool of communication.

Phases of an Interview

According to James M. Lahiff*, an interview consists of six phases: (1) preliminary planning, (2) clarification of purpose, (3) preview of topics, (4) motivation of interviewee, (5) body of interview and (6) summary and conclusions.

Although interviewer and interviewee are coming together at the same time and place, their reasons are not quite the same. Each must prepare for the interview in a slightly different manner. Eavesdropping on the interviewer's thoughts, here is what we should hear:

Preliminary Planning of An Interviewer (Phase 1)

1. Have I chosen the best possible location for this interview?
2. How shall I put this interviewee at ease?
3. Have I reviewed this interviewee's file (résumé, cover letter, application)?
4. Have I allowed sufficient time for this interview?
5. Have I taken the necessary precautions to reduce the number of interruptions during this interview.
6. Have I made certain that this interviewee is being interviewed for the position he/she applied?
7. Have I reminded myself to listen more than talk since the primary purpose of this interview is to get information about the interviewee?
8. Am I in a suitable frame of mind and mood to conduct this interview; might my mood contaminate this interview?
9. Do I entertain any thoughts of matching the job to the person, rather than the person to the job?
10. If the interviewee avoids answering a specific question, should I persist until I get the desired information?
11. Am I clearly aware that I can get more information about this interviewee by using open-ended questions rather than direct ones which can be answered with a yes or no, a few words, or a brief sentence?

*James M. Lahiff, "Interviewing for Results," in Richard C. Huseman, Cal M. Logue, and Dwight L. Freshley (ed) *Readings in Interpersonal & Organizational Communication.* 2nd edition (Boston, Mass.: Hollbrook Press, Inc., 1974), pp. 347–50.

12. Once I have decided to hire the interviewee [provided I have the authority to do so], have I made every attempt to "sell" the applicant on this organization and the benefits of working here?
13. Will I remember to allow a few seconds after the interviewee is seemingly finished answering a question before asking the next question?
14. If I want the interviewee to elaborate on something, I must repeat parts of the key sentence in a questioning tone.
15. Have I a tendency to ask more than one question at a time?
16. I must avoid asking personal questions before an appropriate rapport has been established with the interviewee.
17. Instead of abruptly bringing an interviewee back from a point from which he/she has strayed, do it gently, but firmly.
18. I must make no promises I cannot keep.
19. Making secret notes during the interview is not a good idea. I must openly make only those memoranda I feel are absolutely necessary.
20. It is generally wise to avoid the use of first names on an initial interview.
21. If I am late for the interview, I may give the interview the impression that tardiness is tolerated in my company. I must try to get there as close to the appointed hour as possible; ideally, on time!
22. My appearance should set a visual example for the interviewee.
23. So that I can be aware of the time without abruptly looking at my wristwatch, I must have a timepiece facing me, but not the interviewee.
24. Under no curcumstances should I badmouth another organization, particularly the interviewee's former employer.
25. To get the information I seek, I must maximize the needs and desires of the interviewee.
26. Regardless of what the interviewee says or does, I must not become emotional.
27. Make no value judgments during the interview—only observations.
28. Should interruptions get out of hand, I must instruct my secretary (in front of the interviewee) that I do not wish to be disturbed again for the remainder of the interview.
29. Under no circumstances am I to eat or drink while conducting an interview unless, of course, the interviewee is invited to join me.
30. Try not to allow the interviewee to leave with too many unasked and, therefore, unanswered questions. At some point near the close of the conversation, ask, "Do you have any questions or is there something about which you are still not clear?"

Preliminary Planning of an Interviewee (Phase I)

Because we are talking about people communicating with one another, it is reasonable to expect that several of the plans entertained by the interviewer will likewise be held by the interviewee. Each, either consciously or unconsciously, would like to impress the other. Having evesdropped on the interviewer, it is now time to do the same with the interviewee:

1. How can I make this interviewer like me?
2. I must remember to be confident—to act as though I already have the job.
3. Since a person's office communicates a great deal about the person working in it, I must not forget to look it over carefully for clues to the interviewer's personality and character.
4. Staying on the subject reflects a disciplined mind. I must stay on the subject.
5. Within reason and psychological comfort, I must at all times try to "be myself."
6. When feasable, I must refrain from answering questions with "yes" or "no." Interviewer's appreciate explanations.
7. Inasmuch as eye contact and self-confidence usually go together, I must look at the interviewer when I speak.
8. I must not be reluctant to ask questions if I am asked if I have any questions.
9. The interviewer must not be permitted to "rattle my nerves."
10. It is a good idea to be on the lookout for clues to what interests the interviewer. When I discover one, play up to it discretely.
11. If I fail to get the position, I must not feel personally rejected. A very large number of people fail to get jobs for which they are eminently qualified.

Because the interviewer generally retains the controlling share of any interview, it puts the interviewee at a distinct disadvantage. The interviewer knows where the interview is going, the interviewee doesn't. As a result, preliminary planning becomes that much more difficult. Familiar evidence of this is captured by the following scene.

A young woman, recently graduated from college, had an appointment for an interview concerning a job. Understandably nervous, she asked a friend to go with her. After 45 minutes had passed, she returned to the street where her friend was waiting. "Well, how did it go Mary Ann?" asked the friend. "OK, I guess," she answered. "What do you mean, OK? Did you get the job?" Mary Ann, embarrassed that she couldn't give her friend a straight answer, mumbled, "Well, the man didn't actually say-whether I had the job or not." But this was not the only question for which Mary Ann had no clear-cut answers. To questions from her friend about such things as *salary, hours, benefits, promotions, responsibilities,* and a *starting* date, all she could do was plead ignorance. The interviewer had successfully extracted a great deal of information from Mary Ann. She, on the other hand, had come away with practically no information about the position for which she was interviewed.

There is obviously only one solution to this kind of happening. In planning for an interview, the subject must go in with a checklist of information to be acquired and come out with that information in hand.

> *If you were going on an interview for a job tomorrow, make a checklist here of the information you would want to come away with.*

_____________________ _____________________

_____________________ _____________________

_____________________ _____________________

Clarification of Purpose (Phase II).

One of the more dangerous practices occurring in an interview is that of "making assumptions." As you shall soon discover, there are many different types of interviews and, as a consequence, people are not always clear on the exact purpose of the interview. It is the responsibility of every interviewer to state clearly, at the outset of any interview, its purpose. If this is not done, the interviewee must take the initiative to ask, "What is the purpose of this interview?" At no time should either the interviewer or interviewee assume the purpose of an interview; it must be made explicitly clear so that both parties are there for the same reason.

Preview of Topics (Phase III)

Parties to an interview should come armed with a list of items to be covered—a "shopping list," so to speak. The most persuasive reason for this is that when people communicate, there is a strong tendency to wander off the subject. When personalities clash, this tendency is even greater. From the standpoint of the interviewee, knowing the topics to be covered in an interview beforehand is the best insurance against forgetting to bring specific information or documents, straying from a subject, or overlooking it entirely.

Another cogent argument favoring the announcement of topics in advance concerns a behavior called *selective retention.* Simply, it is the phenomenon whereby an individual recalls only what he or she considers important. It grows out of the typically human inclination to dwell on those subject areas holding some strong personal interest. Consider the interviewer who happens to be hooked on golf. Further consider what might happen if, during an interview, the interviewee just happens to mention a similiar addiction to the game. If they follow true to form, it would not take much to lure them away from the reason for the interview. After such an interview, it would not be surprising if the high point of the conversation was recalled to be golf—a product of selective retention. There are, however, interviews in which the previewing of topics is inadvisable. Talk shows with celebrity guests on radio and television, interrogation of witnesses by lawyers and law enforcement officers, and certain political debates are but a few examples.

Motivation of an Interviewee (Phase IV)

Few things boggle the mind of an interviewer more than an interviewee who doesn't say much. You have probaly seen such an interview on television where getting an answer or an opinion from an interviewee is like pulling teeth. Although it is comforting to rationalize with the cliché, "There are some people who have something to say and some who have to say something," it does little to change the reality of the situation. This, dilemma works a similiar hardship on the interviewee confronted by an interviewer who is equally tightlipped. If information is to flow comfortably during the course of an interview, both participants must help one another.

Although talking is a useful means of motivating people to move from question to answer and answer to question, excessive talking can produce the opposite results. If an interviewer finds herself talking uninterruptedly for as long as two minutes, she very likely is failing to get through to her interviewee. By the same token, it is reasonable to assume that an interviewee who talks too much runs the risk of robbing an interviewer of any previously held motivation. As with everyday street-corner or living room conversations, too much or too little talking has the reputation of dampening one person's interest in what another is saying. Some of the more successful ways of communicating a *positive interest* in what someone is saying include the following verbal and nonverbal cues:

Verbal Cues

1. "That's very interesting. Tell me more."
2. "Yes, I see what you mean."
3. "Good. Very good!"
4. "I would appreciate that a great deal. Thank you."
5. "You are very kind."

Nonverbal Cues

1. Occasional affirmative nodding of the head.
2. Leaning forward.
3. Sitting with hands, feet, and arms unfolded.
4. Smiling appropriately.
5. Sitting erect in chair.

Among the verbal and nonverbal ways of communicating *negative interest* in what someone is saying, there are:

Verbal Cues

1. "That may be true, but I never heard of it."
2. "Is that all you have to say on the subject?"

3. "What has that got to do with what we are discussing?"
4. "I'm terribly sorry. What was that you just said?"
5. "Is it really that important?"

Nonverbal Cues

1. Drumming fingers on desk or tapping foot on floor.
2. Frowning.
3. Squirming in seat or sitting on edge of chair.
4. Looking at one's wristwatch.
5. Gazing out of window or around the room.
6. Playing with some object; (e.g., ring, pen, handbag, clothing, keys)

Any one or a combination of these cues can modify the outcome of an interview by increasing or decreasing the motivation experienced and displayed by its participants.

Body of the Interview (Phase V)

Phase V of the interview is the segment in which members pursue their primary objective. To avoid careless omissions and oversights, both parties are encouraged to adhere closely to their preconceived checklists. Inasmuch as the interviewer's main function is to ask questions, it is not the only function. The responsible interviewer must also answer questions and, when necessary, anticipate them. In the majority of instances, the interviewer is expected to control the interview by asking questions, monitoring answers given to them, and soliciting whatever qualification is needed to make their meaning absolutely clear. Hence, the interviewer's task is to give and obtain information relevant to his/her preconceived objectives. The interviewee, in kind, must make every effort to fulfill his/her objectives during the body of the interview.

Summary and Conclusion (Phase VI)

By the time stage VI has been reached in an interview, a great deal of information will have been exchanged. Some of it relevant, most of it, irrelevant. The less planning that has gone into an interview, the more irrelevancies tend to creep into it. There are exceptions but they are rare. Another source of drain upon the reaching of reliable conclusions following an interview is *redundancy*. Plainly, to be redundant in an interview is to go over the same point(s) more than once. Common causes of this tendency are interruptions, nervousness, egocentricity, poor listening habits and inexperience. Because of these irrelevancies, and redundancies, it is important that an interviewer summarize the conclusions he/she feels were reached in the interview. This will provide the interviewee with an opportunity to compare those conclusions with his/her own. An interview lacking a summary and conclusion almost invariably breeds ambiguity—the stuff from which faulty communication seems to take nourishment.

Types of Interviews

There are a number of different kinds of interviews. Most of them have been designed to either give information, get information, or solve problems. They can also be grouped according to three classes of response:

1 *Limited,* where specific questions are asked and brief answers are given.
2. *Free,* where, because a greater amount of freedom is permitted, the nature and extent of any answer is left to the discretion of the interviewee.
3. *Defensive,* cases in which the interviewer tries to maneuver the interviewee into a psychological corner on a number of different topics for the expressed purpose of seeing how well questions are fielded under pressure.

Study the following interviews carefully and determine which of the aforementioned categories they fit best. Also, try to identify those fitting into more than one category. As an added means of making these interviews clear to the reader, an occasional Interview Simulation will be offered. In it, students are afforded an opportunity to act out an interview using their own imagination, experience and creativity.

Employment Interview

The employment interview is probably the best known interview. It consists of an employer or an employment representative engaged in conversation with an applicant. The main objective of the employer is to hire the best possible applicant and the applicant, to get the job, must meet certain personnel needs. This form of interview varies in length according to the importance of the position it represents. While far from perfect, it has the advantage of being one of the most effective methods of observing a candidate at close range. The average employer, in addition to having a written profile on an individual in the form of an application, cover letter, or résumé, prefers to meet a prospect face to face. The types of questions asked will depend on such factors as the interviewer's personality, preferences, needs, and experience. The kinds of questions used in an employment interview tend to be rather direct. It has been found that interviewers who use a structured approach—adhering to a predetermined set of questions—conduct the more successful interviews. Although they may, at their discretion, stray from their guidelines by allowing an interviewee to speak freely, openly, and without formal control, they are more apt to advocate the closer-knit question-and-answer format. Regardless of how the employment interview is managed, there is always one overriding goal: *to match up an individual with an organization to their mutual advantage.*

Interview Simulation

Procedure:

Step 1. All members of the class are to pair off, face each other, and sit ready with pen and sheet of blank paper.

Step 2. Quickly, each pair should decide which member will take the role of the interviewee and which the interviewer.

Step 3. The following jobs should be written on the blackboard and each interviewer is to select one for which the interviewee will be interviewed.

a. High School English teacher
b. Counselor at a day camp.
c. Salesperson at a local department store
d. Hotel manager
e. Bank teller
f. Police officer

Step 4. At a signal from the teacher, interviews are to begin and last 12 minutes. Roles should then be reversed and, again, a job should be selected by the interviewer and pursued for another 12 minutes.

Step 5. An open discussion should then take place during which students are invited to comment on what happened.

Suggested discussion questions:

1. What were your reactions to being the interviewee, the interviewer?
2. If you had this simulation to do over, what would you say or do differently?
3. What type of questions do you like best in an interview; what kind do you dislike most? Explain your answer.

Selection Interview

The selection interview, also known as the recruiting interview, is conducted to fill a position. Although it has many characteristics in common with the employment interview, it differs in that it is used to select one candidate from among many. With the employment interview, it is possible to have only one applicant for a position, and a hiring decision may be based on that person's qualifications alone. With the selection interview, decisions are based on comparative qualifications involving several individuals. Thus, the purpose of this type of interview is twofold: (1) to choose the best qualified candidate, and (2) motivate that person to accept the position.

Interview Simulation

Procedure:

Step 1. Two chairs should be placed in each corner of the room. The rest of the chairs should be pushed to the center.

Step 2. The teacher should then select four students and send one to each corner to be seated. They should again be equipped with pen and paper.

Step 3. Those seated in each corner of the room will represent interviewers. The teacher should then assign three to five students (depending on the size of the class) to each interviewer. One at a time, for a period of 5 minutes, each is to be interviewed for the position of recreation director at a senior citizen's center.

Stpe 4. After the interviewers in each corner of the room have screened the applicants assigned to them, they must select one person whom they consider most suitable for the position.

Step 5. In sequence, interviewers are then to announce their choice to the class and explain how they arrived at it. Other members of the class are permitted to cross-examine any interviewer concerning the basis used in making any given selection.

Step 6. The entire simulation should now be examined in open discussion.

Suggested discussion questions:

1. Interviewers, to what extent did your "liking" the person you selected influence your decision?
2. Interviewees, do you think you were judged more on the strength of your qualifications or personality? Explain.
3. What makes a selection interview fair or unfair?

Appraisal Interview

The appraisal is an on-the-job interview to evaluate the progress of an employee. It seeks to determine such things as whether employees are fulfilling their potential, are being duly motivated, have the proper job attitude, or can be assigned greater responsibility. It provides them with an opportunity to meet with their superiors and discuss the quality of their work. There often seems to be a disagreement between how employees evaluate their work and how their employers evaluate it. The health of any organization demands that its employees get some feedback from management as to how they are doing. If they are doing a good job, they should be told. If they aren't, they should be apprised of ways to improve. The appraisal interview supplies such feedback.

Placement Interview

In the labor market, when positions are tight and good employees are difficult to find, the placement interview plays an important role. Unlike the employment interview where a decision is made whether or not to hire someone, the placement interview involves a decision concerning where such an individual should be placed in an organization. This position may not, however, be permanent. Employees are often moved around within a company and they perform different jobs at different times. Instead of firing employees whose performance has not met certain standards, they might be transferred to another department or assigned another job. By the same token, the placement interview would come into play in the case of an employee who had become handicapped on the job. Rather than let such an employee go, responsible management might see fit to find another position within the company. Good business sense directs attention to the fact that everyone benefits when people are doing the job for which they are best suited. The placement interview has this responsibility.

Discipline Interview

Organizations operate according to rules. Some are written (company policy) and some are unwritten (personal demands or requirements imposed by those in charge). Employees not adhering to such rules run the risk of being called in for a discipline interview. In it, they are usually told in a rather formal way what they have done, why they shouldn't do it again, and what will happen if they do it.

Not everyone can conduct a disciplinary interview. It seems to take a special kind of personality. To say the least, those who conduct such an interview seldom win popularity contests.

Interview Simulation

Procedure:

Step 1. All members of the class should pair off and sit facing one another.

Step 2. A decision should be made quickly as to which member of the pair will be disciplined first.

Step 3. At a signal from the teacher, the first round will consist of one student conducting a disciplinary interview with the other acting the part of an employee who has done something which management considers to be wrong. The student doing the disciplining should make up some imaginary wrong that has been committed. *Time limit*: 5 minutes.

Step 4. Round two should consist of the same procedure except with different partners and with students assuming the opposite role.

Step 5. Open discussion dealing with what took place in the simulation.

Suggested Discussion questions:

1. What special personality traits do you think a person conducting disciplinary interviews should possess? Why?
2. Do you think this type of interview does any good? Explain.
3. What went through your mind while you were disciplining or being disciplined?

Exit Interview

The exit interview is used to dismiss employees whose services are no longer required. They are told why they are being dismissed and are given an opportunity to defend themselves, if they wish. No company wants to have its reputation marred by a former employee who wants to get back at it for firing them. They would much rather have an employee leave with a pleasant taste in his mouth. It is during the exit interview that an employee and a company should part friends—with no hard feelings, no grudges. New employers are frequently interested in the circumstances under which a prior job was left. Letters of recommendation may depend heavily on the outcome of an exit interview. If angry words were exchanged, a letter of recommendation can be expected to reflect it in a negative way. If the words were cordial and pleasant, a positive letter of recommendation can be expected.

From an organizational viewpoint, a great deal can be learned from this type of interview. For example, employees who are leaving have a tendency to speak frankly about the company and its employees. This provides management with an unthreatened opinion of the job and its duties from the perception of an incumbent. It may also spark ideas for future improvement of the job and its relationship within the department. Because certain fields have the reputation of being very closely knit, the importance of the exit interview should not be underestimated. It is a time when diplomacy is an indispensible tool of communication. Neither employer nor employee can afford the luxury of mismanaging this type of interview.

Stress Interview

Certain jobs require nerves of steel. The purpose of the stress interview is to measure a person's ability to stand up under psychological strain. It was devised during World War II by the Office of Strategic Service to help select candidates for such positions as saboteurs, propoganda experts, spies, and resistance leaders. Naturally, if these people were caught by the enemy and interrogated for information, they had to be able to withstand the mental strain. A more familiar type of stress interview, one closer to home, is a witness being cross-examined by an extremely capable, clever, and talented attorney. Suspects brought into a local police precinct might likewise undergo a stress interview by the detectives on duty. All these interviews have one thing in common–*stress.*

A variation of the stress interview is the *chaotic interview*, in which an applicant is tossed from one interviewer to another. Beside the continuous bombardment of questions, outside noise, telephone calls, and people walking in and out of the room further add to the stress. Then, there is the *Freudian interview* where stress is provided by an invasion of privacy. Questions of a very personal nature are asked; such as, "Are you on the pill;" "Are you a homosexual?" "What would you do if your boss made advances toward you?"

Interview Simulation

Procedure:

Step 1. Six members of the class are needed for this simulation. Three must be volunteers who consider themselves able to conduct a lively and intensive stress interview of a subject; three must be volunteers who consider themselves capable of standing up under a stress type interview.

Step 2. The six volunteers, in pairs, are to sit facing each other at the front of the room. The remainder of the class may gather around as observers.

Step 3. At a signal from the teacher, the stress interview should begin. The interviewers may stand if they wish but the interviewees must remain seated throughout. All three stress interviews will be going on simultaneously. Observers are encouraged to take written or mental notes. *Time limit*: 8 minutes.

Step 4. The position for which the three subjects are being interviewed is a clerk at the refund window of an extremely busy downtown department store.

Step 5. Open discussion of what happened in the simulation.

Suggested discussion questions:

1. What forms of stress did you experience or witness?
2. Are certain people better able to withstand stress than others? Why?
3. What precautions would you take to protect yourself in a stress interview? Explain.

Board Interview

When one person is interviewed by several, it could be termed a board interview. In some of the larger organizations when an individual is being considered for a high position, that person may be obliged to appear before a board of directors. During such an interview, the person in the hot seat may be asked practically anything by any member of the board. Questions generally come from every direction. A similar type of interview occurs in many colleges and universities where candidates must defend their theses and dissertations in order to earn their master's and doctoral degrees. Seated before a committee or board, they are expected to answer questions put to them. After a committee or board has been satisfied that a candidate has been thoroughly interrogated, the candidate is asked to leave and the committee or board begins its deliberation. Shortly thereafter, a decision is handed down concerning the fate of the candidate.

Interview Simulation

Procedure:

Step 1. Five members of the class are chosen by the teacher to represent the Board of Directors of the institution they are attending. *Their objective*: to interview a new addition to the faculty.

Step 2. One member of the class having a clearly defined major area of interest should volunteer to represent the new applicant. If the student offering to play this role in the simulation is a biology major, then the position will be one involving the teaching of biology, if it is political science, then the position will be teaching political science.

Step 3. The students playing the role of board members should sit in a row at the front of the room with their backs to the blackboard. Several feet in front of and facing them should be the candidate, seated and ready to be interviewed.

Step 4. At a signal from the teacher, the board members should proceed to examine the subject applying for the post at their institution. *Time limit:* 8–10 minutes.

Step 5. Open discussion of what happened in the simulation.

Suggested discussion questions:

1. How is being interviewed by several people at one time different from being interviewed by only one person?
2. If you had to be interviewed, would you prefer one person or several? Why?
3. What strategy would you use if you were going to be interviewed by a board or committee tomorrow morning?

Group Interview

Also known as the *oral performance test* and the leaderless group discussion technique, the group interview quite simply consists of 6 to 8 candidates for a job, seated in a circle. They are given either a subject to discuss or a problem to solve by the person in charge. Those whose responsibility it is to make a decision do not participate, but sit nearby and observe. Participants are judged or rated on such qualities as leadership, poise, aggressiveness, initiative, adaptability, tact, social awareness, alertness to group attitudes, self-control, nonverbal behavior, and sense of humor. Several large corporations have found the group interview extremely successful. It took less time and, overall, produced no unfavorable reactions.

Interview Simulation

Procedure:

Step 1. The class should be equally divided into two groups and seated in two circles—one within the other, a circle within a circle. All chairs are to face inward.

Step 2. The inner circle will represent the group being interviewed by the outer circle. *Objective*: to choose one person from the inner circle who would be best suited for a position as personnel director with a leading insurance company.

Step 3. At a signal from the teacher, the inner circle is to begin discussing the topic of "personal problems are no excuse for incompetency on the job." At no time are members of the outer circle to participate in the discussion—only to make observations of the proceedings in the inner circle. *Time limit*: 20 minutes.

Step 4. Each member of the outer circle is to vote for one person in the inner circle.

Step 5. Open discussion should reveal the board's vote.

Counseling Interview

The counseling interview is geared to assist the worker in personal problems inside and outside the organization. In it, management sheds its bureaucratic behavior and attempts to deal with the human condition—people who make up our businesses and professions. Of all the interviews, this is the only one which confronts human values head on. It takes full notice of the fact that people do not leave their private problems in a locker when they arrive at work and pick them up when they leave each day. Your problems may hurt not only yourself, but your fellow employees as well. What is more, they can influence your work, family, and friends. Therefore, the benefit of a counseling interview has the capacity to help not only the individual, but a large measure of the life outside of the job as well.

The work people do often reflects their health, moods, prejudices, biases, energy levels, social habits, intelligence, and neatness. Consider the executive who is a borderline alcoholic and who, with lunch, consumes four martinis—perhaps five. Unless such a person is exceptional, chances are little work will get done on returning to the office. Then there are those employees who suffer from insomnia, who have their hands full staying awake at work. The list of things that could interfere with an individual's work is extensive. Unfortunately, few of them are ever brought to the surface. Only after some conspicuous event draws attention to them is something done.

It is the responsibility of management to take action whenever it becomes aware of an employee who seems to need help. A counseling interview should be the first step. Assistant Professor Laniff of the University of Georgia touches on an important reason why counseling interviews are needed*:

> A recent survey in England found mental illness to be the second fastest growing cause of absence from work . . . . Some of the most frequently reported causes of such stress among executives are inability to cope with sudden change, failure to accept thwarted ambitions, promotion to jobs beyond one's capacity. Such problems of course are not restricted to executives nor are other common ones such as marital discord and fear about one's impending retirement.

Although there is a fine line between where an employee's private life begins and ends in relation to the organization for which he or she works, there is little doubt that one influences the other. When a worker cannot stay awake on the job, it is perfectly within the rights of an employer to inquire into the matter. Whereas it could be argued that it is none of an employer's business what an employee does after work, it could also be argued that it is important to know if insufficient sleep prevents an employee from putting in a full day's work for which a full day's salary is being paid. Whatever the problem, large or small, new or old, effort should be made to arrange a counseling interview at which it can be discussed.

Information-Seeking Interview

There are several types of interviews that fall into the information-seeking category. The host of a late night talk show on TV puts questions to his

*Iain Carson, "What are the causes of executive stress?" *International Management*, Jan. 1972, p. 16.

guests in an effort to ellicit information that his audience will find entertaining and interesting; the census taker who asks you questions about your family and job, or the newspaper reporter trying to get information from an eye witness to a bank hold-up are all examples of information-seeking interviews. Although the primary purpose of the interviewer in each case is to collect facts and opinions, there is often a secondary purpose—to entertain, inform, persuade, educate, sensitize, or promote some financial gain.

From your own life experience, name as many situations as you can in which you have been involved in information-seeking interviews.

Let's-Discuss-It-Over-Lunch Interview

Since the advent of credit cards, computers, and expense accounts, discussing business over lunch has become big business. There does not seem to be anything that cannot be discussed over a coffee, gin and tonic, scotch and soda, martini or a complete business luncheon. With tongue in cheek, perhaps, one sometimes gets the feeling that dining out is "the Business," and the actual business an excuse for dining out. As the cynic said, "What's the good of being a success, if you have to *work*?"

In most instances, job interviews conducted over lunch are for positions higher up in an organization. Rarely will an applicant for the position of file clerk or switchboard operator be invited out to discuss the job over lunch. Exceptions do exist when a person will be working very closely with an administrator, manager, or supervisor of a company (secretary, receptionist, management trainee).

One of the most important reasons for being invited to lunch by an employer is to find out how you behave in an informal setting. Most interviewees tend to be extremely tense, anxious, and guarded when questioned across a desk in formal surroundings. After a drink and a good meal, a feeling of relaxation often prompts a person to speak more freely. Although this is indeed a pleasant way to be interviewed for a job, it can be very tricky if you are not prepared to communicate in an informal setting. Take the simple act of salting your food before tasting it. One corporation executive interprets salting food before tasting it as a sign of impetuousness. By not waiting to see whether one's food needs salt, it could suggest that such an individual makes hasty decisions. Although anyone who makes a decision about another person on the basis of whether food is salted before or after it has been tasted is equally impetuous, it is an example of the kind of judgment certain employers are prone to make from time to time. We all have pet quirks. Why should a prospective employer be different? Hence, as insurance against your becoming the object of such a quirk, here is a list of things you should *not* do when being interviewed over lunch:

Be late.
Rush.
Talk only business.
Hoard the food.
Talk with your mouth full.
Spread papers on the table.
Look at your wristwatch.
Talk too loud.
Ask the other person a question when his/her mouth is full.
Order a heavy meal if the other person is eating a light one.
Monopolize the conversation.
Let the food appear to be more important than the other person.
Demonstrate anything at the table.
Smoke without asking the other person if it is all right (especially a cigar).
Drink over your limit.
Complain about the food or choice of restaurant.
Talk about things you know little or nothing about.
Ask personal questions.
Use profanity.
Jump around from subject to subject.
Be a phoney.
Overeat.
Be a know-it-all.
Be overconfident.
Be noisy when you eat.

In the more positive vein, here is a list of things you *should* do when being interviewed over lunch:

Call if you are going to be late.
Dress appropriately.
Let the interviewer do the interviewing.
Maintain good eye contact—especially when the other person is talking.
Let what your host orders be your guide as to what you should order.
If you arrive first, tell the head waiter or hostess that you are expecting to meet someone.
Be an attentive listener.
Speak to the point.
Stand up when your prospective employer approaches the table if you are already seated.
Maintain a pleasant look on your face.
Be optimistic about things in general.
Make the other person feel as though he/she were the only person in the room.
Be flexible and agreeable, but not obsequious.
Give clues to your agressiveness and initiative (examples).
Show signs of your willingness to learn.
Speak clearly and distinctly.
Be alert.
Display a special interest in your employer's company or firm.
Illustrate your ability to communicate effectively.
Indicate that you are more interested in duties than working conditions and hours.
When it is time to leave, don't linger. Leave promptly.
Graciously thank your host for the luncheon.
Be sure to leave your telephone number and address.
Once you leave, don't look back.

These are only suggested recommendations with regard to your behavior during an interview over lunch. They are neither presented in their order of importance nor according to some magic formula. Each must be used according to a particular time, place, and circumstance. For their full value, an open classroom discussion in which each is evaluated separately would be extremely helpful.

Cross-cultural Interview

Because people are able to get around so much easier, the planet we live on seems to be getting smaller and smaller. No longer are people reared in one culture destined to live out their lives and die in it. Major cities throughout the world are experiencing a mixing of cultures. In New York, for example, growing numbers of people from India, China, Japan, Arabia, Africa, Korea, Thailand, and South America are filtering into the job market. The result: more and more people from differing cultures are being required to get along with one another—to communicate. America, in general, has been known as the melting pot, a nation to which people from all parts of the world have immigrated. Today, millions who were born into another culture now boast citizenship papers and proudly declare themselves Americans.

Although genes and chromosomes determine the physical self, culture seems to shape and direct the behavioral self. Have you ever wondered to what extent those born and reared in another culture and who now live in the United States have shed cultural imprints made on them during their formative years; how many of the attitudes, values, and beliefs spawned in their native culture still remain with them? Such questions bring us to the phenomenon of the cross-cultural interview. Take something as fundamental as eye contact. Young men and women who grew up in Latin Cultures were taught that it is impolite, improper, and rude to engage someone in authority or of higher status in direct eye contact. In the United States, this does not seem to apply. People who avoid direct eye contact during a conversation or interview are considered to suffer from low self-esteem, lack self-confidence, and a deficiency in assertiveness. This is but one of the many culturally

determined traits that may surface in an interview, particularly one in which participating members are culturally different.

Ward H. Goodenough, a cultural anthropoligist, defines culture as, "Whatever it is one has to know or believe in order to behave in a manner acceptable to members of that culture,"* Thus, to provide you with a broader understanding how culture can influence communication in the interview situation, here are some interesting culture-specific characteristics.

Latin Culture

Authority in the home, church and community are emphasized. Within the organization, this produces a built-in hesitency about speaking up to one's superiors.

In Latin America, you should expect to spend hours waiting in outer offices. If you bring your American interpretation of what constitutes punctuality to a Latin-American office, you will fray your temper and elevate your blood pressure. A 45-minute wait is not unusual—or more unusual than a 5-minute wait would be in the United States; in the United States, a consistently tardy person would be undependable, whereas judging a Latin American by such a standard would constitute a major error.

In Central America, local custom does not permit a salesman to land in town, call on the customer and walk away with an order, no matter how badly your prospect wants and needs your product. It is traditional there that you must see your man at least three times before you can discuss the nature of your business.

To a Latin American, with his cultural traditions and habits, a distance of two feet seems to him approximately what five feet would be to us. To him, we seem distant and cold. To us, he gives an impression of a pushiness. In short, Latins tend to stand much closer to one another than we do.

Arab Culture

The mere mention of a deadline to an Arab is like waving a red flag before a bull. In his culture, your emphasis on a deadline has the emotional effect on him that his backing you into a corner and threatening you with a club would have on you.

Every culture has its own way of bringing pressure to get results. The usual Arab way is one Americans avoid as "bad manners," It is needling. If you haven't been needled by an Arab, you just haven't been needled. An Arab businessman whose car broke down explained it this way:*

> First, I go to the garage and tell the mechanic what is wrong with my car. I wouldn't want to give him the idea that I didn't know. After that, I leave the car and walk around the block. When I come back to the garage, I ask him if he has started to work yet. On my way home from lunch I stop in and ask

*Ward H. Goodenough, "Cultural Anthropoligy and Linguistics," in *Language in Culture and Society: A Reader in Linguistics and Anthropology*, edited by Dell Hymes (New York: Harper & Row, 1964) p. 36.

*Edward T. Hall and William Foote Whyte, "Intercultural communication: A guide to men of action," in *Communication and Culture*, edited by Alfred G. Smith (New York: Holt, Rinehart & Winston, 1966), pp. 567–576.

him how things are going. When I go back to the office I stop by again. In the evening, I return and peer over his shoulder for a while. If I didn't keep this up, he'd be off working on someone else's car.

Some societies often converse closely enough to smell one another's breath and body odor. They employ subtle differences in odor to learn something about emotions and personality of even casual acquaintances. In the United States, only the refreshing smell of a lively mouthwash is acceptable, and then only among intimates.

Americans are largely a hands-off culture in which physical contact is a clear sign of intimacy, except in certain stylized expressions of friendship. For Arabs, however, touching colleagues or even strangers in the street is perfectly permissible.*

Japanese Culture

The American desire to get down to business (a "hit-and-run" school of business behavior) and on with other things works to our disadvantage in other parts of the world. The head of a large Japanese firm commented, "You Americans have a terrible weakness. We Japanese know about it and exploit it every chance we get. You are impatient. We have learned that if we just make you wait long enough, you'll agree to anything."

In the United States, we would rarely think it necessary or proper to call on a customer in a group. He might well be antagonized by the hard sell. In Japan, as an example, the importance of the occasion and of the man is measured by whom he takes along.

Even when a group is involved in the United States, the head man is spokesman and sets the tone. This is not always the case in Japan. Two young Japanese once requested an older American widely respected in Tokyo to accompany them so that they could "stand on his face." He was not expected to enter into the negotiations; his function was simply to be present as an indication that their intentions were serious.

These cultural variations in behavior are by no means complete. An interest in them will be sure to turn up many others. However, regardless of how many you uncover, the point of view set forth by Glazer and Moynihan appears to be sound: "Ethnic groups beyond the second generation have retained many of the traits which their forebearers brought with them from other cultures."* Edward Hall adds additional force to this view by suggesting that ethnic groups tend to retain their key assumptions about nonverbal communication: "Superficially, these groups may look alike and sound somewhat alike but beneath the surface there lie manifold unstated, unformulated differences in the structuring of time, space, materials, and relationships."

*Edward Hall, *Hidden Dimension* (Garden City, N.Y.: Doubleday, 1966), pp. 16–25, 156.

†Nathan Glazer and Daniel Moynihan, *Beyond the Melting Pot* (Cambridge Mass.: The M.I.T. Press, 1963), pp. v–vi, 13.

Based on each of these cultural differences, see whether you can relate them to the interview situation. Explain.

Perhaps the most persuasive argument favoring the need to understand cross-cultural interviewing can be made with the following story.

One day, a Spanish speaking man was brought into the psychiatric wing of a large city hospital for observation. Less than a minute into the psychiatric interview had elapsed when it became apparent that the patient spoke very little English and the psysician, very little Spanish. Using bits and pieces of English and Spanish and a variety of poorly understood hand gestures, the exchange went down in the hospital records as a psychiatric interview. The most frightening part of it was the doctor's diagnosis: *schizophrenia.* This most serious diagnosis was arrived at on the basis of many vague assumptions, presumptions, and inferences recklessly made across cultural and linguistic lines. But the story is not over. After being admitted to the hospital, this patient was re-evaluated a week later by a Spanish-speaking psychiatrist. Yes, if you are thinking that he was found to be normal when interviewed in his native tongue, you are correct. Naturally, this case is both extreme and infrequent. It does, however, forcefully drive home the importance of understanding the pitfalls of cross cultural interviewing.

A final note that pertains to the subject of interviewing across cultural boundaries concerns members of subcultures. Briefly, a subculture consists of a group of people who have found commonality among themselves. Examples include alcoholics, nudists, prostitutes, criminals, and even the mentally or physically retarded. Interaction among members of a subculture is known as subcultural communication–a process whereby one gains and maintains the ability to communicate effectively and meaningfully with members of a subculture.* What problems, if any, do you think members of these subcultures encounter when they apply for a position and have to be interviewed by someone who is not a member of that subculture? How would you react if you were an interviewer and, during the course of the interview, the person you were interviewing mentioned that he was a homosexual, ex-convict, former psychiatric patient or rehabilitated alcoholic? Do you honestly believe that your line and level of communication would remain unchanged? Go one step further and ask yourself how you would feel about interviewing a midget or dwarf–or someone who was physically handicapped.

Write a short essay on how you think and feel about interviewing members of the subcultures just mentioned. Be specific in your description of what you would say, how you would say it, and how you look while saying it.

*Fred E. Jandt, *The Process of Interpersonal Communication* (New York: Harper & Row, 1976) pp. 221–243.

Whether one is engaged in an interview involving cross-cultural or subcultural elements, one truth stands out. We are social animals who, if we are to work together, must become aware of and sensitive to one another's differences as well as our similiarities. One member of our specie put it this way through an interesting analogy: Like colors, together the differences of Man create a beautiful image only because of their differences as do the colors of the rainbow. There would be no rainbow without differences.

SELF-EXAMINATION QUIZ

Having read this chapter, my answers to the following questions reflect my understanding of its contents.

1. What is the role of interviewing in business?

2. Why is an interview said to be multidimensional in nature?

3. Tell why so many people are afraid of interviews.

4. What are some of the ways you can prepare for an interview?

5. Explain why qualified people occasionally do poorly on an interview.

6. What is the basis for fearing an interview?

7. Why are questions so important in an interview?

8. Differentiate *perspective* and *perception* as they apply in an interview.

9. What is the function of an interview in an organization?

10. List the phases of an interview.

11. List as many different types of interviews as you can.

12. What are some of the differences between an interviewer and an interviewee?

Asher, J. J., "How the applicant's appearance affects the reliability and validity of the interview," *Educational and Psychological Measurement,* **30**, 687–695 (1970).

Blackburn, J. R., "The efficacy of modeled self-disclosure on subject's response in an interview," *Dissertation Abstracts International,* **31** (3-B), 1529–1530 (1970).

Bolton, D. L., and M. E. Hickey, "Effects of interviews on teacher selection decisions," *Journal of Applied Psychology,* **53**(6), 33–38, (1969)

Carlson, R. E., and D. R. Schwab, and H. G. Heneman, "Agreement among styles of selection interviewing," *Journal of Industrial Psychology,* 5(1), 8–17 (1970).

Delahanty, D., "Three aspects of nonverbal communication in the interview," *Personnel Journal,* **49**, 757–759 (1970).

Dohenwend, B. S., "An experimental study of directive interviewing," *Public Opinion Quarterly,* **34**(1), 117–125 (1970).

Guion, R. M., and R. F. Gottier, "Validity of personality measurers in personnel selection," *Personnel Psychology,* **18**, 136–164 (1965).

Hawes, L. C., "The effects of interviewer style on patterns of dyadic communication," *Speech Monographs,* 39, 114–123 (1972).

McClelland, L., "Effects of interviewer-respondent race relations on household interview measures of motivation and intelligence," *Journal of Personality and Social Psychology,* 29, 392–297 (1974).

Siegman, A. W., and B. Pope, and T. Blass, "Effects of interviewer status and duration of interviewer messages on interviewee productivity," *Proceedings of the 77th Annual Convention of the American Psychological Association,* 1969, 4(pt. 2), 541–542.

Smith, Arthur Lee, *How to Talk to People of Other Races, Ethnic Groups, and Cultures* (Trans-Ethnic Education Communication Foundation, 1971.

WORK AREA FOR CHAPTER 4

Chapter 5

Coping in Groups

Don't be misled. As often as people urge you to tell them the truth about themselves, they rarely want to hear it.

MEMO

TO: Reader

FROM: Author

After reading this chapter, you should have a better understanding of:

1. Why group life on the job is important.
2. How involved you currently are with groups.
3. What physical and psychological needs are served by a group.
4. How each person brings a variety of personal attitudes, values, and beliefs to a group.
5. How obstructive and cooperative behavior function in a group.
6. Why the concept of leadership and leaders is important in a group context.
7. How group situations, goals, and customs affect leadership.
8. How alterations in a group's geography can influence the behavior of its members.
9. What types of people are commonly found in groups.
10. How to cope with people who are slightly different from yourself.

Chapter 5

You have performed an intrapersonal and interpersonal self-inventory, have been exposed to the dynamics of investigating a career, and have been interviewed for a position. Thinking positively, you have been hired. It is now Monday morning, and you are on your way to your new job. You didn't get too much sleep last night because your mind was busily conjuring up images of what the new position would be like. It is 9:00 A.M., and you have arrived, are greeted by a secretary and are told where to hang your coat. The secretary then calls someone on the telephone and says, "Mr. Tatum is here." A woman in her early forties soon appears, looks you squarely in the eye, extends a handshake, and says, "Glad to have you aboard, Mr. Tatum. My name is Alice." With this remark, you have been initiated into the coping process of the small business or professional group. From this point forward, you will find yourself moving deeper and deeper into the organization. But, as you will repeatedly be reminded by this text, there is no such thing as an organization in the "real" sense—only people interacting with people—usually in small groups.

Every member of a business or profession, directly or indirectly, contributes to its character and personality. Common sense would dictate that the smaller the organization, the greater such contributions would be felt; that is, the impact of an obnoxious employee on other personnel in a small business would be greater than in an organization employing thousands. This is not generally true. Why? Because large organizations are made up of smaller units, each of which could easily be likened to the small business. In spite of the fact that General Motors, IBM, and the Macmillan Book Publishing Corporation are each administrated by an overriding set of company rules and regulations, their respective divisions, subdivisions, and numerous departments often seem to manifest an identity of their own. Anyone who has ever worked for a large corporation and has been transferred from one of its departments to another is familiar with these separate identities. These are times when such a transfer makes one wonder whether the two departments are part of the same organization. An expression like, "Now just forget what they told you up on the third floor, here we do things a little differently" is enough to raise some serious doubt.

Contrary to what some people might think, job competency alone is not an absolute guarantee of job security. In more cases than you may be willing to believe, people who are liked by their employers and co-workers, but whose proficiency leaves something to be desired, are more apt to be retained than those who are disliked by their employers and co-workers, but whose proficiency is extremely high. Granted that there are jobs in which a person's personality and interpersonal communication play only a small part, the majority of them are not that impersonal. The message here is both simple and direct: Either you get along and remain on the job, or you don't get along and are asked to leave. Thus, for communication in the business community to operate at maximum efficiency, interactions in the small group must generate some degree of satisfaction for all concerned.

Basically, you will spend the bulk of your productive years either working alone or working with others. Most positions involve working with others.

It shall be the objective of this chapter to increase your awareness of what is involved in the process of coping with people in a small group through communication. To begin, you must understand that the bulk of communication on the job is NOT job-specific; i.e., it is not about the job being done. It is largely composed of people talking about people. While such talk may be indirectly related to the job, it seems to focus rather heavily on the people doing the job. While most individuals have been trained to do their jobs, few have been specifically trained to get along with their co-workers. Consequently, they are strong on mechanical skills and weak on human skills.

Some of the most important events of your life take place in small groups. To give you some idea of just how much you have already become involved in group life, try this exercise:

Name of Exercise: I Belong.

Purpose: To find out how much of an individual's life is involved with various kinds of groups.

Procedure:

Step 1. Each member of the class is to take out of a wallet or purse, anything indicating membership in an organization, club, fraternity, or sorority, etc.

Step 2. Next, a paragraph or two should be written explaining why the individual joined that particular group, whether it was joined voluntarily, and what need it was considered to serve.

Step 3. All papers should be passed to the front of the room and redistributed to give each student an opportunity to read someone else's paper.

Step 4. An open discussion should now take place. Students are invited to give their opinions about how belonging to different groups influences their lives. They should try to answer these questions:

a. Are those who belong to groups generally happier than those who do not?
b. Are people who join groups more apt to be followers?
c. Does group life rob people of their individuality?

Types of Groups

There are four basic groups into which the majority of people fall: (1) family group, (2) school group, (3) career group, and (4) social group. You probably had no choice about joining your family group. You were either born into it, or were adopted by it. There was equally little choice when it came to your school group. You were simply put into it by either your parents or guardians. You will probably have some choice when it comes to the career and social groups you join in the future. From the looks of things, you will be spending the greater part of your life in some sort of group.

Subgroups

In addition to the basic groups just mentioned, there are a number of other situations in which people come together for some common reason. In the family group, for instance, you have the immediate family, which usually includes mother, father, sisters and brothers, grandfathers and grandmothers. Next come the cousins, aunts and uncles, nephews and nieces and, finally, a variety of distant relatives. If a group of cousins were to form a cousin's club, it would be an example of a subgroup. At school, subgroups would include: Leader's Club, Drama Club, Honor Society, school teams, and the many extracurricular organizations to which students belong. In career life, there are unions, professional clubs and organizations, company bowling teams, and so forth. Finally, subgroups in social circles would take in such things as fraternal organizations (Masons, Knights of Pythias, Knights of Columbus, Elks), Political clubs (Democratic and Republican), PTA, religious organizations (Newman's Club, B'nai Brith), and therapeutic groups (group psychoanalysis, encounter groups, sensitivity-training groups).

Needs Served by the Group

Thousands of years ago, cave dwellers and their children were able to survive because they lived and traveled in groups. There seems to have been safety in numbers. The moment one member became separated from the group, that person's chances of survival became very slim. Interestingly enough, the basic needs that existed among the cave dwellers still exist in us today. With a little stretch of the imagination, the basic need categories outlined by the famous psychologist, Abraham Maslow, in his book, *Motivation and Personality*, could just as easily have applied to the cave dweller. Dr. Maslow indicates that a person is motivated by personal needs, as he or she sees them. These needs have been categorized into five levels of importance. Read them and see if you agree.

Level 5. *Self-actualization needs.* For self-fulfillment, to actually become what one potentially can be; desire to actualize one's essential nature; what a person *can* be, he/she *must* be.

Level 4. *Esteem needs.* Desire for self-esteem, based on achievement, mastery, competence, independence; also, the desire for esteem of others (reputation, prestige, recognition, status).

Level 3. *Belongingness and love needs.* For abiding devotion and warm affection with spouse, children, parents, and close friends; the need to feel that one is part of social groups; the need for acceptance and approval.

Level 2. *Safety needs.* For security, stability, protection from harm or injury; the need for structure, orderliness, law, and predictability in one's environment; freedom from fear and chaos.

Level 1. *Physiological needs.* For food, drink, air, sleep, shelter, exercises; the basic bodily "tissue" requirements.

Without worrying whether you understand all the words in Maslow's need categories, you should be able to see that our basic needs have not changed much since the time of the cave dweller. We can satisfy some of these needs by ourselves, but most of them require the help of others. Of course, there have been, and always will be, those who say, "I don't need anyone," but sooner or later, these very people find themselves reaching out for someone.

Groups serve both personal and public needs, and in most instances, needs are a mixture of both. Take the case of an employee moving into a new position or, as mentioned earlier, from one department to another within an organization. Until that person has established some kind of meaningful rapport with the new group, the newcomer experiences a lonely feeling—of being left out, unwanted, or of being different from the others. When acceptance by members of the group finally comes, it heals not only emotional wounds of a personal nature, but also those related to the organization itself. In many ways, both the individual and the company stands to benefit from any uplifting of its employee's physical and/or mental state of well-being.

Attitude of Group Member

At sometime in your life, someone has said, "I don't like your attitude!" Again, someone has probably said, "I like your attitude." What do you think they meant when they spoke of your attitude? People have attitudes toward practically everything: education, religion, politics, love, work, marriage, sex, and health. A person's attitude toward something tells you the way they feel about it. It is almost impossible for you to communicate with people without bumping into their attitudes. And, to make things more complicated, each person has not only one attitude but, perhaps, hundreds of them. Every time you hear the words, "I think," or "I feel," an attitude toward something is sure to follow. Multiply the number of attitudes in any one person's head by the number of people in the average group and you can get some idea of how attitudes can affect and infect their communication.

Attitudes are like mental baggage. Whenever you take a trip, you take along baggage containing the things you will need. Occasionally, you take things you do not need. A similiar happening may occur in your head. Stored in your brain is all of the information you have gathered in a lifetime. Some of it, you use; some of it, you don't use. All of it, in some way, helps shape your attitudes. To find out what kind of attitudes or mental baggage you have stored inside your head, try this exercise:

Name of Exercise: The Fortune Cookie Message

Purpose: To get some idea about the kinds of attitudes which cause people to think, speak, and act in a certain way.

Procedure:

Step 1. Each member of the class is to tear a sheet of paper out of a notebook and tear it again into 16 smaller pieces.

Step 2. Like the little messages found in fortune cookies, each student is to write a different fortune cookie message on each of the 16 squares of paper. Some examples of the Chinese messages contained in the fortune cookies sound like this:

> He who is fond of bravery but complains of poverty is going to create disorder. (Confucius)
>
> Leading an uninstructed people to war is to throw them away. (Confucius)
>
> It is not enough that one's words express fully one's thought. (Confucius)
>
> Study as if you were never to master it; as if in fear of losing it. (Confucius)

Step 3. All the folded pieces of paper are then placed in a hat or a large bowl and passed around the room. Each student should reach in and take out five fortune cookie messages.

Step 4. After all the papers have been read, students should try to figure out the attitude(s) behind each message. An open discussion should consist of students volunteering to read a fortune cookie message and telling what they think the attitude was behind it.

Example: Fortune Cookie Message

I have yet to meet a man who, on observing his own faults, blamed himself.

Possible attitudes behind fortune cookie message:

1. People are quick to blame others.
2. It is difficult to admit your own faults.
3. Few of us see ourselves as others see us.
4. It takes courage to be a responsible person.
5. A sign of "growing up" is being able to admit when you are wrong.

Having sketched certain aspects of group life, you should now be getting some insight into the importance of being able to function comfortably among new co-workers. Unfortunately, just looking at them will not tell you too much unless you happen to be a mind-reader. Although you may get some nonverbal clues to their personality from the way they look and behave, you can't really be sure until they speak—and even then, their words may deceive you. The sooner you discover the attitudes they harbor, the better will be your chances of communicating effectively within the organizational complex.

Behavior in a Group

Whether you are willing to admit it or not, most of your behavior in a group is a matter of self-defense. Although you may feel strongly about the group, its goals, and the people in it, there is a constant urge to say and do things which will make you look good or protect you from being hurt. There are those who believe that it is human nature to behave this way.

How people communicate in a group on the job often depends on three factors: (1) what they bring to the group, (2) what they put into it, and (3) how other members of the group respond to them. Whatever happens, most people seem to dislike having to surrender their personal identity to a group. The idea of being just another spoke in the wheel doesn't appear to be as attractive as playing a major role in a group. Whereas the concepts of a group mind, group effort, and group identity are certainly worthwhile, the success of any group seems, once again, to depend on the individual satisfaction and contentment of each of its members, that is, achieving satisfaction through interaction. Seldom will you find a group of people doing good things whose members are miserable. Generally, groups that do good things are made up of people who feel good about themselves and what they are doing.

Human behavior is shaped and directed by *how people think* (their attitudes, values, and beliefs), *what they say* (their verbal communication), *how they say things* (vocal communication), and *how they look* (nonverbal communication). Individually or in combination, these behaviors may be considered **cooperative** or **obstructive.** Cooperative behavior in a group takes in any action or reaction serving a useful purpose for either the entire group or one of its members. In contrast, obstructive behavior takes in any action or reaction not serving a useful purpose for either the group or one of its members.

Verbal, Vocal, and Nonverbal Characteristics of Cooperative and Obstructive Behavior in Small Groups.

Cooperative Behavior

Verbal

1. Refer to others by name.
2. Ask questions if you are not clear on a point.
3. Do not prejudge others or their ideas.
4. Allow people to finish their thoughts.
5. Encourage others to speak.
6. Use the words *we–our–us*, rather than *I–me–my.*
7. Be polite.
8. Try to build on what others say.
9. Use simple, straightforward language.
10. Compliment others freely.

Vocal

1. Use a pleasant tone of voice.
2. Speak up so that you can be heard.
3. Try to avoid the use of *ers, ahs,* and *uh-huhs.*
4. Stress all important words or ideas with your voice.
5. Avoid mumbling.

Nonverbal

1. Look at the people to whom you are talking.
2. Sit as though you were interested, leaning forward.

3. Move toward, rather than away from, other speakers.
4. Occasionally nod agreeably or smile at other speakers.
5. Wear clothes that will tell others that you care enough about the group to dress appropriately.

Obstructive Behavior

Verbal

1. Cracking jokes that distract the group's attention.
2. Using big words just to show off.
3. Interrupting others.
4. Changing the subject for no good reason.
5. Monopolizing the conversation.
6. Trying to make other people look stupid or silly.
7. Repeating the same thing several times.
8. Making self-centered remarks.
9. Using foul language that offends others.
10. Ignoring what others have to say.

Vocal

1. Shouting unnecessarily
2. Speaking in a monotone (the voice sounds the same all the time).
3. Talking too fast or too slow.
4. Using such phrases as, You know? Right? Do you see what I mean? OK?
5. Mispronouncing certain very familiar words.

Nonverbal

1. Having a bored look on your face.
2. Doing something else while another person is talking.
3. Fidgeting around in your seat.
4. Making purposeless gestures while you are talking.
5. Moving your head from side to side while someone else is trying to make a point.

> *List as many cooperative and obstructive forms of behavior you have observed in the groups to which you have belonged or now belong.*

No single behavior is a consistent sign of cooperation or obstruction. A great deal may depend on the situation in which it occurs. What can and should be said is that, for the majority of situations, behavior seems to exhibit a dominant pattern. If, as mentioned in an earlier chapter, an exception does occur in which there is a contradiction between an individual's verbal, vocal, and nonverbal behavior, it qualifies as pseudoaffective behavior.

The boss who, in one moment, tells you to take your time and, in another, stands over you and nervously taps his fingers on the desk or repeatedly looks at the clock on the wall, is a classic example of pseudoaffective behavior, a conflict between what is being said and what is being done, verbal versus nonverbal.

To see how changes in a person's attitude and behavior can lead to changes in his or her communication in a group situation, try this exercise:

Name of Exercise: The Imposter

Purpose: To illustrate what happens to the way a person communicates as a result of taking on another's behavior, attitude, values and beliefs.

Procedure:

Step 1. The teacher sets a date on which each member of the class will attend as an imposter. The characters chosen to be impersonated by the students may be male or female, fictional or nonfictional, and male students may assume female characters, or vice versa. They may choose whomever they wish, but some suggestions are: Napoleon, Jesus Christ, Adolph Hitler, Martin Luther King, Voltaire, Dante, W. C. Fields, Queen Victoria, Thomas Paine, Alice in Wonderland, Rudyard Kipling, and Edgar Allen Poe. All that is required of the imposters is that they research the lives of their characters or read a biography to get some idea of their attitudes, values, and beliefs toward the world in which they lived. Costumes and props are encouraged.

Step 2. On the day set aside for this exercise, students are to have an open discussion on any one of the following topics:

1. The meaning of life.
2. Are all people equal?
3. What should all children be taught?

The only firm rule during this discussion is that the impostors speak and act as if they were the characters they chose to impersonate. *Time Limit:* 15–20 minutes.

Step 3. Another discussion should follow in which students, returning to their own identities, should tell how it felt communicating on the basis of someone else's behavior, attitudes, values and beliefs.

Leadership

Do you remember a game from your childhood called, Follow the Leader? Each player had to do whatever the leader did, and those who didn't were out. Although there were some who never wanted to lead, others fought hard to become leaders. What went on in that children's game takes place, to various degrees, in most business group situations. Almost invariably, you will find those who lead and those who are led. Do you think you can tell whether someone is a "leader type" by the way that person looks?

Name of Exercise: The Leader Type

Purpose: To find out why certain people look like leaders.

Procedure:

Step 1. Entire class should sit in a large circle. Each student is then to tear a sheet of paper from a notebook and print his or her name on it in large block letters (only first names).

Step 2. At a signal from the teacher, everyone in the class should look around the group and jot down the names of those who look like "leader types." Under each name picked as a potential leader, the reasons for such a choice should be given. Remember, the choice is to be based, as much as possible, on the person's looks. One selected as a "leader type" might read:

John

Looks intelligent
Has honest eyes
Has a good build
Sits tall and hold his head high

Step 3. After everyone has finished choosing these leader types, each should take turns reading aloud the names listed on their papers. As a name is read, that person should step to the front of the room. After all of the names have been read, those picked as "leader types" should be standing at the front of the classroom, facing those seated.

Step 4. One at a time, each of the selected leader types should step forward and announce his or her name to the class. After this, any student who selected that particular person may volunteer an explanation as to why. This process should be repeated with each leader type.

Step 5. An open discussion should follow in which members of the class are invited to make any comments they wish on the subject of leaders and the characteristics that have been assigned to them in this exercise.

For some time, a number of those who studied the question of leaders and leadership have embraced the belief that leaders possessed certain qualities. Some went so far as to say that leaders were born, not made. Here are some of the qualities that are attributed to the leader type.

1. Greater intelligence
2. Freedom from anxiety
3. Better informed
4. More honest
5. Achieved more prior to assuming role of leader
6. A strong desire to influence others
7. Self-confidence
8. More responsible
9. Emotionally secure
10. Able to help others in practical ways
11. Warm, sensitive, sympathetic
12. Consistent in performing leadership functions
13. Ability to adjust to different situations
14. Highly motivated
15. Initiative

It would be foolish to expect any leader to possess *all* these qualities. This is especially true because leadership, rather than being strictly a matter of qualities or traits, is more a function of the relationship between the various members of a group. Frequently, a would-be leader will say or do something that is acceptable to a group and, as a result, members of that group will tend to see him or her as the kind of person they want to lead them. In effect, it is often the group that decides whom it will follow, how much power it will vest in a leader, and how long it will continue to follow that leader.

Function

It is difficult to talk about leadership without talking about leaders. By the same token, it is difficult to talk about leaders without discussing leadership. Keeping this fact in mind, let us discuss some of a leader's functions. To begin with, a leader must represent a positive force in any group. Furthermore, a leader must be concerned with where a group has been, where it is at the present time and, finally, where it is going. Anything to do with each of these considerations must be the leader's business. They are the general goals which should concern a good leader. Among the more specific functions of a responsible leader are: (1) creating a pleasant and cooperative mood in the group, (2) seeing to it that any member of the group is not abused or ignored, (3) keeping order and helping the group stay on the subject, (4) raising important questions, such as, "Now that we have seen the effects of inflation, wouldn't it be helpful to examine some of the causes of this problem?" (5) clarifying contributions made by members of the group, (6) offering encouragement and praise to elevate group morale, (7) resolving differences that might arise between members of the group, and (8) bringing the discussion to a satisfactory conclusion.

Until now, we have been talking about leaders. Perhaps, this would be a good time to define the term leadership: A verbal or nonverbal interpersonal process capable of shaping how people think and act in a particular way; influencing a group of people so as to help them complete a task or reach a specific goal.

Styles

There are three popular styles of leadership: *authoritarian, democratic,* and *laissez-faire*. Each has its good and bad points. These will often depend on the types of people who comprise the group, the group's task or goal, and the specific circumstances under which the group must function. Here is a brief description of each leadership style.

Authoritarian This style involves a leader who is power-hungry—someone who controls every aspect of a group's behavior and thought. Autocratic leaders rule with an iron fist, make all decisions, and hold themselves above all other members of the group.

> *List as many autocratic leaders as you can (living or dead).*

Democratic The democratic style of leadership is the most common. It seems to encourage the greatest amount of fair play and sharing of ideas. It also appears to be responsible for the most success when it comes to a group effort at reaching its goal or completing an assigned task. Although a leader who employs a democratic style plays an active role in a group, its members seem to appreciate the freedom of participation featured by this style of leadership. As the word democratic suggests, a group experiences a sense of equality and freedom under its governing influence. Team work thrives best when this style of leadership is at work.

> *List as many teachers in your school whom you would consider to employ the democratic style of leadership in their classrooms.*

*Laissez-Faire** All the laissez-faire style of leadership does is supply information and material when asked. Such a leader does not take part in or direct decision making in the group. Group members enjoy complete freedom to do practically anything they want to do (within reason). The principle behind this type of leadership is that every member of the group is believed to have the capacity to lead and, therefore, the ability to determine personal

**Laissez-faire:* Loosely translated from the French, it means to let people in a group do whatever they please.

goals. In other words, laissez-faire leadership is a leadership shared by all members of a group. This style, however, reportedly produces the lowest-quality perhaps because the "group" functions as a nongroup; it lacks esprit de corps.

Influential Factors

Situation A leader in one situation will not necessarily function as a leader under another set of circumstances. For example, the leader of a street gang whose main interest in life seems to be getting into trouble and starting fights would probably need to be physically strong and have a lot of nerve to commit acts which were against the law. Characteristics like these would have little or no meaning to a leader of a literary book club. Knowing the situation in which a group exists will give you a good idea as to the type of leader it would find attractive. Take a situation in which you have to vote for a department head. What leadership traits or qualities would you consider necessary? Would you be on the lookout for someone who is a good talker or someone who hardly talks at all, someone with brains or brawn, a worker or a dreamer? From a situational standpoint, it would probably depend largely upon the needs of your department.

Group Goals Most groups have goals—something they would like to achieve or have happen. There are short-term and long-term goals. An example of a short-term goal would be the desire of a fund-raising group to raise $1 million on a local television telethon for a worthy cause. It's long-term goal, to establish such telethons on a yearly basis over a 10-year period. How do you think a group with such long-term goals would fare with a leader having very little patience.

Another factor that has the capacity to affect leadership is whether the leader is goal-oriented or process-oriented. Goal-oriented leaders have but one objective—to get where they are going. Process-oriented leaders are less interested in where they are going, but are greatly interested in how they get there. Assume, if you will, that there are two political groups working for votes that will get their candidate into office. They couldn't care less how they get the votes as long as they get them. Having a process-oriented leader in this situation might hurt rather than help their candidate's chances of getting into office. Such a leader would probably spend too much time and energy worrying *how* the votes were gotten. On the other hand, a goal-oriented leader would have only one thing in mind—getting votes and worrying very little about how. Realizing, of course, that these are both extreme attitudes, they, nevertheless, have been used merely to illustrate the differences between them.

Group Customs Groups, like people, have personalities. Some are noisy, others are quiet; some groups approve of smoking pot and drinking alcoholic beverages, others disapprove of both. When it comes to leadership, groups tend to search out leaders whose personalities and life styles agree with their own. It is highly unlikely that you will find a group whose customs stress religious devotion with an atheist as its leader. Likewise, you are not apt to find a revolutionary group with a coward for a leader.

For a broader understanding of how communication can be affected by altering the relationship between a group and its leader, try this activity.

Name of Exercise: Changing Leaders

Purpose: To demonstrate what happens in a group when its leader is removed and replaced by another.

Procedure:

Step 1. The class is subdivided into small groups of equal members.

Step 2. At a signal from the teacher, each group is to begin a discussion on the topic of: *How to establish an individual's "worth" in a business.*

Step 3. After 10 minutes of dicussion, a vote should be taken in each group to discover which member was considered to have emerged as a leader. If there is a tie, the group is to continue voting until the tie is broken.

Step 4. At another signal from the teacher, each group is to change leaders and continue the discussion where it left off with the former leader.

Step 5. After another 10 minutes have elapsed, all group leaders are again to be changed and the same discussion topic continued.

Step 6. After each group has had two new leaders, the exercise should stop.

Step 7. At this point, the entire class should respond to the following questions:

1. How did members of your group feel about losing its leader?
2. How did members of your group feel about the new leaders it got?
3. How did the leaders feel about being shifted from one group to another?
4. Did all the leaders continue to remain leaders in whichever group they joined?
5. Did the act of changing leaders cause any other group members to experience a noticeable change in their behavior?

Write a one-page composition on leadership.

Group Geography

Tonight, if you eat supper with your family, sit in your father's chair. Don't say a word–just sit down and see what happens. If your father runs true to form, he will order you to move to your regular seat.

In our society, roles and status are often defined by where a person sits, stands, eats, sleeps, or works. Most offices are arranged so that the chair occupied by the person of highest rank or status is set apart from the others. In certain parts of the South, where segregation used to exist, blacks were required to stand at the back of the bus. Many organizations provide their executives with a separate dining room for their eating pleasure. Master bedrooms in the majority of homes sleep the head of the household. Finally, many large corporations house their entire administrative staff on a separate floor.

The study of where people sit, stand, eat, sleep, and work in relationship to one another is called *proxemics* (coined by anthropologist, Edward Hall). Also operating under the name of Microecology, the subject of human spatial relationships has attracted the attention of a number of researchers. Here are some of the things they have turned up, thus far:

1. Nonviolent prisoners in a penitentiary can tolerate up to 18 inches of interpersonal distance; whereas, violent ones, 34 inches. In simpler terms, nonviolent prisoners will let people get closer to them than violent prisoners.
2. Most people stand closer to each other while waiting in line to see an X-rated movie than while waiting to see one that is rated GP.
3. People stand closer to those they like than to those they dislike.
4. People communicate more with one another in a circle because they can all see one another face to face.
5. People tend to stand closer to those nearer their own age.
6. Students will sit closer to a teacher they expect to be praised by than one they expect to criticize them.
7. In conversation, men stand almost twice as far apart from each other than women do.
8. People stand closer to those they trust than those they distrust.
9. Marriages, generally, occur among those who are more closely associated in terms of distance.
10. Extroverts (outgoing and aggressive people) stand closer to others than introverts (shy and retiring people) do.
11. Leader types, if they have a choice, will sit at the head of a table.
12. When blacks move closer to whites in conversation, whites consider this aggressive behavior. However, when whites back away from blacks in conversation, blacks consider such behavior cold and standoffish.

To get some idea about your own proxemic habits, take the following quiz:

Your Proxemic Personality

Where would you sit in the following situations?

1. In the Dean's office:

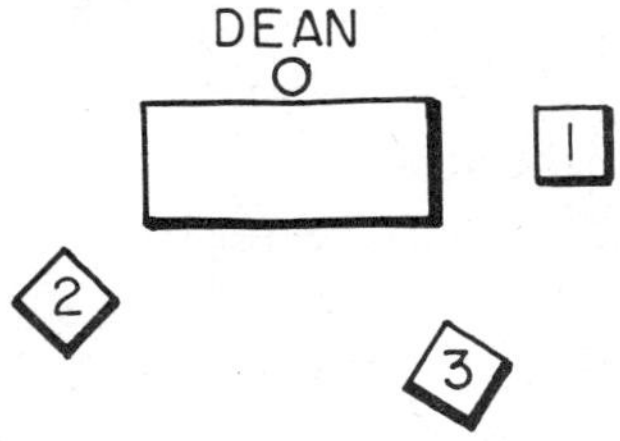

2. In an interview for a job you want very much:

3. In the library, helping your best friend prepare for a difficult exam:

4. In a coffee house with someone you have been seeing regularly and whom you like a great deal:

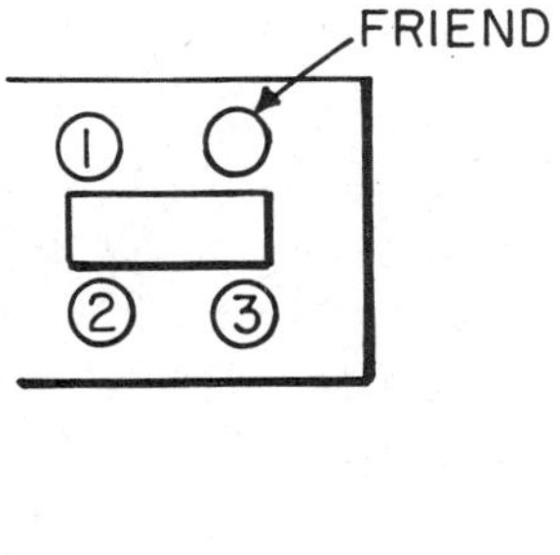

5. In a classroom taking a course you are very interested in and with a teacher you consider to be terriffic:

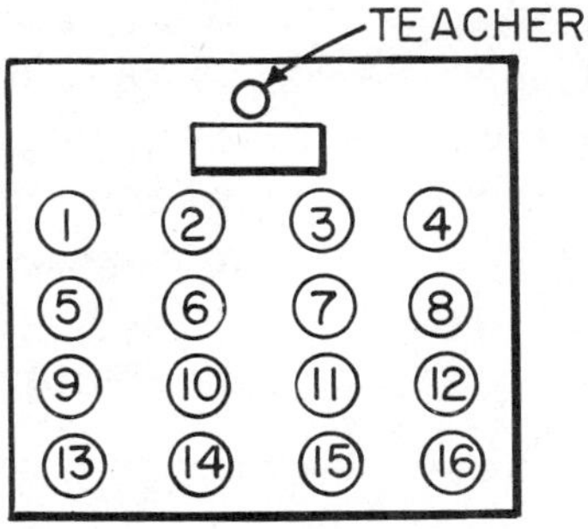

6. At a conference table:

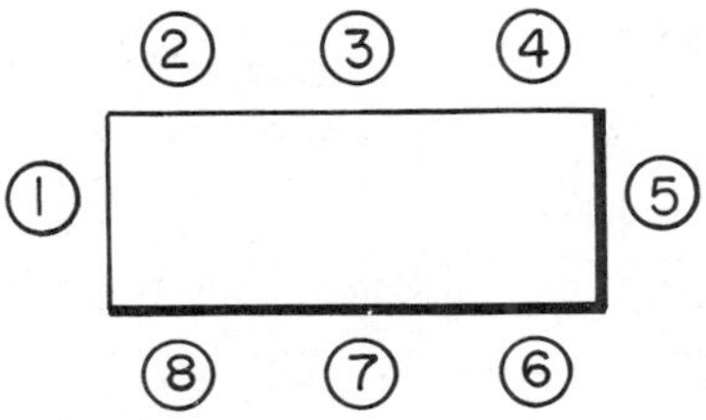

Prepare a brief paper in which you explain why you chose the seats you did.

It's amazing how much you can tell about people by noticing the distance between them. For instance, imagine yourself sitting in the last row of a neighborhood movie house. Out of the corner of your eye, you see a pretty young girl walk down the center aisle to the middle row, slip in about ten seats, and sit down. Ten minutes later, you see a nice looking young man do the same thing except that he sits about five seats away from her. So far, everything seems quite normal and you get involved in the movie. After another 10 or 15 minutes, you happen to notice that the young man is now three seats away from the young girl. Another five minutes pass and he is one seat from her. Finally, you see him sitting right next to her. Again you pay little attention to them and return to your movie. Then, after about half an hour, you happen to look at them again and guess what, the young man is back where he started–five seats away from the young girl. From the changes in distance between them, you probably guessed what was going on in both their minds.

The distance we keep from others varies with the situation and our personalities. Some of us like crowds, others prefer the wide open spaces. Did you know, for example, that every person has his or her own private bubble or personal space? You should recall it from an earlier chapter as the invisible circle that surrounds every person. Have you ever been on a bus that was practically empty and have someone come over and sit right next to you? There were plenty of empty seats and the person had to sit in the seat right next to you. Did you mind? The same thing might have happened to you in an elevator. You were the only passenger in the car and the next one to enter had to stand with his arm against yours. In both of these situations, on the bus and in the elevator, people invaded your "personal bubble." To make matters worse, they did it without your permission. To find out how big your personal bubble is, try this exercise.

Name of Exercise: How Big Is Your Bubble?

Purpose: To find out at what point another person's closeness makes you uncomfortable.

Procedure:

Step 1. Class members are to stand up, pair off, and face one another about five feet apart.

Step 2. At a signal from the teacher, one member of each pair of students should slowly begin to inch toward the other who is to remain motionless.

Step 3. As soon as the advancing student reaches a point where the other one feels uncomfortable, the student should call out the word, *stop*. The nose to nose distance between them should then be estimated. It represents that person's private bubble size.

Step 4. The other student's bubble size should now be tested.

Step 5. At a second signal from the teacher, all students should change partners and take turns checking out each other's bubble size.

Step 6. A general discussion should now begin in which all students should volunteer to tell what they thought and felt during and after doing this exercise.

For an entire day, stand 4 to 6 inches closer to everyone you meet. Notice both your own reactions and the reactions of others. Then, write a 1-page reaction paper on it.

Edward Hall describes four distances we use in our everyday lives. When we whisper, tell secrets, wrestle, hug, kiss, and comfort each other, we do it at what is called an *intimate distance*, which extends about 18 inches away from the surface of our skin. When we conduct normal interpersonal activities such as chatting, shaking hands, and casually looking at one another, it is our *personal distance* (or *space*). It ranges from 1½ to 4 feet out from our bodies.

Next, there is social distance at which most business transactions are carried on such as the man seated behind a desk talking with a visitor. It occurs between 4 and 12 feet. Last is *public distance*, which may cover any interpersonal relationships that exceed 12 feet from person-to-person. A typical example would be a speaker and an audience or people standing around at a bus or train station.

There is something else beside the space existing between people in groups that you should know about. It is the angle at which people approach each other*. Professors Donn Byrne and Jeffrey Fisher, from their studies, discovered that men and women have "good and bad" sides. For example, if you want to get on a stranger's good side, you must approach a woman from the front and a man from the side. They found out something else. When communicating with friends, women like them to come from the side and men preferred that they come at them from the front. Another researcher found that the angle of people's feet while in conversation can indicate whether or not they are interruptable. If their feet are arranged like this:

it suggests a "closed conversation". and should not be interrupted. If, on the hand, their feet are arranged like this:

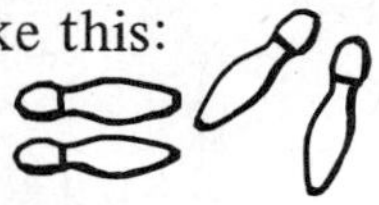

it suggests an "open conversation" which is interruptable.

If you are expecting some sure-fire formula to grow out of this brief discussion of group geography, you will be disappointed. It would be extremely misleading to suggest that if you sit or stand in a particular relationship to someone, it will cause the interaction to move in a given direction. You may then rightfully ask, "Why all this talk about proxemics?" The explanation goes something like this. As you already know, people bring to a relationship a set of notions about themselves and about that relationship to others. These notions are not by any means static—they vary dynamically according to time, place, and circumstances. By allowing yourself to become sensitized to these interpersonal spatial relationships, your awareness of proxemics will become noticeably elevated. In the process, you will discover those positions, angles, and distances you maintain which are to your best communicative advantage. Think of yourself as a walking, talking, feeling laboratory with but a single target—to notice how people position themselves in relation to one another in groups.

Group Personalities

Into whatever field you should go in the years ahead, you will meet all types of people. Some you will get to know rather well; others will remain

*Don Hyman, "Re: Apt angles of approach," *Long Island Press,* (Feb. 16, 1976), p. 11.

strangers. Knowing how to get along with them is an art you must learn, and the earlier you start studying people and how they communicate in groups, the better your chances of being happy and successful in your chosen line of work.

Many relationships begin and end because someone possesses one special and unique quality. There are also times when you meet someone who is terrific in almost every way—except for one small thing. The people to be described in these pages were selected because they each possess that one special trait. Down the line, you will notice that they all have a unique way of behaving which sets them apart from others. Since it is not practical to examine them individually, we shall collect and discuss those with similiar traits as a group. Bear in mind, however, that whether you are dealing with physicians, lawyers, bankers, industrialists, fish-peddlars, or prostitutes, their primary identities are those of "human beings." Learning to cope with them as people will require your time, patience, and, above all, your understanding of where they are coming from in their heads.

Because we are all mixtures of one another, you will probably see reflections of yourself in each of the personality types soon to be described. Thus, out of fairness to them (as they cannot defend themselves here), put the kind of person you are on record by taking the following quiz;

Are you the kind of person who:

Seems very concerned about how things used to be?	Yes ___	No ___
Is inclined to tell others what they can look forward to?	Yes ___	No ___
Tends to throw cold water on other people's ideas?	Yes ___	No ___
Often finds yourself saying just the opposite of what others have said?	Yes ___	No ___
Has the reputation of explaining what other people mean?	Yes ___	No ___
Doesn't take an umbrella, even though the weather bureau forecasted rain?	Yes ___	No ___
Studies like crazy for every little examination or quiz?	Yes ___	No ___
Can't resist telling others what you have just learned or read?	Yes ___	No ___
Is always quoting famous people?	Yes ___	No ___
Insists that people stick to whatever subject they are discussing?	Yes ___	No ___
Is annoyed by people who do not let other people finish what they are saying?	Yes ___	No ___
Demands that people be specific when they discuss a particular subject?	Yes ___	No ___
Likes to write things down?	Yes ___	No ___
Always seems to find yourself caught in the middle?	Yes ___	No ___
Helps people who cannot express themselves clearly?	Yes ___	No ___
Thinks you know more than the average person when it comes to general knowledge?	Yes ___	No ___
Is surprised at what most people say?	Yes ___	No ___
Giggles a lot?	Yes ___	No ___
Doesn't say much at parties?	Yes ___	No ___
Catches yourself repeating what others have said?	Yes ___	No ___

These questions do not represent a scientific test or quiz. There is no right or wrong. How you answered them does not mean that you fall into any special category. All they have been designed to do is provide you with some self-feedback. The point has already been made that most people see themselves, not as they really are, but as they have "learned" to see themselves. Reading this section, together with how these questions were answered, may help you get a clearer picture of yourself as you really are.

An important thing to remember is that few people behave a certain way—all the time. Their behavior seems to form patterns; i.e., people who talk a lot can be found, on most occasions, to be talkative, those who speak in a loud voices do it most of the time. The characters developed here were conceived on the basis of these patterns. Hopefully, by providing you with insights into their behavior, it will enable you to better cope with them in whichever organizational group situation they might emerge. Now, without further delay, here they are:

Time-Bound People

Among time-bound people are the *historians* and the *prophets.* The historian is always talking about how things used to be. You get the feeling when talking with this type of person that you are still living in the past. They begin so many sentences with *I remember when ______, if only they would bring back the ______,* and *they just don't make 'em like they did in the good ole days.*

Prophets, on the other hand, talk as if they were living in the future rather than the present. Their pet phrases usually begin with: You watch. One of these days. Mark my words. Ten years from now.

Your greatest difficulty in dealing with either the historian or the prophet is getting them to communicate in the present. They persist in ignoring how things are now and dwell on how they were in the past or how they will be in the future. The best way to handle them is to ask questions. Force them to adjust their remarks to the present. If the historian says, "I remember when the hot dog was only a nickel," ask, "How does the value of a dollar today compare with the value of a dollar when a hot dog was only a nickel?" Use this same technique with the prophet—except, in reverse. If the prophet says, "Watch, in 20 years, we'll have a dictatorship in this country," ask, "What specific trends do you observe in government today that lead you to believe that in 20 years we'll have a dictatorship in this country?" With the historian and the prophet, make every effort to work the present into the conversation. Should this technique fail, politely withdraw from the conversation as quickly as possible.

The Hostile Ones

Hostility is their business. They upset others whenever, wherever, and however they can. They consist of *blockers, contraries,* and *district attorneys.* In conversation, the blockers are known to throw cold water on any new ideas or opinions other people have. If you were to say, "Hey, why don't we advertise our line in one of those foreign language newspapers," the blocker would probably butt in and say, "Are you kidding, that would be a waste of time. The people who read them haven't got a dime." The contraries, no matter what you say, take the opposite point of view. If you say *up,* they say *down*; if you say *right*, they say *wrong*. The district attorneys complete your list. They are the types of people who cross-examine you on whatever you say. Imagine that you have just given your opinion on the current state of the stock market. Without warning, some self-appointed district attorney will fire a bunch of questions at you; such as, Are you an economist? Have you ever played the stock market? What is your definition of economy? They rarely have opinions of their own. All they do is attack the opinions of others. Individually or together, the hostile ones usually do more harm than good when it comes to communication.

There is a way of dealing with hostile people. It is not very different from the way you deal with getting rid of ants in a kitchen. You simply remove whatever it is that ants thrive on. In the case of the hostile ones, it is the reactions of others that they feed on. If you don't snap at their bait, they are usually lost.

Picture this scene. You are sitting around at some friend's house with a few old and a few new acquaintances. In the course of conversation, you happen to mention how excited you are about a new job you've just started. The hostile one smells blood and throws out the bait. It comes in the form of a remark like, "Sounds to me as if you're wasting your time. Why don't you go back to school and study something worthwhile?" At this point, you must make a decision. Should you get into an argument with this person or just let the remark go by. Remember, if you snap at the bait by answering, you must be ready for some emotionally loaded communication that will probably go nowhere fast. By the same token, if you decide to ignore the remark, you have indicated to both the hostile one and everyone else in the room that the remark is not worthy of an answer.

Bloomer 'n Gloomers

Members of the special group of bloomers 'n gloomers come in two varieties: *optimists* and *pessimists.* The optimist is the bloomer who has mastered the art of positive thinking; the pessimist has mastered the art of negative thinking. For the bloomer, life is a bowl of cherries. The gloomer sees life as a bowl of doubt, dispair, sadness, decay and tears. From this description, you should be able to spot either one of these types in a matter of minutes. Here is an example of how each would be inclined to think in relation to a midterm examination. The optimist would say, "Wow, I really breezed through that examination. It was like taking candy from a baby." The pessimist would say, "Boy, I really messed that one up. It was like being buried alive."

Once you have established whether a person is a bloomer or gloomer, it makes conversation much easier. Before they open their mouths on practically any subject, you can generally predict what their attitude toward it will be. With this insight, you might find it useful to anticipate them once in awhile. Assume you are confronted by a bloomer. Following true to form, this bloomer should treat almost anything you say to be loaded with goodies, whoopies, and happy days. Prepared for this kind of positive response, you might wish to begin whatever you are going to say with, "Even though I just know that everything is going to turn out fine, . . ." and, then, continue with what you wanted to say. Whereas this optimistic remark may not completely satisfy the bloomer's compulsive need to see the world through rose-colored glasses, it will, at least, sound the alert that you are also thinking positively. Do the same thing with the gloomer, but in reverse. Say something like, "I realize all of this work may be completely useless, but . . ." and finish whatever you were going to say.

Under no circumstance should you be getting the impression that a bloomer or gloomer can be controlled with only one sentence. However, the fact that you display a sensitivity toward their way of thinking and monitor your remarks accordingly, a great many breakdowns in communication with them may be avoided.

Town Criers

Here are a couple of characters I am sure you have met: *the information-giver* and *the according-to-___freak.* Without being asked, these two go around telling people things. Like encyclopedias, they pass along the ideas and opinions of others. With one minor difference—the information-giver and the according-to-___freak have about the same line. The information-giver will give out any kind of information, regardless of who said it; whereas, the according-to-___freak is hung up on who said it. To illustrate, the information-giver would probably say, "Did you know that dreams play an important part in our lives?" In contrast, the according-to-___freak would say the same thing, except for one small item—who said it! It would sound like this: "According to the famous psychoanalyst, Sigmund Freud, dreams play an important part in our lives."

Dealing with these two types of people depends a great deal on your own personality. If you are at a cocktail party and some according-to-___freak begins to annoy you by showing off how much he knows, it might very well please you to expose him as being a phoney. To do this, you will have to put him on the defensive by asking such questions as: How does what you are telling me relate to what we are discussing? Why are you telling me all this? Did the person you just quoted say anything else in his or her writings that might contradict what you have just said? How can I be sure that your quote is accurate? Needless to say, these questions should only be used if you find it necessary to defend yourself against one of these types. Otherwise, relax and enjoy yourself.

Regulators

There are three kinds of regulators: *gatekeepers, police officers,* and *leaders.* All three share the compulsive need to influence what others say, think, and do. Let's look at them separately. Gatekeepers take it upon themselves to decide what should or should not be said in a group. If someone is talking about Christmas vacations and another person happens to bring up the subject of final examinations, the gatekeeper would probably interrupt and say, "Just hold on a minute, we're talking about Christmas vacations and you bring up final examinations. Would you mind if we stick to the subject of Christmas vacations?" Under these same circumstances, the police officer in the discussion might jump in with, "Alright, alright, everyone quiet down. We're not going to get anywhere with everyone talking at the same time. Let's have a little order, OK?" Finally, if there had been a leader type present, a remark like this might have been heard. "Hey, how about cutting all this chatter about vacations and examinations and going into town? I know a place that serves the best pizza in the whole world."

As you can see, regulators are people who take it upon themselves to manipulate others in some way. Whether they are good or bad, helpful or destructive, will depend on the individual situation and the other people involved.

In almost every class, there is at least one regulator. Make it a point to watch for them in your classes for the next few days. You will know you are on their trail if you hear, while sitting in, perhaps, an English class, this remark from the rear of the room: "Come on, Phil, give someone else a chance to get a word into the discussion, will ya? "Such a remark could come from either a police officer or a leader type. Generally speaking, regulators are not dangerous unless they get out of hand and behave in some extreme manner.

Attention Addicts

We all need attention. Because of this, we employ different ways of getting it. As children, we did certain things that pleased our parents and other things that made them angry. Unable or unwilling to use many of these methods as young adults, we had to figure out alternative ways of getting attention. Thus, using various forms of communication as tools, some of us developed into *martyrs, playboys* and *playgirls,* and *situationists.* Martyrs get attention by playing the role of injured parties. If everyone in a group wants to go on a picnic and the martyr doesn't feel like it, you will probably hear something like, "Gee, I really don't feel like going on a picnic; but, don't let me spoil your fun. You all go ahead without me and have a good time. I'll find something to do by myself." Meanwhile, a playboy or playgirl might emerge as the individual who is always fooling around and telling jokes. Situationists have their own special gimmick. No matter what anyone says, they get attention by saying, "Well, that really depends upon the situation." As an attention-getter, it almost never fails because it fits in practically anywhere. No matter what anyone says, it will always depend on something else. Can you think of any case in which it does not apply?

Situationists, as a group, are not harmful. They make their bids for attention, give their reasons why something depends upon something else, and patiently wait for an opportunity to do it again. Martyrs can be a little more disturbing if they overplay their role. After all, who needs someone in a group always crying the blues and bidding for sympathy? The playboy or playgirl also run the risk of offending others by overdoing their jokes, wise-cracks, and fooling around. There are times, however, when these types can, through their use of humor, relieve tension in a group. Try to remember that when dealing with a martyr, playperson, or situationist, they all have one common trait—the need for attention. If they don't get it, they will usually try a little harder. Chances are, after several unsuccessful attempts, they will give up.

Transferites

The word transferites, as used here, applies to the type of people whose only interest is passing on information. Included among them are *recorders* and *go-betweens.* The recorder is quickly recognized in any discussion as being the individual with a pencil and paper. No matter what is being discussed, these people seem unable to resist the temptation of writing things down, making lists, or keeping score. Go-betweens remind us of a game we played as children called "telephone." It consisted of whispering something from one child to another to see whether, after passing through an entire lineup of kids, the information changed from the way it started out.

Recorders are great note-takers. Seldom do they make any oral contributions to a discussion except, perhaps, to have something they didn't get down repeated. Their main contribution to group life is their ability to take down what has been said in any conversation, discussion, meeting or lecture.

Go-betweens carry messages from one person to another. Suppose you and your best friend had an argument and weren't talking to each other. You were both sorry about what happened but, each of you was too stubborn to apologize first. Finally, you decide to break the ice by having another friend give your best friend a message. Whoever delivered that message could be classified under *go-betweens.* This might sound like an easy way to make up, but there is an occasional danger: Although most go-betweens have your best interests at heart, by substituting a word here and there, using a slightly different tone of voice, or wearing an inappropriate facial expression, they could alter the message they are carrying for you.

Recorders or go-betweens generally do not represent any threat to communication. The only thing that bears watching when dealing with them is that they accurately relate the information they receive.

Know-It-Alls

There are two types of know-it-alls: *qualifiers* and *oracles.* Both behave as if they have a direct line to God. No matter what anyone says, they go out of their way to let them know that they know all there is to know on the subject. The qualifier is someone who is always jumping into a conversation to explain what someone else has just said. If you have just answered a question in class, before you are able to finish, the qualifier will interrupt with, "What George is really trying to say is _____." Out of some misguided sense of being helpful, qualifiers sincerely feel that if they don't come to the rescue, the rest of us will not be able to make ourselves understood. Oracles suffer from a similiar superiority complex. They fancy themselves as "Mr. and Mrs. Right." They swim through life casually sweeping aside what others believe as nonsense.

Coping with the qualifier or oracle is by no means an easy task. They seem to have a desperate need to show others how intelligent they are. As a result, they have a stubborn streak. If what they say is ignored or taken lightly, instead of backing off, they frequently bounce back with even greater force. Their biggest weakness seems to be credibility; that is, being believed by others. If the remarks made by an oracle or qualifier are dismissed as being foolish, irrelevant, stupid or meaningless, they suffer the greatest setback. Therefore, if you should have the misfortune to be attached by one of them, do everything in your power to reduce their credibility. Raise as many doubts as you can with regard to whatever they happen to say.

Out-to-Lunchers

Out-to-lunchers is being used here to describe those people who, whenever you talk to them, don't seem to be with you. They seem to be out of touch. There are four types: *intellectual virgins, gigglers, mannequins,* and *parrots.* Intellectual virgins are people who have practically no opinion on anything. No matter what you ask them, they always draw a blank and say, "Gee, I never thought of that!" or, "Wow, that's really fantastic!" Their entire vocabulary appears to consist of little more than a series of wows, gee whizzes, gollys, and no kiddings. They often give the impression of being amazed that the world is round and that bees can fly. Gigglers are individuals who substitute giggling for conversation. Whatever you say to them, they giggle. Mannequins act like store window dummies. Without saying a word, they can go through an entire evening sitting in the same chair. If someone offers them a drink or a sandwich, they take it in complete silence. Some mannequins are smilers, others are frowners, and still others have no expressions on their faces at all. Parrot people repeat what they hear others say. For example, should someone in the room say, "It's stuffy in here. Will someone please open a window?" The parrot person will repeat, "It's stuffy in here—someone open a window." Being around them could make you feel like you like you're in an echo chamber.

Dealing with out-to-lunchers is more a matter of understanding and patience than conflict. Their behavior is most often a question of personality adjustment than an intentional withdrawal from whatever is going on in a group. Most of them feel threatened by people, especially when they are confronted by them in numbers. If you can get an out-to-luncher off to the side, you might be surprised at how some of them open up.

Name of Exercise: Who's Who

Purpose: To give members of the class an opportunity to role play the various types of people described in this section. By doing this, students can acquire a first-hand knowledge of the kinds of communication feedback the characters they are playing might get in real life. Students are also provided with the challenge of being able to correctly identify these characters on the basis of their behavior in a group situation.

Procedure:

Step 1. The names of all the types just described in this section are to be written on small pieces of paper and placed in a hat or bowl (historians, blockers, contraries).

Step 2. One small group of students equal to the number of pieces of paper in the hat or bowl is to be seated in the center of the room (or at the front, if that is more convenient). The others will sit around them as observers.

Step 3. The hat is to be passed around and each participating student picks out a piece of paper. The student must, then, assume the character and personality of whichever name is written on the paper.

Step 4. The teacher will now give the group a discussion topic. Members of the group, using this topic, should then procede with the discussion and behave like the type of person they have chosen (martyr, police officer, district attorney).

Step 5. After approximately 15 minutes, the discussion should be stopped. The observers are to try to identify the roles being played by members of the group.

Having met these various types of people, you may be wondering why "normal people" were not included in this section. An understandable reason is because the word *normal* is semantically very unmanagable; that is, its meaning is extremely difficult to nail down. "Normal" means different things to different people. There may well be as many definitions as there are people.

For your own satisfaction, briefly describe a "normal person."

It has been suggested that we are all mixtures of one another. Do you agree? The opinion being advanced here is that on any job, you will probably be working with people with whom you share a far greater number of similiarities than you might be willing to admit. Furthermore, if you can search out these similiarities and use them as bridges to span differences, your ability to cope with them in groups will be markedly improved.

SELF-EXAMINATION QUIZ

Having read this chapter, my answers to the following questions reflect my understanding of its contents.

1. Why is group life so important on the job?

2. How involved are you with groups? Explain your answer.

3. List some of the psychological and physical needs served by groups.

4. Identify some of the things an·individual brings to any group.

5. What is the difference between *obstructive* and *cooperative* behavior in a group?

6. Describe the concept of *leadership* and *leaders* in a group context.

7. How do group situations, goals, and customs affect leadership?

8. How can altering the location of a group influence the behavior of its members?

9. List, and briefly describe some types of people one encounters in groups.

10. What is one way to cope with someone different from yourself?

Suggested Readings

Brilhart, John K., *Effective Group Discussion* (Dubuque, Iowa: Brown, 1967).
Brislow, H. S., "Employee communication: A personnel man's viewpoint," *Personnel*, **48**, 995 (1969).
Burns, T., "The directions of activity and communication in a departmental executive group," *Human Relations*, 7, 73–97 (1954).
Doll, R. E., and E. K. E. Gunderson, "The influence of group size on perceived compatability and achievement in an extreme environment," *Personnel Psychology*, 24. 305–310 (1971).
Egan, Gerard, *Face to Face: The Small Group Experience.* (Monterey, Calif.: Brooks/Cole, 1973).
Farris, G. F., and F. G. J. Lim, "Effects of performance on leadership, cohesiveness, influence, satisfaction, and subsequent performance," *Journal of Applied Psychology*, 53 491–497 (1969).
Hare, Paul A., "Bibliography of Small Group Research," *Sociometry*, 35, 1–150 (1972).
Kiesler, Charles, A., and Sara B. Kiesler, *Conformity* (Reading, Mass.: Addison-Wesley, 1969).
Maier, Norman R. F., *Problem Solving and Creativity: In Individuals and Groups* (Belmont, Calif.: Brooks/Cole, 1970).
McGregor, D., Leadership and Motivation (Cambridge, Mass.: M.I.T. Press, 1966).
Rosenfeld, L. G., *Human Interaction is a Small Group Setting.* (Columbus, Ohio: Charles Merrill, 1973).

WORK AREA FOR CHAPTER 5

Chapter 6

Listening: A Serious Business

There is more to listening than meets the ear.

MEMO

TO: Reader

FROM: Author

After reading this chapter, you should have a better understanding of:

1. Your own listening aptitude.

2. The various reasons why people listen.

3. The relationship between hearing and listening.

4. Why "paying attention" is so important to the art of listening.

5. What is meant by a "listening philosophy."

6. Why effective listening is such a serious business.

7. Some of the myths commonly associated with listening.

8. How certain listening exercises can help you become a better listener.

9. The expressions: I know that you believe you understand what you think I said, but I am not sure you realize that what you heard is not what I meant.

10. How improving your listenting skill can improve your overall ability to communicate.

Chapter 6

Few things bring people closer to one another than listening. Not only does it tell the next person you care about what they have to say, it also tells them that you care about them as individuals—as human beings. Parents who do not listen to their children, teachers who do not listen to their students, and employers who do not listen to their employees all commit one of the most serious offenses in communication. The crime of *not listening* robs any relationship of its dignity, its participants of their self-respect, and people of the opportunity to share their emotions and experiences. Imagine the empty feeling that comes with landing a terrific job, getting a raise in salary, or being promoted to a higher position and not having anyone to tell the good news. Much of the joy in life is being able to share the good things that happen to us. But what if nobody listens, if people are too busy with their own affairs to pay any attention to yours? It can be very unpleasant. Think of listening as important because it allows you to venture out beyond the safety limits of your inner world and, by so doing, meaningfully share the inner and outer words of others.

Although sloppy listening could have serious consequences in casual conversation, the risk of such consequences seem to run significantly higher in business and professional conversations. The physician or nurse with poor listening habits could result in giving a patient the wrong medication, a salesperson writing up and shipping the wrong merchandise, or an engineer constructing a bridge or building not corresponding to the architect's specifications. The list of situations in which faulty listening has been linked with substantial losses of goods and money is lengthy. Ask anyone in business or who renders a professional service to what extent that business or service would improve if the listening associated with it were better. Although it is common knowledge that some fields depend on listening effectively more than others, the truth of the matter is that all fields depend upon listening to some extent. Would it surprise you to learn that most people, if asked, think they are good listeners, that they grasp the meaning of what is said to them in the majority of situations? If you were being interviewed for a job and asked whether you were a good listener, how would you answer? Before starting to read this chapter, it might be a good idea for you to find out just how good a listener you actually are. To find out, take the following quiz.

LISTENING QUIZ

Instructions:

Read each of the following statements and, on the basis of your judgment, place the word *true* or *false* in the appropriate spaces:

________ 1. The better you can hear, the better you can listen.

________ 2. It takes no effort to listen

_________ 3. Listening is just a matter of understanding the language.

_________ 4. More intelligent people listen better.

_________ 5. The older you get, the more effectively you are able to listen.

_________ 6. In the communication process, speaking is usually more important than listening.

_________ 7. The average person does more talking than listening.

_________ 8. People cannot be taught how to improve their listening ability.

_________ 9. When you learned to read, you learned to listen at the same time.

_________ 10. Listening is simply a matter of being quiet and looking at a speaker.

If you marked all of these statements *false*, you probably have a slightly better sense of communication than most people. If you marked any of them *true*, consider yourself perfectly normal and as someone who should find this chapter rather interesting. Realizing that some of the statements used in this quiz may have had more than one interpretation, a brief comment on each of them is in order.

The better you can hear, the better you can listen. For a very long time, people have gotten *hearing* and *listening* mixed up. They are not the same thing. Hearing refers to the process by which the sounds around you are carried to your brain. It is a physiological process. The word physiological means "how things work" inside your body. In this case, we are talking about the physiology of hearing. Listening, on the other hand, is an emotional and intellectual process. It consists of taking what you hear and giving it meaning. In other words, because you heard something, it doesn't automatically mean that you understood it. Although every time you listen you are also hearing, the opposite is not necessarily true. Every time you are hearing, you are not necessarily listening.

It takes no effort to listen. Every student knows this is completely untrue. Listening requires concentration and concentration generally requires some effort. It demands even more effort when a subject or teacher is boring and uninteresting. Sitting in classes for five or six hours a day often causes the mind to wander. To keep it focused on a particular subject requires a certain amount of discipline. Here is one important reason why this is so. The average person speaks at the rate of about 125–140 words per minute. In contrast, the average thought-speed ranges from 400–600 words per minute. As a result, if you are listening to a lecture where the teacher's speech-speed is 135 words per minute and your thought-speed is 500 words per minute, your mind will obviously have plenty of time to wander—to take little side trips. For this reason alone, you can see that listening requires effort. The amount of effort will, naturally, depend upon several other factors—how you feel on that particular day, your interest in the subject, the time of day, how good the teacher is, etc.

Listening is just a matter of understanding the language. Would you agree that because you know the alphabet, you can automatically spell? Would you also agree that because you know a great many words, you can automatically write poetry or short stories? From reading the earlier chapters in this book, you should already have come to recognize that both of these questions should receive a "no" answer. Listening involves taking the words you hear, decoding them, and coming up with a series of meaningful thoughts. Be reminded once again, that meaning is in people, not in words or language. Occasionally, a student can be overheard to say, "I can't figure it out. I listened so carefully to the lecture and didn't understand what the teacher was talking about." It certainly would appear that there is more to listening than understanding the language.

More intelligent people listen better. In order to appreciate why this statement is wrong, you must first ask yourself why people listen. People listen for different reasons. Can we say that people who are more intelligent have "better reasons" for listening than those who are not as intelligent? There is no basis for even suggesting such a thing. The word that is troublesome in this statement is *better.* What is it supposed to mean in this context? Intelligent people clearly do not have better hearing than those who are less intelligent. By the same token, we cannot say that the more intelligent have better reasons for listening than people who are less intelligent, can we? What we can say, however, is that intelligent people, because they have the reputation of being able to manipulate ideas in a certain way, listen in a slightly different manner. Listening differently, therefore, does not necessarily mean listening better. Regardless of intelligence, the quality of a person's listening ability seems to depend upon how well it serves an overall ability to communicate.

The older you get, the more effectively you are able to listen. Whereas a person's hearing might suffer in later years, listening habits tend to remain essentially the same. Unless there is a serious change in a person's mental or physical health, the way someone listens does not usually change much over the years. Poor listeners in their twenties are apt to be poor listeners in their forties and sixties. There are, of course, those few whom age teaches the wisdom of good listening. However, it is not advisable to wait for Father Time to make you an effective listener. The wiser course is to develop healthy listening habits when you are young which will last you all your life.

In the communication process, speaking is usually more important than listening. We live in a speech-centered society, a country in which the ability to speak up is considered by many to be a desirable trait. Nevertheless, while a great deal of talking goes on, not too many people are listening. In fact, the need to be listened to is so great that professional listening services are now available; i.e., people who get paid to listen. While a persuasive argument could be advanced for the importance of either speaking or listening, the need for more effective listening seems to be slightly greater. Think about it for a moment. Every form of communication, if it is to have meaning, depends on feedback. Listening is a major source of feedback functioning as the radar by which most speakers guide themselves. Without responsible listening, most speaking proceeds rather aimlessly.

The average person does more talking than listening. Whereas the above statement might more rightfully apply to people whose job, business or profession demands that they talk for a living (teachers, salespersons, actors, and actresses), it does apply to the general population. The average individual spends approximately 45% of each day listening. These pursuits include listening to other people, television, radio, records, tapes–plus attending concerts, theater, and films. Actually, you do much less talking than thinking each day. Most of us speak in spurts–in bits and pieces. If you added up (in minutes) all the times you speak in an average day, you would be surprised at how little it amounts to. The remainder of the time, you probably spend reading or writing. Research on the subject has shown that the average adult spends approximately 18 per cent of the time writing, 15 per cent reading, 25 per cent speaking, and 45 per cent listening.*

People cannot be taught how to improve their listening ability. Wrong! Listening ability can be improved through special listening training programs. Dr. Charles Irvin tested 1,400 Michigan State college freshmen before and after listening training. Poor to above-average listeners before training improved the most. Listening-trained students improved from 9 to 12 per cent over nonlistening trained students. Reading this chapter will help you discover several practical ways you can learn to improve your listening ability. The first step in this direction, naturally, is for you to want to become a better listener. You may be a good listener and think you are not or be a poor listener and think you are a good one. In either case, listening training can make you better at it than you are. There appear to be two types of people: (1) those who learn by listening (audio people) and (2) those who learn by reading (video people). Each, for some poorly understood reason, learn better one way or the other.

Listening is simply a matter of being quiet and looking at the speaker. Have you ever had people look you in the eye, remain perfectly quiet, and give you the distinct feeling that they weren't listening to a word you were saying? How can you tell whether someone is really listening to you? Obviously, silence and eye contact are not sufficient proof that a person is not listening to what you are saying. Knowing whether someone is listening to you is especially difficult when talking on the telephone. Without being able to see the other person's eyes, all you often have to go on is their silence and a series of intermittent words and sounds, such as uh huh, right, sure, yeah, hmmmm,

*Donald E. Bird, "Teaching listening comprehension," *Journal of Communication* 3, 127 (1953).

and OK. Without such clues, you are prompted to say, "Are you listening? Are you still on the line?" Learning how to determine whether or not someone is listening is an extremely serious part of business and professional communication.

The listening quiz you have just taken and the comments on its statements you have just read represent a beginning—an introduction to the fascinating art of listening. Now, if you are still listening to me, let us continue.

Why People Listen

People listen for a variety of reasons:

1. *To get information:* The majority of time you spend in a classroom is spent listening for information. At home and after school, you listen to your parents for information about how to get along in society and with other members of your family. If you have a job after school, you listen to your boss for information concerning the most effective way of doing it. Socially, you listen to your friends for information about how they think and feel and compare it with your own thoughts and feelings.

2. *To be amused:* Whether it is a good joke, a spine-tingling horror movie, or a fantastic concert, you listen to be amused. Aware of this, toastmasters, diplomats, politicians, traveling salesmen and teachers often include amusing anecdotes in their opening remarks to get people to listen.

3. *To be polite:* We often listen out of courtesy to older people, those in a higher position, or those from whom we stand to gain some personal benefit. We do this in addition to the fact that what they have to say might be very interesting. If not, we listen to be polite.

4. *To earn money:* Psychologists and psychiatrists, guidance and marriage counselors are but a few examples of people who are paid to listen.

> *Can you think of any others who are paid to listen.*
> *List them.*

5. *To gain an advantage:* In a street-corner argument, a courtroom, or a quarrel on the job, someone is likely to be listening in order to gain an advantage. They wait for something to be said which they can use to make their point or to shoot down someone else's point. Occasionally, an employee can be found waiting for a foreman, manager, or supervisor to make a mistake. This, too, is a case of listening for an advantage. Needless to say, it is very risky to play such games with one's superiors.

6. *To relieve boredom:* There are times when we all listen to someone or something because we haven't anything better to do. Surely you have found yourself listening to a program on the radio or television and saying, "Why on earth am I watching or listening to such garbage." Usually, it is because it is convenient and helps pass the time of day.

7. *Out of fear:* There are many situations in which we listen because we are frightened—afraid of what might happen if we don't listen. This would apply to certain classes where, if we don't force ourselves to listen, there is a good chance we will flunk the course. Another example of listening out of fear occurs in the home where a parent is giving a lecture to a son or daughter. Still another example is the employer–employee relationship; a boss reads the riot act to a worker who, afraid of losing his job, listens without uttering a word.

8. *To compare opinions:* From time to time, some clever and some not-so-clever ideas pop into our heads. Out of curiosity, we sometimes turn them loose on an employer or classroom teacher. Our purpose is to find out how others feel about such an idea. Much of our thinking is based on comparing it with how others feel. Recall how exciting it is to have an employer or teacher come up with an idea you had at home the previous day. Without being fully conscious of it, many of us spend our days listening to others for thoughts and feelings we oursevles have had.

9. *To increase our understanding:* It is normal to be confused occasionally. In fact, it has been said that the more you know about something, the more confused you are apt to be about it. There is nothing in the world about which we have a complete understanding. At best, all we can hope for is a growing understanding of life which can be applied to everyday living. Listening is one method of gathering the information leading to such understanding.

10. *To be nosey:* People who have no business of their own, mind other people's business. Instead of Peeping Toms, let's call them Listening Toms. On buses, trains, elevators, in restaurants, hallways, movie theaters, and locker rooms, these Listening Toms make it their business to listen in on the conversations of others. Some go so far as to become insulted if people walk away without letting them hear the end of a conversation.

11. *In self-defense:* If you listen carefully to someone who is trying to put you down, you will have a better chance of protecting yourself. Instead of tuning them out, listen carefully to what they say, and use it as ammunition against them. Listening this way is one of the superior ways of defending your ego and building a healthier self-image.

12. *To be liked:* None of us likes to be ignored. If we talk, we appreciate being listened to. Listening is perhaps one of the best ways of getting people to like you. It is so good that, at times, after an hour of listening and not saying a word, the other person might say, "Gee, I've really enjoyed talking with you. We must have another chat real soon."

These are some of the more common reasons why people listen. In some instances, you understand, they listen for not one reason but a combination of reasons.

> *List the reasons why you listen and give one example of each.*

Deeper Reasons Why People Listen

In the previous section, you were told the obvious reasons why people listen. There are other reasons that are not so obvious. For instance, people are more inclined to listen to things that are related to their own goals and purposes in life. Take people whose sole purpose in life is to make money—lots of money. Day and night, all they think about are ways of making money. It would be safe to say that such people would listen very attentively to anyone talking about how to make money, or even ways of holding on to it once you've got it.

Another deeper reason why people listen has to do with satisfying their *conceptual* attitudes (how they think or understand things) and *evaluative* (how they rate things) attitudes. Assume that two political candidates will deliver a speech tonight on two different channels. People will be more likely to listen to the candidate whose views most closely agree with their own and of whom they hold a high opinion. This same principle can be found to operate in a work situation. Wouldn't you be more inclined to listen to a superior whom you considered very intelligent and whose opinion on something agreed with your own?

Lastly, people tend to listen to the unexpected. Most of the things we hear each day are fairly predictable. Can you guess, with any accuracy, what each of your close friends will talk about at the next party you attend? Can't you guess, with equal accuracy, what your parents will say in most situations, or what certain teachers will say year after year in their classes? It is when any of these people depart from what you expect them to say that your listening habits are jarred. We tend to perk up our ears when we hear the unexpected.

Paying Attention

Pay attention! Pay attention! Pay attention! Everyone seems to want you to pay attention to what they are saying. Listening cannot occur unless someone pays attention. A story is told about a young man who had to deliver a speech in one of his classes. On the day of the speech, he walked to the front of the room, took a gun out of his pocket, placed it to the side of his head—and fired! He then announced, "The title of my speech is *Suicide*." Naturally, the gun wasn't loaded, but it nearly scared the pants off several members of the class, including the teacher. Of one thing you can be sure—he had their undivided attention. Another student with a curious sense of humor introduced her speech by sprinkling ashes on the floor and saying, "The title of my speech is CREMATION."

The average person's attention span is much shorter than you think. It has been suggested that it lasts from three to four seconds. While listening, your attention is constantly wandering and decreasing in strength. In most cases, it can only cope with four or five objects at a time through your sense of sight and five to eight objects through your sense of hearing. To make this clearer, pretend you are sitting in a public speaking class and the professor is lecturing on audience analysis. Each factor is explained and illustrated. Throughout the lecture, you have been expected to pay close attention. Unless the professor is exceptionally gifted, your attention level is probably somewhat patchy. A student's mind is frequently a crowded place, filled with different ideas each bidding for attention. This confusion becomes compounded when we recognize that certain teachers have the reputation of insisting that their subject is the most important. Consequently, it will warrant that the student pay very close attention. But attention alone is not enough; it must be coupled with concentration, thought, interpretation, and imagination. These are the stepping stones leading to the phenomenon called listening.

Paying attention has the effect on people of making it possible for them to perceive, conceive, distinguish, and remember things. When you perceive something, you are made aware of it through your senses of sight, smell, taste, touch, and hearing. To conceive something is to take that of which you have become aware and formulate it in your mind. The process of distinguishing such thoughts is to compare them with the information you already have acquired. Finally, remembering is the ability to recall that to which you have paid attention previously.

A Listening Philosophy

> I know that you believe you understand what you think I said, but I am not sure you realize that what you heard is not what I meant.

If you were asked to pick out the most important sentence in this chapter, it would have to be the one you have just read. It is so important, you had better read it over a couple of times to be sure you understand its meaning.

In your own words, write your interpretation of the sentence in the spaces below. Then, compare it with what a couple of your classmates have written.

____

____

____

____

What do you think a philosophy of listening means? If your answer suggests that it has something to do with how and why people listen, you are on the right track. It does. Such a philosophy should communicate to anyone going into a business some of the important things associated with good listening.

To begin with, listening takes patience. People who are impatient rarely make good listeners. While others are talking, they usually are straining at the bit and anxiously awaiting the opportunity to say something. Frequently, they interrupt the speaker, preventing him from finishing what he is saying. It is therefore absolutely essential for anyone wanting and willing to become a good listener to work hard at developing patience. They must repeatedly practice saying to themselves, "I must wait until others have finished a thought before I begin to speak." You probably lack patience if people often ask you to wait a minute or beg you to let them finish what they started to say.

A healthy listening philosophy also includes something called *empathy.* It sounds like sympathy but it has a different meaning. Sympathy means feeling sorry for people in trouble; empathy is trying to put yourself into their shoes in an effort to better understand their feelings. Said another way, sympathy is a kind word, a pat on the shoulder, a condolence card, or a tear in the eye. Empathy is feeling with another person an honest attempt to understand what they are going through. Thus, listening backed by empathy is more valuable than that backed by sympathy.

Another characteristic to be considered in any discussion of listening is *selfishness.* Yes, listening that has a purpose could be regarded as selfish. While someone else is speaking, the selfish listener should be saying, "I am going to pay strict attention to what this person is saying, let nothing distract me, and come away with as much meaning as possible."

Here is an example of "selfish listening," which you will recognize in a moment. Do you remember how you carefully listened when one of your teachers reviewed your class for an important final examination and how angry you became when certain students were talking? You were listening selfishly—with a definite purpose. In this context, selfishness must be considered something good rather than bad. It means you were motivated to listen more effectively. Such motivation is the backbone of a well-grounded listening philosophy.

A final element essential to good listening is *involvement*. Unless you live in complete seclusion, you must become involved with other people to some extent. As already pointed out, as a member of the human race, you have a great many things in common with each and every one of its members. You feel pain—they feel pain; you get hungry—they get hungry; you need love—they need love; you need to communicate—they need to communicate. The list is long. If you listen carefully to those around you, you will run into your own thoughts again and again coming out of other people's mouths. All you have to do is listen. This is called *involvement*; it is a way of showing others you care about them and are willing to share, by listening carefully, what they have to say.

Patience, empathy, selfishness, and involvement should be taken as major ingredients in any listening philosophy. Without them, listening can be reduced to an exercise in courtesy—hearing words to which little or no meaning has been assigned. Now, to test the quote:

> I know that you believe you understand what you think I said, but I am not sure you realize that what you heard is not what I meant.

Name of Exercise: If I'm Not Mistaken, You Said _____

Purpose: To find out how well you listen to what others have to say.

Procedure:

Step 1. All members of the class are to sit in a circle.

Step 2. All students are invited to participate in an open discussion on one of the following topics:

Four-day work week
Expense accounts
Sexism in business
Guaranteed minimum annual wage
Unisex clothes on the job
Bilingualism in business
Compulsory retirement at age 65

Step 3. After a signal to begin has been given by the teacher, all members of the class must abide by this rule: *Before anyone can speak, he or she must first repeat, in general, whatever the previous person was believed to have said.* That person must also agree that the interpretation was correct. The discussion should not be permitted to continue unless the meaning intended by one speaker is accurately restated by the next speaker. Naturally, the opening remark will not be a restatement. Keep in mind that a restatement of what a previous speaker said need not be word-for-word, only a paraphrase. *Time limit:* Approximately 15 minutes.

Step 4. A general discussion should now take place in which all participants are expected to volunteer their opinion of the exercise and its consequences.

An exercise such as this puts listening to the test. Properly done, it illustrates how innocently and unintentionally people listen poorly. Without realizing what they are doing, many twist what others say into all kinds of knots. These people fall into three classes.

1. *Additive listeners:* Those who expand or exaggerate what they hear. Example: If a strike action involved 500 workers, the additive listener might report it as involving 5,000 workers.
2 *Subtractive listeners:* Those who make less out of what they hear. Example: If there were 1,000 workers involved in the strike action, they would report it to have involved only 200 workers.
3. *Distortive listeners:* Those who alter what they hear so that it differs significantly from what was originally said. Example: They would report the strike as involving the local police, National Guard, thousands of spectators, five helicoptors, and the governor.

All three types of listeners, in some way, altered the messages they heard. These, of course, are extreme examples. To some extent, we all do similiar things with what others say.

Listening at an Office Party

You have just received an invitation to an office party and you can't wait to go. Finally, the day arrives and you are at the front door of the home at which the party is being held. You ring the bell, the door opens, and you walk in. You are immediately exposed to a variety of sounds—people talking, music playing, bottles and glasses klinking, hands clapping, and the shuffling of dancing feet. You hear them all, but not to the same extent. Why? Because people listen more attentively to things that interest them most.

You have been at the party for about two hours and located yourself in a corner with an interesting stranger, someone who came with your supervisor. The conversation has settled on your favorite subject–*sex*. You have become so involved in the discussion that you no longer hear most of the party sounds you heard when you first walked in. This becomes apparent when a friend walks up and asks, "Hey Marge, did you hear the news? Frank and Ann just announced their engagement." Embarrassed for not hearing the announcement, you realize that you didn't hear it because you were listening to something that was more interesting at the time–*sex*. The following exercise will demonstrate how this process of selective attention operates in a speaker–listener situation.

Name of Exercise: Divided Attention

Purpose: To illustrate how and why people decide to listen to one person and not another.

Procedure:

Step 1. Have two good talkers go to the front of the room and stand approximately 3 feet apart facing the class. They are to stand in immaginary circles approximately 2 feet in diameter.

Step 2. The speakers are then to think of a subject they can talk about comfortably for at least one or two minutes. It could be a hobby, pet gripe, or an interesting person they know.

Step 3. At a signal from the teacher, remaining inside the circles, both speakers are to begin talking at the same time. Their objective is to get the audience to listen to what they are saying rather than what the other speaker is saying. To accomplish this, they may use any attention-getting technique they wish (vocal devices, gestures, eye contact, body movements, colorful language, or an exciting topic.). At all times, they are to completely ignore their fellow speaker.

Step 4. After signaled by the teacher to stop, the entire class should begin an open discussion about what happened during this stereophonic listening exercise. Members of the class should advance as many reasons as they can explaining why they paid attention to one speaker and not to the other at any particular time; also, if their attention shifted back and forth, speculate why it happened.

Most of you have probably not had the experience of sitting in an audience and having two speakers talk to you at the same time. The closest you may have come is having a couple of friends talk to you at the same time at a party or social function. At first, no matter where or when it happens, it feels strange and you wish they would talk one at a time instead of both at once. However, after a while, you get used to it and divide your attention between them. The question this exercises raises is, "What determines to whom you listen?"

Here is a list of the most common things capable of attracting the attention of someone in an audience. They have been arranged in a scrambled order. Look them over and rearrange them according to your evaluation of their importance:

- Gestures
- Eye contact
- Clothing
- Physique
- Loudness of voice
- Pitch of voice
- Posture
- Rhythm of voice
- Enthusiasm
- Topic
- Charisma
- Vocabulary
- Closeness to speaker

There is no correct order for the terms you have just rearranged. Whereas some will be more inclined to get people's attention than others in one situation, they may not in another. The items which happen to catch your attention were unique to you. While you may have been attracted by a speaker's gestures and eye contact, someone else might have been attracted by a speaker's enthusiasm in their topic. The next time you watch T.V., when one of your favorites appears on the screen, try to figure out what it is about their personality that holds your attention. See whether your answer agrees with the list you have just ordered.

Having come this far, you should now be able to appreciate the fact that what you hear and what you listen to are not the same thing; also, that listening carefully to what others say is helpful to the establishment of meaningful communication with them. Now, as an additional assistance toward making you a better listener than you are, here are some valuable secrets.

Secrets of a Good Listener

Secret 1

Learn the name of the person with whom you are communicating and use it. People are more willing to believe that you are listening to what they are saying if you call them by name occasionally. Using name-substitutes such as honey, sweetie, darling, girl, fellah, buddy, or ole pal when you don't remember someone's name is often worse than asking for their name outright. At work, when you ask the manager a question and he answers you by name, it makes you feel good. By so doing, the manager is responding to you, not any other member of the staff; you are a specific person, not just another face in the crowd.

Many people complain that they have a bad memory for names. This need not be. You can learn how to remember 20–30 names at one time, if you want to. This exercise will prove it.

Name of Exercise: I'll never forget what's her name.

Purpose: To prove that you can learn as many as two dozen names at one time with very little effort.

Procedure:

Step 1. Arrange members of the class in a circle (seated).

Step 2. At a signal from the teacher, each person in the circle should say his or her first name out loud. After saying it once, the person should allow 10 seconds to pass and say it again. Only the first name, nothing else.

Step 3. As each group member speaks, everyone else should try to make some association in their minds about it. If the person's name is Mary, the thought of Mary in the Bible might be a good association to use; if it is Henry, one might think of Henry the VIII. Another form of association could be based on a person's looks. Assume someone says his name is David and he happens to be sitting next to someone very tall, the story of David and Goliath should work nicely. The objective is always to connect up the unfamiliar (the person's name) with the familiar (a person, place, or thing you know).

Step 4. As each individual speaks, do not fail to make some kind of an association. Periodically, mentally go back through the names you have already committed to memory.

Step 5. After all members of the class have said their names, volunteers should be asked to try to go around the circle naming everyone in it. As many people as possible should be encouraged to try to do this. Many will be surprised at the number of names they can recall.

Step 6. As an extra source of interest, the entire class should now change their seating arrangement and see if it affects their ability to remember names.

Put this secret of being a good listener to work as soon as possible. Tomorrow, make it a point to lock as many people's names into your memory as you can.

Secret 2

Have you ever been told, "Look at me when I'm talking"? This secret involves eye contact. Without staring, looking into the eyes of someone talking to you is one of the more reliable indicators of listening. By the same token, not looking at someone who is talking immediately arouses suspicion that you are not listening. The value of this secret, then, is in looking at the person talking to you.

> *From this moment on, use good eye contact with every person you talk to. Don't stare, just tell them with your eyes that you are interested in what they have to say.*

Secret 3

This secret concerns nonverbal communication. Using body movements, facial expressions, posture, and certain hand gestures are means of letting others know you are listening. Instead of a screwed up or painful expression on your face, a relaxed look and an occasional smile are positive signs of active listening. With regard to body movements, the more you squirm and fidgit, the less you will appear to be listening. If you sit quietly, it will have the opposite effect; they will think you *are* listening: The best listening posture is the more errect one, not slouched in your seat or hunched over. As far as hand gestures are concerned, a general rule is to gesture very little while others are speaking. It can be distracting and create the impression that you are not concentrating on what is being said.

Secret 4

Ask questions! That is your final secret. A surefire sign that you are listening is to ask a question. This is particularly true when the question deals with what the person is saying. Although most people seem to resent being told things, they often enjoy being asked questions–questions usually give their egos a lift. It makes them feels that you consider them intelligent enough to supply a worthwhile answer. This should not be taken to mean that you should go overboard and ask a battery of questions designed to mow someone down. A question now and then can do wonders toward making you a better listener.

Listening Around

What do the words grapevine, rumor, tattletale, scuttlebutt, busybody, prattle, and gossip have in common? They all involve listening—but not in the ordinary sense. In each field, there is *formal* and *informal* listening. Formal listening occurs in the line of duty and is properly associated with the performance of certain tasks and the reaching of certain personal and organizational goals. By contrast, informal listening occurs outside the line of duty and is generally incidental to the performance of certain tasks and the reaching of certain personal and organizational goals. Until now, this chapter has addressed itself to formal listening. It will shift that focus at this point to informal listening.

Few businesses and professions are without their "Gossips in Residence." These are people who usually take it upon themselves to keep others apprised of matters they consider worthwhile knowing. Whether these gossips are born or made has not as yet been established. What is known, however, is that they exist and play an active role in practically every orgnaization.

A human chain along which information travels is called a "grapevine." Gossips keep this chain alive. They do it by selectively listening around for information they decide warrants being spread and faithfully pass it on. If others should refuse to listen to them, they are out of business. There is some controversy over whether grapevines are an asset or liability to an organization Most authorities seem to agree that they are capable of contributing to the overall well-being of any organization's communication system by accommodating information not normally transmitted through regular channels. In short, the grapevine is an underground listening network whose ears are sensitive to the currents of thoughts, feelings, and ideas customarily found to circulate through most businesses.

Many employers, acquainted with the potential of the grapevine, use it to their advantage. With strategically placed listening agents located within its network, they are supplied with a continuous flow of information about their employees. Through such feedback, these employers are able to keep a thumb on the pulse of their organization. To them, listening is a serious business, often a profitable one. The same grapevine, likewise, serves a useful purpose to employees by supplying them with information about the activities of their employers.

In a final effort to maintain the perspective of this chapter, here are a few brief descriptions of the more common situations in which people find themselves.

Listening Situations

Medical

A common complaint about doctors is that they don't listen. If they do listen, it is with half an ear, on the run, or while attending to something else.

For whatever reason, these doctors make their patients feel rushed—as though they have to sputter what they want to say quickly and to the point. The office or hospital nurse is also a sometime culprit of spotty listening. But, lest you get the impression that lazy listening is unique to doctors and nurses, patients also share a large measure of this practice. By not listening to a doctor's instruction for taking a particular medication, considerable harm can be done.

Whether it is a doctor, nurse, or patient who is guilty of lazy listening, each, in some way, detracts from the practice of medicine.

Legal

In the field of law, the principal characters are the client, lawyer, judge, and jury. Lawyers must listen to their clients carefully, as it constitutes the basis upon which a case is founded. Clients, in turn, must listen attentively to their lawyer's questions so as to furnish accurate information. If the case goes to court, in addition to listening to their clients, lawyers must also listen to the presiding judge. Should it be a trial by jury, 12 jurors must listen carefully to the proceedings if they are to reach a fair verdict. Court reporters or stenotypists must also listen well if they are to take down whatever has been said during a trial. Obviously, listening plays a major role in the courtroom.

Secretarial

It is frightening to think what would happen in the business and professional world if all of the secretaries in it entered into a conspiracy. Those who know can appreciate the possible consequences. Some employers dictate to a secretary directly, others dictate into a tape recorder or dictaphone and the secretary transcribes it later. Whatever the method, secretaries must listen carefully if they are to preserve the meanings intended by their employers.

Although listening to a tape recorder or dictaphone has the advantage of being played over and over again, there are no facial expressions, body movements, or gestures to reinforce or color the spoken word. This shortcoming places a greater demand upon a secretary. Then, there is the question of an employer's speech pattern—dialect, nonfluencies, pitch, rhythm, speed. Any of these could represent a listening barrier to the most well-intentioned secretary.

Another listening chore for the average secretary is taking telephone messages. Occasionally, embarassed to ask a caller to repeat a message, a secretary will repeat it to her employer in an incomplete form. This could be extremely costly in certain businesses; (e.g., stock and bonds, banking, importing and exporting goods across continents, etc.). Language differences in any of these cross-cultural transactions make a secretary's job that much more difficult. The very last thing any secretary should do is underestimate the importance of "listening on the job."

Psychotherapeutic

Working with a depressed person who is bent on self-destruction is an awesome responsbility. How frightening it is to realize that one wrong word might cause another individual's death. Yet, psychotherapists have long realized the value of listening more and talking less.* When a person has a disgust for life, he needs desperately to ventialte his burdensome feelings. This means that those who are concerned could be of invaluable assistance by responsive listening, by giving their full attention to what the distraught person is saying.

Suicide, of course, is an extreme case in which listening could be crucial. Although the majority of people who seek psychological help are not suicidal, they, nevertheless, need the benefits therapeutic listening can provide. Psychologists tell us that the more we attempt to understand one another, the better we become and the better we communicate. And, to extend this idea even further, the better we communicate through listening, the better we shall be able to live and work together in harmony.

Educational

Perhaps one of the largest single bodies of listeners in this country are the thousands of young boys and girls, men and women, who daily fill the seats

*Earl A. Grollman, *Suicide: Prevention, Intervention, Postvention.* (Boston, Mass.: Beacon Press, Universalist Association, March 1969), p. 90.

in our schools. Teachers often complain that students don't listen. Students, in rebuttal, charge that teachers don't listen. The truth of the matter is that both are guilty from time to time; they frequently fail to appreciate the importance of what they hear. If the educational grapevine speaks the truth, examinations are the bane of a student's existence. Many educators have speculated that a substantial number of students do poorly on their examinations because they do not listen to the teacher's preexamination instructions. Similiar speculation has been advanced by serious students that if one listens attentively in class, less homework is necessary in most courses. Teachers and students both stand to benefit from listening to one another. The degree to which either falls down on this responsibility contributes, in part, to many of the deficiencies in our educational system.

Theatrical

To the naive among us, television and stage productions are predominantly a matter of memorizing scripts and dramatically speaking lines for the entertainment of audiences. In musical comedy and opera, the lines from a score are sung. In each of these instances, the emphasis is thought to be on delivery rather than reception. Experienced members of the theatrical profession know differently. Take, if you will, the subject of cues. A cue is a signal one performer gives another. It may occur in verbal, nonverbal, vocal or musical form. The failure to pick up on a cue could easily disrupt both the flow and meaning of any performance. While there are exclusively visual cues (e.g., closing a door, raising an arm or banner, etc.), most cues are acoustic in nature and have to be carefully listened for by a performer. Even more complex are those theatrical listening situations in which word and musical cues are designed to mesh.

All members of any cast, including the director, stage manager, choreographer and musical conductor, are professionally expected to be good listeners. No production can afford the luxury of a lazy listener. Thus, whether we are talking about radio, television, stage, screen or opera, effective listening should always be among those qualities given top billing.

Sales

Few things can kill a sale more quickly than a failure to listen. Millions of dollars are spent each day on the basis of a telephone call from a salesperson to a buyer or a buyer to a salesperson. Prices are often quoted, shipping dates mentioned, commodities described, purposes explained and sales features stressed. Each of these elements of a commercial transaction will be found to represent varying degrees of importance to the people involved. What is unimportant to one person—and casually glossed over, may be of paramount importance to another. Ask anyone heavily involved in sales which is more important, speaking or listening. Whereas on the surface it is tempting to say *speaking*, you may find those who say otherwise. For example, it has been suggested that most people persuade themselves to buy an

item. All the salesperson does is provide that individual with the psychological information with which to do it. It would be foolhearty to give the impression that speaking is not important in selling; it is very important. But, the stepchild of communication—*listening*, must again not be shortchanged here. You would be surprised how many people "sell themselves." All they often require is the patient ear of a salesperson willing to listen to them expound on how they feel about a product.

Regardless of what is being sold or who is doing the buying, each must be aware of what the other is bringing to the transaction. This can only be accomplished by listening. Some experienced salespeople have gone as far as implying that if listened to carefully, customers often will reveal what is needed to sell them: "If I were to buy this, it would have to ___," or "In order for you to close this deal, you would have to show me ___." Attentive listening, by no means a panacea in the business world, is certainly one of the most powerful instruments available to those actively engaged in sales.

Neither this chapter nor any other words on a printed page will ever make you a good listener. Only you can do that. You must first, however, be ready to listen. It is entirely possible that you are still too busy talking to listen. Perhaps you have to "talk out" a few more million words before starting to listen. If you think you are ready to listen, apply some of the listening suggestions offered in the chapter. If you are not ready, come back to it when you are. Until then, bear in mind the words of one listening expert, Larry Barker:*

> A failure to listen probably creates more interpersonal problems than any other aspect of human behavior.

*Larry L. Barker, *Listening Behavior* (Englewood Cliffs, New Jersey: Prentice-Hall, 1971), p. xi.

SELF-EXAMINATION QUIZ

Having read this chapter, my answers to the following questions reflect my understanding of its contents.

1. Describe your own listening skill.

2. List some of the common reasons why people listen.

3. Explain the relationship between *hearing* and *listening.*

4. What is the relationship between *paying attention* and *listening*?

5. State briefly the listening philosophy presented by this chapter.

6. Why is listening referred to as a "serious business"?

7. List some of the popular myths associated with listening.

8. How can performing listening exercises make you a better listener?

9. Analyze the statement: I know that you believe that you understand what you think I said, but I am not sure you realize that what you heard is not what I meant.

10. In what way can improving your ability to listen improve your ability to communicate?

Suggested Readings

Barker, Larry, *Listening Behavior* (Englewood Cliffs, N.J.: Prentice-Hall, 1971).
Dominick, Barbara A., *The Art of Listening* (Springfield, Ill.: Charles C Thomas, 1958).
Duker, Sam, *Listening: Readings*, Vol. 2 (Metuchen, N. J.: Scarecrow Press, 1971).
Kelly, Charles, "Empathetic Listening," in *Small Group Communication: A Reader*, edited by Robert S. Cathcart and Larry A. Samovar (Dubuque, Iowa: William C. Brown, 1974), pp. 340–347.
Mills, Ernest P., *Listening: Key to Communication* (New York: Petrocelli Books, 1974).
Nichols, Ralph G., and Leonard A. Stevens, *Are You Listening*? (New York: McGraw-Hill 1957).
Seibel, R., R. E. Christ, and W. H. Teichner, "Short-term memory under work-load stress," *Journal of Experimental Psychology,* **70**, 154–162 (1965).
Weaver, Carl H., *Human Listening: Processes and Behavior* (New York: Bobbs-Merrill, 1972).
White, W. H., Jr., *Is Anybody Listening*? (New York: Simon and Schuster, 1952).
Yates, F. A., *The Art of Memory* (Chicago, Ill.: Univ. of Chicago Press, 1966).

WORK AREA FOR CHAPTER 6

Chapter 7

Negotiating

The ability to disagree without being disagreeable is indispensable to the success of practically every business transaction.

MEMO

TO: Reader

FROM: Author

After reading this chapter, you should have a better understanding of:

1. What is required of an effective negotiator.
2. What types of people enter into negotiations.
3. How to prepare for negotiations.
4. What stages are involved in the process of negotiation.
5. What kinds of situations require negotiation.
6. What types of negotiation are common to the business and professional world.
7. Which strategies can be used in negotiating.
8. What makes something right or wrong.
9. What different types of proof are used in the negotiating transaction.
10. Which fallacies are common among negotiators.

Chapter 7

Petty differences of opinion in the marketplace over such things as price, property, position, or point of view are usually referred to as haggling, quibbling, and dickering. Slightly more sophisticated differences of opinion are known as arguments, controversies, and confrontations. But by far, the most civilized method of coming to terms on an issue is through the process of negotiation. For negotiation involves communication—exchange of ideas, expressions of goals, debate, and mutual compromise.

Without realizing it, you have been negotiating all your life. *Children negotiate*: "I'll let you ride my bicycle, if you let me play with your water pistol." *Teenagers negotiate*: "Dad, if you let me borrow your car this Saturday night, I promise to mow the lawn." *Husbands and wives negotiate*: "Honey, if you let me sleep late Sunday morning, I'll go with you to that boring dance your lodge is giving next week."

At any given stage of your life, unwillingness to negotiate can cause serious difficulties of an emotional as well as a financial nature. This chapter will help you to recognize some of these difficulties and will suggest ways to manage them. However, skillful negotiation is an art, not a science. The art of negotiation is expressed when people try to resolve their differences without being disagreeable.

As indicated above, negotiations and arguments share the element of controversy. As children, most of us were taught not to argue. Take an informal survey among your friends and see how many of them still harbor a distinct aversion toward arguing. You will find that they lack an education in how to argue constructively, how to disagree without becoming disagreeable. For instance, have you noticed how some of your friends accept abuse in a restaurant by putting up with badly prepared food and remaining silent? Not a word is said about it to the waitress or the manager. Regardless of whether the food isn't fresh, is poorly cooked, or is badly served, arguing is avoided like the plague. It is beyond belief how much abuse many people are willing to endure. If they lack the self-confidence to voice a legitimate gripe, imagine the stumbling blocks to confronting people on purely controversial issues. It may be said that it is not a question of a lack of self-confidence but rather one of politeness. In any case, the person is not entering into any level of negotiation with the staff of the restaurant in an effort to change things for the better. Would such a person argue about a stolen parking space, dispute incorrect change with a cashier, admonish the person who sneaked ahead in line at the box office, or return sour milk to the supermarket?

Each of the above instances involves negotiation on a fairly simple level. How would the same person handle such crucial issues as promotion to a higher rank, expressing preferences in job assignments, and asking about benefits or raises?

> *After listing those things you prefer not to argue about, ask three friends which issues they prefer to avoid in an argument.*

Obviously, the willingness to argue is a personal matter underscored by definite psychological currents of values and beliefs. Again, it boils down to how willing we are to communicate. Basically, we all know how to argue, but few of us know how to do it well. Three of the most common mistakes we make are: (1) talking too much, (2) getting emotional, and (3) arguing conclusions instead of the basis for them.

> In any serious reckoning of inventions and discoveries which have issued from man's earnestness to alter his own condition, negotiation in the conference manner deserves to rank with his finest achievements—with those successes which have habitually been attributed to rare and superior creativity. A thinking person who takes the trouble to explore this field will be bound to wonder how it could have escaped the human discipline so long.*

Qualifications of a Negotiator

Whereas all the following prerequisites are not absolutely indispensable to being a good negotiator, they assuredly increase a person's chance of becoming one.

Ability to plan or organize.
Can think under stress, that is, has a high tolerance for ambiguity and uncertainty.
Practical intelligence (common sense).
Good talker and listener.
A thorough working knowledge of the subject being negotiated.
Integrity (high self-esteem, self-worth).
Courageous (takes carefully conceived risks).
Patience and perseverance.
Open-minded.
Ability to perceive and exploit power.
Observant.
Respect for an opponent and the position that opponent has assumed.
Power of concentration.
Ability to recognize logical relationships.
Can stay on a subject.
Can react quickly to an idea and, if need be, shift mental gears in any direction.

Although these qualities come easily to some people, most of us have to work to acquire them. Go down the list again and check off those abilities and characteristics you honestly feel you possess. Then, begin thinking about how you can best develop the qualities you lack.

For example, if you feel you are not a good talker, take some courses in public and persuasive speaking. If your shortcoming is wandering off the subject, take a course in meditation or yoga to improve your powers of

*Ann Douglas, *Industrial Peacemaking* (New York: Columbia University Press, 1962), pp. 3–4.

concentration. Unless you make up your mind to change, you will continue as you are. If no change takes place, you and you alone are to blame.

Types of Negotiator

At the risk of oversimplification, we can divide negotiators into three categories: (1) aggressors, (2) victims, and (3) instigators.

Aggressors

Aggressive people can not only be found to initiate negotiations, they also tend to carry the action while such negotiations are in progress. Aggressors are the prime movers when it comes to negotiating an issue. In our culture, an aggressive people elicit mixed reactions. Under certain circumstances, aggressive behavior is admired and applauded, but it can also be frowned upon and deplored. If pressed, most of us would be inclined to admit that our judgment of assertive or aggressive behavior would depend on how it was implemented. There are times when an aggressive act, performed with sensitivity and tact, is extremely admirable. International diplomacy often requires a diplomat to behave aggressively, to negotiate world affairs with sensitivity and tact, and to disagree without being disagreeable. The aggressor, therefore, should not automatically be taken to play a negative role in negotiation, but rather one that can move in either direction.

Victims

"Why is it always me?" is a complaint frequently registered by the victim in a negotiation. This is particularly true among those who usually find themselves with the short end of the stick. It is reasonable to assume that in most negotiations some will bear the brunt of it, while others tend to emerge unscathed. A person who repeatedly loses out is the very one who would profit by taking the time to wonder why it happens every time. A convenient excuse for any victim is to blame failure on some inherited trait, circumstance, or just plain "bad luck." All these excuses are clearly nonsensical. Victims of negotiations are made, not born. A careful analysis of any negotiation should turn up specific instances in which a victim made clear-cut mistakes either in judgment or delivery. With little effort, these mistakes can usually be corrected.

Para-victims are people who, out of the direct line of fire, are negatively affected during the course of a negotiation. Occasionally, in large organizations, two department heads and certain members of their staffs come together to negotiate a change in company policy. Most of the negotiating is done by department heads and their immediate aides. The rest of those in attendance generally sit quietly, listen, take notes, and have to be ready to supply specialized information, if requested. Should the outcome of the meeting favor one department over the other, the silent members of the less fortunate department are the para-victims. As indirect participants in, and contributors to, the fate suffered in negotiations, they were not primarily responsible for it.

Instigators

Instigators are people who start trouble during negotiations, but who fail to become involved themselves. To illustrate how some instigators operate, imagine yourself witnessing a roundtable dispute between the city and mass transit. During one of the coffee breaks, you happen to see a man whisper something to one of the principal labor leaders. Upon returning to the bargaining table, this labor leader makes a statement that literally shocks everyone present. You get the distinct impression that the statement was precipitated by what he was told during the coffee break. If, indeed, it was, the one who did the whispering was the instigator.

In a broader sense, the label "instigator" can rightfully be applied to anyone who verbally (snide remark), nonverbally (hostile facial expression), or vocally (obnoxious) introduces a disturbing influence to any negotiation proceedings. Although the actions of an instigator could conceivably have a constructive effect on negotiations, they generally tend to be destructive in nature.

Now that we have been introduced to the three basic types of negotiators, we will need to learn what preparations must be made for negotiating.

Preparing to Negotiate

Just as a problem well-stated is half-solved, being properly prepared for negotiations places the odds of success in your favor. The following preparations should be seriously considered:

1. Keep negotiating committees reasonably small. If they are too large, everyone insists on participating; it will be time-consuming, tempers may be excessively taxed, and much irrelevant material may be introduced.
2. Each side should have only one person in charge. A division of authority ensures orderly procedure and speeds up the decision-making process.
3. Time limits for the proceedings should be set in advance.
4. Parties should exchange demands before bargaining sessions begin.
5. Agreement of negotiating procedures should be established beforehand so as to avert unnecessary quibbling.
6. Negotiators should have the authority to make decisive commitments during the course of the negotiations.
7. Negotiations should begin with a well-planned agenda that includes complete statements of all disputed issues plus a list of proposals and counterproposals on the disputed points.

8. There should be an agreement as to relevant factual information.
9. Negotiators should first eliminate the least controversal issues and commit agreement on these issues to writing before they proceed to negotiation of the tougher issues.
10. Issues may be divided into those which involve money and those which are noneconomic demands.*

Naturally, not every negotiation will require *all* these preparations. Only those appropriate to the particular situation should be incorporated.

Stages of Negotiation

Although no two negotiations are identical, they seem to adhere to fairly similiar stages:

Stage 1: The opening ritual, the first of the meetings, where one of the sides presents their demands.

Stage 2: Exploratory sessions, meetings that allow each side to "feel out" what the other side really wants.

Stage 3: Revelation of issues and position, when both sides begin to sense the priorities in the demands held by the other side.

Stage 4: Deadline crisis, when the set expiration date or strike date draws dangerously near, and the parties get down to brass tacks and some hard bargaining.

Stage 5: Closing ritual, a time when a company or union extends its final offer, during which it is hoped that the final agreement is reached and the two negotiating committees inform their principals as to the contract.†

Whether a negotiation occurs on a one-to-one, one-to-many, or many-to-many basis, the stages it passes through occur in different contexts or situations. Here are some examples of such situations.

Situation-Specific Negotiations

Sexual

A century ago, the role of women in society was clearly established and went virtually unchallenged. Things have changed considerably today. The once-labeled "weaker sex" has raised its social and sexual aspirations to an all-time high; men have been invited to negotiate with women on equal footing in marriage, sports, business, politics, and in practically every professional field. In a successful marriage, both partners gain satisfaction, whereas a relationship that offers too little to one partner or to both culminates in a deadlock.

*Harold W. Davey, *Contemporary Collective Bargaining* (Englewood Cliffs, N.J.: Prentice-Hall, 1959), p. 111.

†J. D. Dunn and Elvis C. Stephens, *Management of Personnel: Manpower Management and Organizations Behavior* (New York: McGraw-Hill, 1972).

Successful marriage negotiation, in the view of Milford Graves, resembles mature collective bargaining more than it does a peace conference, because the problem-solving process in a lasting, valued relationship takes precedence over share bargaining. It would be nice to think that our divorce rate would go down if the marriage vows were changed to read, "love, honor, and negotiate."

Political

Politicians are forever negotiating about one thing or another in an on-going process. Negotiation continues in Congress, between the governments of two countries, and among city, state, and federal governments. Trust in political negotiation is essential. The fear of being cheated or betrayed could cause drastic results. The outcome of political negotiations is so important, it must be set down in a written contract or document.

Sporting

There are various types of negotiation in the world of sports. Players negotiate with each other over positions and strategy, managers negotiate with one another over which players to trade and how much to pay, and every-one tries to negotiate with referees and umpires over the decisions they have made during a game (here, no one gets even a "sporting" chance). The very nature of any sport captures the spirit of negotiation.

Religious

Granted that the term "negotiation" in connection with the Catholic church may seem somewhat alien to the public mind, we do see the parishion-er who "bargains" with a priest in the confessional booth while asking forgive-ness for his sins. The priest is hidden and separated from the "sinner" by a wall or a dark curtain. The sinner confesses the wrongdoing and promises to expiate the sin and never to do it again. The priest then issues a penance, which involves saying prayers to cleanse the soul. Once done, the parishoner's mind, body, and soul are clear, and the religious negotiations have been transacted.

Business

There is hardly an aspect of business that does not involve negotiation. Whether between employers and employees, buyers and sellers, merging businesses, and unions and management, the opportunity to negotiate is the backbone of industry. The rather simple (face-to-face) process of negotiation between employment and worker has been blotted out by today's complex proceedings in which parties no longer represent their own interests. Legal counsel, agents, shop foremen, arbitrators, and mediators have turned negotiation itself into "big business."

Familial

The ability to negotiate at home has disintegrated so badly over the past 30 to 40 years that agencies have sprung up to fill the need. Family-counseling services, child-counseling agencies, marriage-counseling centers, and so forth, are now available for whatever family problems require the benefit of negotiation at the hands of a professional. Although familial negotiations may not be as vital to society as political or business negotiations, they are essential to the survival of the family unit in this country.

Social

Socialization is the process by which we learn social behavior. Stretched another way, it could be viewed as the process by which we survive. From the moment we open our eyes in the monring 'til we close them at night, we are actively engaged in negotiation. As social animals, we strive to satisfy our personal needs, modifying them according to the expectations of others. In so doing, we are, in a way, negotiating our personal wants with our own alter egos. The group situation becomes internalized like the voices in a perfect chorus of social norms, persuading us toward the "give and take" of accommodation and compromise.

Types of Negotiators

Arbitration and Mediation

Arbitration occurs when people agree to let someone else settle an argument for them. The person chosen to settle the argument is called an arbitrator; one who listens to both sides of the argument and then decides who is right and who is wrong. The decision of the arbitrator is called an award. Arbitration is often used to settle arguments and disputes between labor and management, especially for minor, day-by-day disagreements, which neither group feels is worth a major confrontation.

Mediation involves a "third person" (the mediator) who remains attached to a case at the discretion of the two parties involved. It is understood that the disputants reserve judgment until a time of their own choosing on whether to heed or disregard the mediator's counsel. Mediation differs from arbitration in that a mediator cannot make an award—he or she can only help the two sides to agree. If at any point in the proceedings they come to regard the mediator as a *persona non grata* (unacceptable), they are within their rights to dispense with this person's services.*

Collective Bargaining

Collective means "for a group." A labor union, or association of employees, is said to bargain collectively when a few people representing the

*Ducksoo, Chang, *British Methods of Industrial Peace* (New York: AMS Press, 1968), pp. 27, 42–44.

union meet with the employers to agree on wages and working conditions for all the members of the union. It is for this purpose that the union is formed.

During collective bargaining, representatives of the union meet with members of the management (representatives of the owners of the company). They agree on how many hours a week the employees will work, and how much they will receive per hour's work. Often there are different rates of pay for people in different jobs, depending on the skill required.* Pensions, working conditions, medical benefits, and other issues are also subjects for collective bargaining.

Intrapersonal Negotiation

Decision making and problem solving are both manifestations of the intrapersonal process of negotiation. Both processes are more concerned with what is going on inside a person than what is going on outside. Lee Thayer puts it this way:

> "Many writers on problem solving seem to assume that people apprehend problems more or less as they actually exist. But from what we have learned . . . about the nature of communication and the nature of people, we are forced to recognize that this assumption is not a tenable one. People do not apprehend or comprehend anything as it actually exists. The physical event data we perceive may be more or less the same for all of those who look at a situation. But what we actually see, what we actually apprehend, and what those events mean or portend—these are sourced in us, the problem perceivers.†

Thayer's message is clear: Problems exist only in people. Although events and situations do exist "out there," their meaning, significance, "problematicalness" (Thayer's term) is a property of people, not of the event or situation. This distinction between people and problems is central not only to Thayer's thesis, but to this book as well; that is, no organization or profession exists out there, per se—only people interacting with one another. It is in this context that we are examining the process of people engaged in decision making and problem solving.

Every business or profession uses intrapersonal negotiations. Whether it is a secretary deciding which letter to type first or a vice-president deciding the fate of a sizable account, the process is essentially a private one. Each comprehends the specific problem or decision on the basis of personal perception. Extending this thought even further, whatever notions people carry around in their heads about their external environment seem to influence the sorts of problems they will have and the kinds of decisions they will make in relation to them. Put this way, you will find it an advantage to think of problem-solving and decision-making as simply adjusting to one's environment.

*P. Ford, *The Economics of Collective Bargaining* (Oxford, England: Blackwell Press, 1958), pp. 2–4.

†Lee Thayer, Communication and Communication Systems, In Organization, *Management, and Interpersonal Relations* (Homewood, Ill.: Richard D. Irwin, Inc., 1968), p. 67.

If the adjustment you have made favorably alters your perception of what you formerly pinpointed as a problem, your intrapersonal negotiations have been successful. If, beyond this, you have also favorably modified your external environment, the degree of success will be even greater.

Few people realize that "Those actively involved in decision-making usually know little about it. They possess neither the elementary skills of decision making nor the ability to communicate effectively in order to achieve that goal."* Ask yourself this question: How do I go about making decisions? Is there a right and a wrong way? Authorities speak of a rational and an irrational method and, as they favor the former, you should be aware of it. One method is called the **autocratic method**, in which decisions are made by a single person. Throughout history, the bravest, cleverest, most capable made the decisions. Another method is referred to as the **adversary method**, in which two sides of a question are represented and argued. A good example of this method of decision-making is in our court system. Opposing lawyers present their cases, and a judge or jury makes a decision in favor of one and opposed to the other. Finally, there is the **inquisitory method**, wherein one seeks to find the best answer from all that may be available. Groups, boards, panels, and committees everywhere employ this method. Obviously, none of these methods is right or wrong. Their rightness or wrongness must be determined both by the principles involved and their perception of the situation and its consequences.†

When you are confronted by the need either to make a decision or solve a problem, do not make the mistake of thinking that they are the same. "Problem-solving involves discovering previous unknown alternatives or solutions, whereas decision-making involves choosing between two or more solutions. Thus, problem-solving generates the material on which decisions are made."‡ Think back for an example to the chapter on interviewing (Chapter 4). Imagine that you have been interviewed for a most desirable position and are faced with the need to make up your mind. When your intrapersonal negotiation focused on the various aspects of the interview in terms of figuring out its various meanings and implications, you were solving a problem. When your attention shifted to the question of whether to take the position, you were making a decision. However, the process does not end there, for it is an ongoing process of decisions giving rise to problems, problems to more decisions, and so forth.

It seems only proper to mention that the charge suggesting that people know little about decision-making should also be levied against problem-

*James C. McCroskey and Lawrence R. Wheeless, *Introduction to Human Communication* (Boston: allyn and Bacon, 1976), p. 394.

†John Hasling, *Group Discussion and Decision Making* (New York: Thomas Y. Crowell, 1975), pp. 21–28.

‡Michael Burgoon, *Approaching Speech/Communication* (New York: Holt, Rinehart and Winston, 1974), p. 219.

solving. Again the question: How do you go about solving problems? Compare the method you use with that of John Dewey, the famous educator. Dewey recommended the following five steps:*

Step 1. *Locating and defining* the problem—sensing a felt difficulty.
Step 2. *Exploring* the problem—defining, delimiting, analyzing the difficulty.
Step 3. *Examining* suggested solutions—exploring each suggested solution.
Step 4. *Choosing* the best solution—through evidence and reasoning.
Step 5. *Securing acceptance* of the best solution—testing its efficacy.

Select a problem you have had recently, or are now grappling with. Write a brief essay explaining your method of solving it. Do the same with a decision you have had to make recently, or are in the process of making now.

Problem-solving and decision-making are tasks for which most people are woefully unprepared. But, this need not be so. There is a great deal of readily available material on these subjects. Read as much as you can and, from a practical standpoint, seize upon every opportunity you can to make your own decisions and solve your own problems. You will feel the satisfaction of dealing with your daily work load in a personal and fulfilling way, shaping and tailoring your own priorities.

Plea Bargaining

Plea bargaining is a form of negotiation common to the legal profession. The term refers to a prearraignment deal between the prosecution and the defense in which the defendant is offered a reduced charge, carrying a lighter penalty, if he or she is willing to plead guilty. For example, the state may agree to reduce a charge of burglary to criminal trespass, just to save the time and expense of a trial. Because plea negotiations are not entirely accepted, they are conducted informally and off the record in most jurisdictions. Plea negotiations are sometimes conducted in hurried whispers in the courtroom or through jail bars. "It's like sex before Freud," said Steve Sachs, a former U.S. Attorney from Maryland. "Everybody did it, but few discussed it."

Treaties

Treaties are the result of negotiation between countries. Written international law consists of treaties signed by two or more countries. A treaty

*John Dewey, *How We Think* (Boston: Heath, 1933).

involves a promise on the part of each country to do, or not to do, certain things (for example, if one country is attacked, the other will come to its rescue, or, both countries might agree not to trade with a third country). But a treaty is not like the law of a single country or state, because there are no international police to make countries obey. Most countries adhere to international law most of the time because they find it in their *national* interest to do so. Cuba agreed to deny asylum to airline highjackers, for example, because of the obvious inconvenience of attracting a large population of psychopathic armed extortionists.

Debates

Negotiation through debate is a formal discussion carried on between two persons or teams of opponents. Before a debate begins, a topic is chosen on which both sides agree to disagree. The topic chosen to be debated is usually stated in the form of a resolution, such as "*Resolved*, that Democracy is a better form of government than Fascism." Sometimes the topic of debate is presented in the form of a question: "Should the voting age in this country be lowered?" In a debate, one side is called the *affirmative,* the other, *negative.* Both sides try to gain agreement with their point of view by presenting arguments stronger than their opponent's.

Thus far in this chapter, you have been introduced to (1) the human phenomenon of negotiation, (2) the qualifications of an effective negotiator, (3) several different types of people who negotiate, (4) just how one prepares for the negotiating process, (5) the stages involved, (6) some situation-specific forms of negotiation, and (7) the most common types of negotiation. All this information has been of a *descriptive* nature. The balance of the chapter, in contrast, is *prescriptive*—that is, it is concerned with telling you more about *how* to negotiate.

Strategies of Negotiation

Without resorting to the use of bombs, guns, clubs, fists, fire, or torture, how do you win someone over to your point of view? Obviously, the method being recommended here is negotiation through rational and nonviolent means. It can be done, but not without great difficulty in most cases. The ability to change others' minds is a unique art possessed by very few. Most of those engaged in mind-changing or persuasive endeavors are, at best, of average competence. Experts in the field of persuasion, argumentation, and negotiation have intimated that people's minds are *not* generally changed from the outside. What people seem to require is the necessary information to persuade themselves to enter into a change of mind. To repeat: This form of independent mind changing does not apply when any kind of force is used. The following are some recommended methods capable of leading to successful negotiations.

Piecemeal Approach

In the piecemeal method, efforts are made to settle issues one by one in some prearranged order, such as "easiest" first or from the beginning to the end of a list of demands. As it arises, each item is treated as a separate issue, argued out, and disposed of. Attention is then turned to the next issue.

Total Approach

The total approach is the opposite of the piecemeal approach. Nothing is regarded as settled until everything is settled. Bargaining points are raised and discussed, then laid aside as others are brought forth. Every question remains open until the entire complex of issues is ready to crystallize into total agreement.*

Compromise

Every negotiator is aware of the power inherent in compromise. Simply put, it is a matter of each side giving a little ground. The familiar prison scene in which several convicts take some guards as hostages clearly illustrates the persuasiveness of compromise. At the risk of jeopardizing the lives of the guards being held hostage, the warden frequently tries to make a deal with the prisoners; such as "If you let the guards go, you won't be harmed or punished for what you have done." Likewise, the prisoners offer a compromise: "If you open the gates, get us a car, and tell your guards to lay down their weapons, we will release the hostages." Both the warden and prisoners in this situation are attempting to negotiate through the use of compromise.

Most compromising operates on a cost/benefit basis. This means that both sides of a controversy must carefully weigh the cost they will sustain in relation to the benefits they will enjoy from whatever compromise they elect. Once the compromise is made, however, the negotiator must be prepared to deal intelligently with any consequences it might spark. At best, each compromise is accompanied by some degree of risk.

Submission

To give in, to submit, to surrender, all adds up to submission, wherein one faction, in a negotiation yields to another. Many factors can be responsible for the submission of one group to another—financial embarrassment, fear, weakness, lack of leadership, poor timing, intimidation, apathy, inadequate planning, or expedience. Furthermore, submission is not always a sign of inferiority. There are times when the act of submission takes a great deal of courage. This phenomenon can be witnessed in a situation where a

*Edwin F. Beal and Edward D. Wickersham, *The Practice of Collective Bargaining* (Homewood, Ill.: Richard D. Irwin, 1967), p. 174.

department head of a big corporation, rather than have his entire department phased out, willingly submits to a severe cut in personnel and budget.

Stalemate

When negotiations are brought to a complete stand still, the result is referred to as a *stalemate*. What is interesting about a situation like this is that, although there is seemingly no movement in any direction, things do undergo change. Consider what happens during a strike. Workers on a picket line are not receiving their usual wages and production has stopped. How can things remain the same? Certain private functions must continue—bills must be paid, people must eat, children must be clothed. And all the while, the company's customers are buying from competitors.

Another characteristic of the stalemate is that its effects are often felt by people far removed from the immediate situation. When workers at General Motors go out on strike, the entire country feels repercussions. Suppliers of raw materials and parts are forced to lay off workers. Public pressure is applied to both sides to resolve settlement. By no means should you think that when negotiations become locked in a stalemate, everything stops. The situation merely takes a different direction.

Coercion

A popular example of coercion is captured by the expression, "I made him an offer he just couldn't refuse." In the minds of certain people, practically everyone can be persuaded to behave in a particular way, make specific decisions, and support definite ideologies. For centuries, people have been coerced by money, position, rewards, favors, blackmail, physical violence, and property damage.

Gerard Nierenberg, in his exciting book, *The Art of Negotiating*, offers these strategies:*

Forbearance: By avoiding a direct conflict, you can eventually achieve a settlement. Needless to say, the technique of forbearance requires a patient negotiator.

Surprise: The element of surprise demands a sudden shift in method, argument, or approach. To be effective, it must take your opponent off guard.

Bland withdrawal: A refusal to defend an error, bland withdrawal helps maintain your integrity. (Who, me?)

Apparent withdrawal: Apparent withdrawal, on the other hand, is a mixture of forebearance and a little deception. Its aim is to convince your opponent that you have withdrawn when, in reality, you haven't.

Reversal: Acting in opposition to what may be considered the most popular trend or goal is called reversal.

*Gerard I. Nierenberg, *Art of Negotiation* (New York: Hawthorn Books, Inc., 1968).

Limits: Imposing limits implies that you will not negotiate on more than one subject, or that you will only negotiate in one manner.

Feigning: Making a move in a direction to divert your opponent's attention from the real goal or objective is known as feigning.

To these strategies of Nierenberg, you might also wish to add:

Table pounding: Making loud noises is both useful and limiting, for each negotiator pounds loudest when making assertions about which they are least certain.

Bluffing: Card players are familiar with the technique of bluffing. In negotiating, both sides make demands and threats with no serious intention. They both realize that their public may be better satisfied with results that appear to be compromises. Some negotiators also have the need to impress their sponsors with their devotion to the sponsors' cause—bluffing can accomplish this.

Soft shoe: A strategem in which both parties put on an act of playing it calm and cool is the old soft shoe. They look at their situation, see that it is not that bad, and strive to keep what they already have.

Pat hand: The pat hand is where one side gives a ready-made comprehensive offer, usually based on an extensive preliminary study. For example, an employer may determine what is fair and appropriate, announce the results publically, and start an advance campaign to sell the plan to individual employees.

Trade-off and Buy-out: Each party may have the idea that anything can be agreed upon if "the price is right." For instance, a union may accept a lesser wage increase in return for a better pension plan and more paid holidays. This technique is often used in response to the "pat hand"; the company has already indicated the total cost of the package it is prepared to offer. The union negotiators can then consult the rank and file on which elements of the company plan the individual workers would like modified.

What Makes Something Right or Wrong?

Around every corner, there are people ready to label certain things "right' and other things "wrong." It is not difficult to understand the basis for these opinions when it comes to the length of a room, a person's weight, or the temperature of a swimming pool. All that is needed is a tape measure, scale, and thermometer to determine whether someone is right or wrong. But, what kind of an instrument would you need to determine whether an idea is right or wrong? For example, did you know there was a time in history when the following beliefs were considered to be wrong?

1. Blood circulates. *Wrong*
2. Bacteria causes disease. *Wrong*
3. Humans can travel through outer space. *Wrong*
4. The human voice can travel over a wire. *Wrong*
5. The human heart can be transplanted from one person to another. *Wrong*

List as many other beliefs as you can that are now labeled right, which were once labeled wrong.

If the preceding statements were on an examination you had taken last week, and you had marked them wrong, your teacher would have marked you wrong. Today, the correct answer to each of them would be *right*. Now consider these statements and decide whether they should be answered *right* or *wrong:*

1. People are basically good. ____________
2. Spare the rod and spoil the child. ____________
3. Hard work never killed anyone. ____________
4. A joking physician seldom succeeds. ____________
5. Abstract art is ugly. __________
6. The meek shall inherit the Earth. ____________
7. The end justifies the means. ____________
8. Ignorance is bliss. ____________
9. Money makes money. ____________
10. Success breeds success. ____________

Did you mark all of these statements *right* or *wrong*? If you marked some right and others wrong, why? Compare your reasons for marking each question right or wrong with a classmate who answered the same way. Are you beginning to understand why it is easier to judge those things you can see, hear, feel, taste, and touch than those you cannot? If so, you are at the very heart of negotiation—the necessity to make judgments about attitudes, values, and beliefs—things that cannot be proved through the senses.

Proof of the Pudding

Most people entertain the genuine belief that in any form of negotiation, the person who is right should win. Although this may happen most of the time, it does not happen all the time. What determined who was right in the negotiations you have had. Was it because you had superior proof, were more intelligent, talked louder, or was it because your opponent gave in to you? Proof, as you may have already gathered, changes both in time and form. Yesterday's proof may well be today's folly. Here are some examples of the more common proof people are likely to accept today.

Logical

Logic is not a natural phenomenon like rain, lightning, thunder, or cyclones. It is artificial. Logic is a way of reasoning, or processing information, and, as with most activities in life, has its own rules. Hence, any proof used in a negotiation employing logic that breaks these rules should be immediately marked as unacceptable. Be on your guard, however, against logical proof. Wartime generals have been known (quite logically) to figure out how to take a particular town or village and, by so doing, cause the deaths of hundreds of people. In a similiar vein, it wasn't too long ago that courts of law (also using logic) found certain people guilty of crimes and ordered them executed by gas, hanging, or the electric chair. Are such forms of logic right or wrong?

On the more pleasant side, there is the matter of love. It is logical? What do you think happens to love when logic is forced upon it? Anything? It certainly would appear that logic, as proof, should be carefully examined before being accepted.

> *Go to the library and gather as many definitions of the term "logic" as you can. Then, on the basis of what you have learned, write a one-page impression of the meaning of logic as proof.*

Scientific

If you heard someone on the radio or television say that something was "scientific," would you consider it good or bad? The poison gas used in

World War I or the Atomic Bomb dropped on Hiroshima in World War II were both scientifically executed and used on human beings. As with logic, why must something scientific necessarily be "good?" Although most of the proof arrived at scientifically is quite reliable, it can be manipulated to serve any master. It, too, must be kept under careful scrutiny along with logic.

> *A scientist spent his life studying frogs. One day, he conducted the following experiment: He placed a frog on a table and proceeded (very scientifically) to remove its legs, one by one. After the removal of each leg, he would command the frog to "jump," Each time, it jumped, albeit a bit wobbly. After its last leg was removed and it was commanded to jump, the frog remained motionless. This brought the scientist to the following conclusion: "Removing a frog's legs renders him deaf."*

Authoritative

Every business or profession has its experts. Following close behind them are the pseudo-experts—those who *think* they are experts. Whether genuine or impostors, for every opinion these "experts" express, there is another expert available to volunteer an opposite opinion. Prove this to yourself by asking anyone you consider an expert whether all the experts in that particular field agree with one another.

When dealing with negotiators who offer you authoritative proof, special care should be taken. One phenomenon to be on the lookout for is the *halo effect,* which is said to apply when an expert in one field makes a remark about another field and is believed simply on the basis of being "an expert." Television advertisers take advantage of the halo effect when they use a movie star in a commercial. Their psychology is that people will buy a product if they hear their movie idol say she uses it and that it is good. Authoritative proof is only as valid as the authority. Obviously, not everything a bona fide expert says should automatically be taken as gospel.

Journalistic

Do you generally believe everything you read? A staggering number of people do without question. Those who report what they read in newspapers, magazines, textbooks, and trade journals as truth are using journalistic proof. Not infrequently, in the negotiations related to collective bargaining, arbitration, or mediation, proof in support of a participant's point of view is offered in the form of a newspaper article. When challenged, the user will often parry with, "Are you suggesting that this newspaper would print something that wasn't true?" Since the invention of the printing press, a large segment of the population have continued to assign a kind of infallability to the "printed word." This tendency is a lapse no negotiator can afford.

Screening journalistic proof for validity and reliability requires that you ask four important questions: (1) Who wrote the piece? (2) What did it say in its entirety? (3) Where was it published? (4) When? To illustrate, imagine that you have just read an article about the stock market in the *Wall Street Journal* and the same article in *Mad Magazine.* Which source would you consider the more reliable? Obviously, the *Wall Street Journal*, because it concerns the stock market. On the other hand, if the article were a "put-on" about life on a college campus, *Mad Magazine* might be a wiser choice.

Because we live in a mass age, the printed word has enormous influence over our lives. As such, it would be extremely helpful if we all had a better understanding of how easily and how often journalistic proof guides the lives of millions in deciding what is right and what is wrong.

Historical

Evidence used in any negotiation on the basis of what has happened in the past constitutes historical proof. Because humanity uses language, both written and spoken, it enables us to keep the past alive. This ability to pass information on from generation to generation has been designated as "time binding." Not only are we aware of what happened yesterday in Los Angeles or Detroit, we are also aware of what took place in Egypt 5000 years ago. This ability to take liberal helpings of history could play an important role wherever and whenever people negotiate.

The two things to watch for when dealing with historical proof are: (1) meaning compromised by translation from one language to another, and (2) the context in which the item was set. Although there are other conditional factors, these two should be established as quickly as possible. It would seem that the longer a unit of historical proof goes unchallenged, the more apt it is to survive.

Statistical

Like the written word, numbers also seem to attract legions of disciples. This is especially true when the numbers bear decimal places. For example, which of the following statistics sound more credible to you: (68 per cent), (68.4 per cent), (68.72 per cent), or (68.001 per cent)? Would you agree that the latter–68.001 per cent would possess the greatest credibility? For some curious reason, the more complex a computation, the more readily it is accepted by the majority of people not otherwise trained–it seems more authentic to the layman.

Somewhat facetiously, it has been said, "Figures don't lie, but liars figure." It has also been said that any statistician of competence can make figures sit up, roll over, beg, or play dead. Whereas the dishonest use of statistical proof is largely a matter of conscience, in the hands of those with character and integrity, it has proved one of the more reliable means of determining whether something is right or wrong.

Keeping numbers in line (statistical proof) can best be accomplished with these questions:

1. Who did the study?
2. Why was it done?
3. Who paid for it?
4. Where was it done?
5. How was it done?
6. How large a sample was used?
7. Who interpreted the findings?
8. What were the credentials of those who interpreted it?
9. When was it done?
10. Was the study continuous or interrupted?

Statistical proof that can stand up to these questions without buckling warrants the respect of any negotiator.

Personal

Of all the types of proof mentioned, personal proof carries the greatest emotional charge. Have you noticed how many of your friends get very upset when they tell you something and you don't believe them? They snap back with, "Would I lie to you?" They make you feel as though you were rejecting them, not what they said. Personal proof, by far, is the most commonly used form of proof, perhaps because it requires the least amount of effort and is the most readily accessible. Personal proof can best be recognized by the fact that it generally comes without any outside support. It rests entirely on expressions, such as, I think, I feel, I believe, I know—rarely anything more.

There you have it: logical, scientific, authorative, journalistic, statistical, and personal proof. Having been exposed to them, chances are excellent that the statements you answered earlier with right and wrong were based on one, or a combination, of these proofs. Bear in mind that although evidence is the raw material from which proof is derived, proof, in turn, is the foundation upon which constructive negotiation is built. Shoot down your opponent's proof and you are well on your way to winning your case. The question you should now be asking is: How will I know which of my opponent's arguments I should shoot down? Before you answer this question, there is a marvelous classroom exercise designed to get you in a shooting mood.

Name of Exercise: You Have Met the Enemy and It Is "You."

Purpose: To discover how it feels to negotiate against yourself.

Procedure:

Step 1. All members of the class should think of a subject on which they agree or disagree (capital punishment, open marriage, sexism).

Step 2. Either a volunteer or someone chosen by the teacher should then go to the front of the class and, at a signal from the teacher, begin talking on the subject selected by the speaker.

Step 3. After talking for one minute, the speaker should then "switch sides," that is, argue against him/herself. For example, if the person attempted to negotiate in favor of capitol punishment, the opposing view should be presented for one minute.

Step 4. When a speaker has finished, the class should be polled to determine which of the two points of view presented corresponded with how the speaker really felt. The poll should be conducted by a show of hands.

Step 5. After several speakers have presented oppossing views on various subjects, an open discussion should address the question: *How does your ability to negotiate with yourself influence your ability to negotiate with others?*

It should be clearly evident to you now that we must communicate or, in this context, negotiate with ourselves before, during, and after we negotiate with others. Take the very page you are reading: I negotiated with myself before writing it, while writing it, and certainly after writing it. Bits and pieces of ideas, whole ones, and remnants of those once discarded all scrambled through my brain in search of meaning and appropriateness to my purpose. Thinking is an act of negotiation. We shall now carry that process to bear on shooting down an opponent's argument.

Fallacies in Negotiation

What constitutes a fallacy? A fallacy exists when "wrong reasoning" is used. If negotiations rest on their proof, that proof must be shot down. The best way to accomplish this is to expose any fallacies that might exist in your opponent's proof. Because there are a great many fallacies of reasoning, only those commonly committed are discussed in this section. After considering each fallacy, try to make up a dialogue of your own.

Fallacy 1: Attacking the Person

Store Manager: Come here, you kids. What are you doing?
Teenagers: We're shopping. Is there any law against it?
Store Manager: Do you have any money?
Teenagers: Excuse me, sir, but if we were adults, would you ask us that question?
Store Manager: Come on, both of you—out, outside, you look like a couple of troublemakers, anyway. Out!

The store manager in this dialogue didn't seem interested in what the teenagers had to say, did he? From the manager's point of view, the teenagers were young and didn't look as if they had any money with which to buy merchandise. The fact that the store was open to the general public and the teenagers had as much right to be there as any adult didn't seem to matter to the manager. The fallacy in this situation consisted of the attack on the teenagers, rather than the real issue: Their legal right to be in the store. Whenever an attack is made on a person instead of what that person said, it constitutes the fallacy known as *attacking the person.* Young adults are often victimized by this fallacy whenever an older person says, "Just hold on a moment, young lady. How old are you?" Instead of taking issue with what the young adult actually said, such things as her age, manner of dress, or way of speaking become the topic of conversation—the target. The reverse is also a common occurrence. Senior citizens are frequently victimized in an altercation on the basis of their age, rather than what they actually said or did. Tell the truth. When you see an automobile accident in which one of the drivers is in his middle seventies and the other in his thirties, what is your reaction with regard to the cause? Many people would be quick to say, "What's the old geezer doing driving a car, anyway?"

In negotiations of any kind, be on the alert for people who attack people and not their ideas. If it happens to you, get your opponent back to the issues without delay.

Fallacy 2: It Doesn't Follow

Salesman: How many dozen can you use this month, Mr. Jones?

Customer: I haven't used up the ones you sold me last month, Mr. Smith.

Salesman: I know, but this season they are expecting them to sell like crazy.

Customer: Tell you what. As soon as my brother gets up, we'll send next door for something to eat and watch the ball game on T.V.

If you were to overhear this conversation, that last remark by the customer didn't make much sense in relation to what the salesman was saying. This is characteristic of the *it doesn't follow fallacy.* When someone veers off the subject or makes a remark that has absolutely nothing whatever to do with what has been said before, this type of fallacy has been committed. If an opponent of yours does this, politely interrupt and get negotiations back on course as quickly as possible.

Fallacy 3: Seen One, Seen Them All

Regional Sales Manager: That gal we took on last month to work the Southwest sure isn't working out too well, Bob.

National Sales Manager:	Really? She sounded like an eager beaver when we interviewed her for the position.
Regional Sales Manager:	I know that, Bob, but somehow using women in the field always seems to backfire on us.
National Sales Manager:	You said it, buddy. Women in the field is downright bad business. Seen one of them gals, seen 'em all.

This fallacy is rooted in prejudice and stereotyping. In our dialogue the bias is clearly sexist. To make such a sweeping generalization about women, as though to know one woman is to know all women, is patently absurd. Yet, as absurd as it is, many men find it awkward to conduct hard-nosed bargaining with members of the opposite sex. So they conveniently deal with women as negotiators by dismissing all of them as incompetent. Generally speaking, anyone whose behavior suggests the belief that what is true of a part is true of the whole must be carefully watched. The "seen one, seen 'em all" fallacy is widespread in business circles and is, by no means, limited to men against women. The prejudice clearly works in both directions.

Fallacy 4: Everyone Knows That . . . .

First Wrestling Fan:	Did you see that last match? Wasn't it the wildest thing you ever saw?
Second Fan:	Are you kidding? It was fixed.
First Fan:	Fixed? You're out of your mind. Every one of these wrestling matches is completely honest and aboveboard.
Second Fan:	I guess you were born yesterday, friend. Everyone knows they're rigged.

This is one of the more persuasive fallacies. Because so many people want to conform to the majority opinion about anything, certain negotiators rely on it to strengthen their case. Whatever point they happen to be making, they preface it with the words, "Everyone knows that . . . ." If taken to task, the fact of the matter is that everyone doesn't know a great many things mentioned in everyday conversation. Defend yourself against this fallacy by challenging anyone using it to explain the basis on which it is being applied.

Fallacy 5: The Excluded Middle

Patron:	Waiter, how many pancakes do you get in a full order?
Waiter:	Four, Ma'm.
Patron:	I can't eat four. Could I get an order of just two pancakes?
Waiter:	Sorry Ma'm, we only serve complete orders—no half orders.
Patron:	Why not? Just have the chef make two pancakes, put them on a plate, and you charge me half the regular price.

Waiter: Sorry Ma'm, I can't do that. I don't make the rules–I only work here.

Perhaps you have not had this particular pancake experience, but you have probably had similar ones. The fallacy of the Excluded Middle is a situation in which someone negotiates on the basis of two extremes. In our dialogue, the waiter is negotiating with the patron from an all-or-none position–either she orders four pancakes or none! The patron also commits this fallacy if she insists on being served two pancakes or she will leave the restaurant. When dealing with this kind of fallacy, it is essential that alternatives to the extremes on both sides be known. For example, the patron may elect to: (1) demand what she wants, (2) order four pancakes and leave two on her plate, (3) order four pancakes and deduct half the price from the waiter's tip, (4) perhaps share a full order with someone else, or (5) send for the manager and try to have an exception made.

Options also exist from the standpoint of the waiter. He could elect to: (1) serve a full order and charge her for half (which would be dishonest), (2) attempt to persuade her to order something else, (3) suggest that she accept four smaller pancakes, or (4) let the manager decide the matter.

Whereas many of these alternatives may strike you as unrealistic or impractical, they clearly illustrate the nature of this fallacy–people thinking in terms of extremes, black or white, this or that, all or none. It can be combatted by raising options that fall between the extremes.

Fallacy 6: Mistaken Causation

Junior Senator: It sure looks like this country is headed for another depression.

Senior Senator: How did you arrive at that optimistic conclusion?

Junior Senator: Have you noticed how shaky the stock market is lately? If the bottom drops out like it did back in 1929, we'll have another crash on our hands.

Senior Senator: I don't follow your reasoning. Are you saying that the depression in the '30s was caused by the stock market crash?

Junior Senator: Exactly! No stock market crash, no depression.

It would be a neat trick if negotiations could be made on the basis of such simple logic. For anyone to set up an arbitrary cause-and-effect relationship between the stock market crash and the depression is to ignore the existence of any other factors, such as world trade at the time, the morality of the people, national leadership, internal business cycles, and so forth. Those who commit this fallacy have been known to suffer from tunnel vision, a phenomenon in which a person sees nothing to the right or to the left–only what lies straight ahead. Having such a limited perspective on any subject establishes a perfect climate for a one-cause/one-effect conclusion. To show you how easily one can be lured into committing this fallacy, complete the following statements without too much thought. Write your answers down quickly, to reflect as much spontaneity as possible.

1. Pain in the left side of the chest means ______________

2. People who have difficulty breathing suffer from ______________

To a physician, chest pain on the left side could mean a dozen different things. No competent doctor would dare make a diagnosis on the basis of one symptom alone. Nor should you when engaged in negotiating. Although most of you probably answered statement number one something to the effect of heart disease, the pain could have been attributable to gas, muscle spasm, arthritis, pulled ligament, an inflamation of cartilage, or even a psychosomatic problem. Any one of these and several others could be responsible for left chest pain. Therefore, to jump at heart disease without considering the other possibilities could easily qualify as fallacy of mistaken causation.

The second statement generally elicits some reference to asthma whenever difficult breathing is mentioned. It, too, could have such diverse causes as anxiety, fear, overexertion, or high altitude. These are but two examples of how easy it is to arrive at a hasty conclusion about practically anything. Guard against this tendency in others by avoiding it yourself.

Fallacy 7: It Was Alright Until . . . .

Customer:	Hi. My name is Mr. Faber. You gave my car a complete tune-up last Friday.
Garage Mechanic:	Yes, Mr. Faber, what can we do for you?
Customer:	Well, I'm only getting about 9 miles to a gallon.
Garage Mechanic:	That's about right for a car like yours, Mr. Faber.
Customer:	Then, how come before I brought it to you to have it tuned, I used to get at least 13 to 14 miles to a gallon? It was alright until you tuned it.

The striking force of this fallacy comes from placing blame on whatever came after on the basis of what came before. In this dialogue, Mr. Faber claimed that having his car tuned caused it to get less mileage per gallon. Similar examples are often cited when dealing with changes in personnel, such as, "Everything was going just great guns until we hired Mrs. Portnoy. Then everything that could go wrong, went wrong."

Part of the negotiation process involves manipulating events in time. Things happen in an order or sequence. Assigning some special cause or importance to an event often supplies a negotiator with the ingredients for perpetrating this fallacy.

Fallacy 8: Round 'n' Round We Go

Patient:	Doctor, why doesn't my son, Jerry, listen to me?
Psychiatrist:	Because you are always shouting at him.
Patient:	But why am I always shouting at him?
Psychiatrist:	Because he doesn't listen to you.

In this fallacy, people, like dogs chasing their tails, negotiate in circles. If you were Jerry's parent, would you find another psychiatrist? Whereas the exchange of question and answer between doctor and patient is probably a serious one, it comes off as comic. But it's as amusing as going for a job, being asked if you have experience, telling them you haven't any, and then being refused. How in the world are you supposed to have experience if nobody will give you a job? Not a very funny fallacy when the person look-for the job happens to be *you.*

A rule of thumb for detecting the *Round 'n' round We Go* fallacy is to note the presence of two or more unsupported claims, each of which supposedly proves the other.

Fallacy 9: Count Your Blessings

Commentator:	Commissioner, is it true that our city has one of the highest crime rates in the country?
Police Commissioner:	Yes, but our neighboring state to the north has a 9 per cent higher crime rate than we have.
Commentator:	Really, then I guess we aren't that bad off after all.

This is a fallacy of false consolation. The fact that another state has a nine per cent higher crime rate doesn't for one second make rapes, muggings, and murder any easier to take. Politicians frequently employ this fallacy when comparing one set of intolerable circumstances to another comparatively worse situation. Whether arguing for more funds, public housing, or increased police protection, negotiators can always find people who are better or worse off than others. Don't allow yourself to be deceived by this fallacy. All it attempts to do is cause people to sit back and say, "I guess we're not as bad off as the next fellow." This gives them a false sense of security that often prevents them from doing something about their predicament.

Fallacy 10: Appealing to Pity

Motorcycle Policeman:	May I see your driver's license, please?
Motorist:	What's wrong, officer?
Motorcycle policeman:	You were speeding–going 15 miles over the limit.

Motorist:	Give me a break, officer. I have six kids, I'm a diabetic, my wife is in the hospital having her gallbladder removed, and I'm a veteran of the Korean and Viet Nam Wars.

Many an attorney attempting to negotiate an acquittal for his clients will employ this fallacy with a jury The motorist in our dialogue sure used it on the policeman who stopped him for speeding. It may not help, but it sure can't hurt his cause. Defending yourself against those who would use it on you consists of staying close to the hard facts in the case and far away from anything designed to play on your sympathy. Pity is the working agent of this fallacy.

Fallacy 11: Good Breeds Good–Bad Breeds Bad

Mailman:	Good morning. How are you today?
Shopkeeper:	Fine, and you?
Mailman:	O.K. Say, did you hear about the head teller down at the bank? They arrested him for shooting heroin.
Shopkeeper:	You don't mean Mr. Prendol? I can't believe it. He's the nicest man over there. As far as I'm concerned, a good person like him just wouldn't do anything like that, especially something that was against the law.

In this fallacy, the assumption is made that a good person wouldn't do something bad. If, on the other hand, Mr. Prendol had a reputation for being an obnoxious, rude, and unkind person, hearing that he was arrested for shooting heroin would come as no surprise to many who would fall prey to the workings of this fallacy. They would simply say, "It figures. He was a bad man, and bad men tend to do bad things. It's just a matter of time until they're caught."

Reputations in any business or profession are frequently used as a basis for judging a person's behavior. A forerunner of this has its roots in primary and secondary school. There, certain teachers have been known to label a student a "bad boy or girl," and the label is merely passed on from teacher to teacher. The unfortunate result is that other teachers often tend to match the student with the reputation; that is, good boys and girls do good things, bad boys and girls do bad things.

The mainspring of this fallacy is that people and their deeds are inseparable. This notion must be dispelled if negotiations are to be kept on an even keel. This is accomplished by judging people and the acts they commit separately. Ironically, newspaper reports have occasionally described people guilty of multiple murders as quiet, mild mannered, soft spoken, and gentle. Obviously, the criteria society often uses as an indicator of a "nice" person only touches the surface. (In fact, the word "nice" comes from a contraction of the Latin *ne scio*, "I don't know.") Thus, we must not be misled by these glib labels and what they have come to mean in everyday life.

Fallacy 12: It's Brand New

New Car Dealer:	Isn't she a beauty? Just came in yesterday.
Old Timer:	They just don't have it, Sonny. In my day, cars were built to withstand all kinds of abuse. Today, they are made out of cardboard. Ever see how they fold up in an accident?
New Car Dealer:	You may have a point, Pop, but have you noticed what the newer models have that cars in your day didn't have: engines with over 400 horsepower, power steering and brakes, air conditioning, tape decks for stereophonic radio, puncture-proof tires? There can be little doubt about it, Pop, the newer the car, the better.

When a negotiator attempts to convince you that whatever is newer is better, a fallacy is being committed. If manufacturers are to stay in business, they must constantly come out with a newer this and a better that. Furthermore, their advertising must convince the general public that the latest product is necessarily the best. Although there are undoubtedly advantages to many of the more recent developments in every field, life experience should not let you ignore the fact that the characteristics of many older products and methods have withstood the test of time. Advocates of this fallacy will try to persuade you that whatever is new is decidely an improvement over what is old. Watch them carefully, and make them justify every claim they make.

You have just been introduced to 12 of the more common pitfalls of negotiation. Through experience, you will become more adept at recognizing them without too much difficulty. As a first step in the direction of that experience, try this exercise:

Name of Exercise: Mock Negotiation

Purpose: To experience some of the dynamics of negotiation which tend to occur in a simulation of it.

Procedure:

Step 1. The class should be subdivided into five equal-sized units. Each should represent one of the following groups: (1) the mayor's committee, (2) law enforcement officers, (3) teachers, (4) welfare recipients, and (5) senior citizens.

Step 2. Simulating real life happenings, each of the last four groups should research the needs of their group and prepare a formal list of demands to be submitted to the mayor's committee.

Step 3. Upon receiving such a list from each group, the mayor's committee is to prepare a formal reply to each list, and then return it to the group from which it came.

Step 4. On the basis of the reply each group receives from the mayor's committee, plans to negotiate should be made by *all* groups.

Step 5. On specific, prearranged days, each group should confront the mayor's committee and enter into negotiations on the basis of the demands it made and the responses it had received.

Step 6. After all five groups have negotiated, an open discussion should take place in which all members of the class are invited to make comments on what happened and to offer suggestions as to methods of improvement for the future.

SELF-EXAMINATION QUIZ

Having read this chapter, my answers to the following questions will reflect my understanding of its contents.

1. What are some of the qualities required of an effective negotiator?

2. Describe some of the types of people who negotiate.

3. How does one prepare for negotiations?

4. List the various stages of negotiation.

5. What business or professional situations tend to require negotiation?

6. List various types of negotiation found in the business world.

7. Name some of the strategies that can be used in negotiating.

8. What makes something *right* or *wrong*?

9. What are three types of proof used in negotiation?

10. List as many fallacies as you can·that might arise during the course of negotiation.

Suggested Readings

Boulding, Kenneth E., *Conflict and Defense: A General Theory* (New York: Harper & Row, 1962).

Jandt, R. E., ed. *Conflict Resolution Through Communication* (New York: Harper & Row, 1973).

Kelly, Harold H., "Experimental Studies of Threats in Interpersonal Negotiations," *Journal of Conflict Resolution*, **9**, 79–105 (1965).

Kelly, J., "Make Conflict Work For You," *Harvard Business Review*, **48**, 103–113 (1970).

Keltner, J. W., "Communication and the Labor–Management Mediation Process: Some Aspects and Hypotheses," *Journal of Communications*, **15**, 64–80 (1965).

Lomas, Charles W., *The Agitator in American Society* (Englewood Cliffs, N.J.: Prentice-Hall, 1968).

Smith, D., "Communication and Negotiation Outcome," *Journal of Communication*, **19**, 248–256 (1969).

Stagner, R., and H. Rosen, *Psychology of Union–Management Relations* (Belmont, Calif.: Wadsworth, 1966).

Walton, R. E., Interpersonal Confrontation and Basic Third-Party Roles," *Journal of Applied Behavioral Sciences*, **4**, 20–31 (1968).

WORK AREA FOR CHAPTER 7

Chapter 8

Influencing Others

Provide people with the necessary information, and they will often persuade themselves.

MEMO

TO: Reader

FROM: Author

After reading this chapter, you should have a better understanding of:

1. What the relationship is between how the society in which you live influences you, and how you influence it.
2. How much you are influenced in your life, both privately and publicly.
3. How people's beliefs tend to dictate their behavior.
4. Why people believe the things they do.
5. Why people resist being influenced.
6. What motives lie behind the process of influence.
7. How various con games operate.
8. How propaganda and brainwashing work.
9. What the difference is between what is true and what is false.
10. What lying is about.
11. How rumors spread over a grapevine.
12. How an audience should be analyzed.
13. How people influence each other without words.
14. How people resist being influenced by others.

Chapter 8

> We know that some form of control of influence over one another is an inescapable part of human living. That's part of Saturday night dates, marriage, and the rearing of children; the supervision of employees, the making of group decisions, and the sale of products; the running of political campaigns, and any other human effort that involves the actions of others. That's why we can't live and work unless we learn how to design human communications that will get others to think and act in conformity with out wishes.*

What you should eat, wear, and do with your life are but a few of the behaviors influenced by the society in which you live. Think about it for a moment. There aren't many things that you do that are completely of your own free will. Although they may seem to be voluntary acts over which you have absolute control, each can probably be traced back to some form of prior environmental influence or conditioning.

This chapter holds to the belief that today, more than ever before, people are preoccupied with influencing others. This is evidenced by our rapidly growing knowledge about controlling human behavior. The mass media appears to have one paramount objective—to influence how people think, feel, and act. Books, magazines, newspapers, films, tape recordings, radio, and television all play a part in this influential process generated and regulated by the mass media. Although some might find the words *persuasion* or *manipulation* to have a rather shady connotation, these words have one thing in common—the power to influence.

Two types of influence have attended humanity throughout the pages of history—private and public influence. Private influence refers to those incidents that shape a life on a one-to-one basis. Public influence does this through the collective efforts of people, that is, through the influence of city, state, local, and federal governments on the citizens they govern, the influence exerted by business and professional sectors of society, and so forth. The fact of the matter is that we seem to be living in a country with the greatest "influencing density" in the world. Manufacturing and manipulating public opinion and behavior has become big business. The individual can no longer hide from it. To hide, or to behave as though it doesn't exist, can only lead to a weak and vulnerable state. Too many people are already delcaring themselves helpless victims of an overbearing society: "What's the use? Nothing can be done about it anyway." Such a submissive attitude is not only wrong, it is unnecessary. By understanding how and why you influence others, as well as how and why they influence you, your ability to communicate will be markedly enriched. Arthur Schlessinger's words support this attitude: "If man or mechanism were infallible, there would be no need for persuasion; but because they are not, the discipline of consent is indispensible to civilized society.†

*Otto Lerbinger, *Designs for Persuasive Communication* (Englewood Cliffs, N.J.: Prentice-Hall, 1972), p. 3.

To survive as a people, we must work together for the common good, keep open minds to new ideas, and be able to differentiate the good ones from the bad. Without the opportunity to influence or persuade one another, growth and progress would be brought to a standstill. The pages to follow will thus attempt to persuade or influence you to accept his point of view—not a bad thing in this case.

Why People Believe

No discussion of influence, whether going under the name of persuasion, coercion, manipulation, or propaganda should take place without seriously considering the question: Why do people believe? Philosophers, educators, heads of state, industrialists, and military leaders have grappled with this question for centuries. One plausible reason for such interest seems to be the relationship between what people believe and how they behave as a result of those beliefs. For example, if someone entertains a strong belief in making money, chances are excellent that such a person's work habits will reflect that belief; strong religious beliefs are often coupled with devoted worshiping practices, hedonistic beliefs, with a dashing life-style. These generalizations are admittedly sweeping in nature, but they tend to elicit affirmative nods from the public mind. Putting it even more squarely, *people's beliefs tend to dictate their behavior.* Although this concept should not be taken as absolute, there are many professional influencers who use it as a rule of thumb.

Loaded Influences

Apart from technical advances, people haven't changed much over the past few thousand years. They continue to believe things about themselves and their environment much as the ancients did. Subjects dealing with the purpose of humankind, ways of achieving personal happiness, and the meaning of life are still being met with answers that remain substantially unchanged. The basis for their believing today, as in the past, falls into three categories: (1) emotional influence, (2) logical influence, and (3) status influence.

Influencing Through Emotions

There are certain people who, given a sob story, will believe practically anything. On the streets of any large city, people like these make perfect targets for a variety of con games. Whether they have a psychological need to believe, aren't terribly bright, or have a genuine compassion for their fellow human beings isn't the issue here. What is important for you to realize is that their inclination to believe is based, to a large extent, on the type of influence being brought to bear upon them. In this instance, it is any appeal directed at the emotions.

Influencing Through Logic

If, in order for you to believe something you hear or read, you require that it be logical, then logical influence is your Achilles heel. Little else matters to those who fall into this category. They are often equally impressed by anything having a statistical or mathematical foundation. Emotional influence rarely makes an impression on them. Reason is the deity worshipped by such people.

Influencing Through Status

Emotional and logical appeals have little or no effect on people who are influenced by status. Status influence is based on *who* is to be believed. Messages from people in high places (presidents, governors, mayors, police commissioners, famous personalities of stage, screen, and film) are believed because of their status, instead of what they actually have to say. Qualities such as competence, integrity, good will, trust, worthiness, personal dynamism, expertise, knowledge, ability and attitude, in combination or separately, make up the stockpile from which this type of influence is drawn.

Genesis of Influence

Influence begins at birth. There are even those who would argue that it begins before birth, while the fetus is in the mother's womb. Whether the latter is true or not is irrelevant to this discussion. What we know for certain is that as soon as an infant is brought home from the hospital, it is exposed to an ongoing series of verbal, nonverbal, and vocal stimuli. And, as the definition of a stimulus is *anything capable of evoking a response*, these stimuli clearly qualify as sources of influence on the growing child. As these stimuli are repeated over and over again, becoming routinized, they begin to form patterns of thought which in time, develop into attitudes, values, and beliefs. Psychologically speaking, all this information or knowledge lumped together makes up an organized and integrated set of thoughts and feelings about any given object, idea, or event. The extent to which we understand these organized sets of cognitions people have about themselves and their surroundings often acts as a yardstick as to how they will react to new information.

To keep our mental balance, it seems necessary that we screen what we believe. If we didn't, the enormous amounts of information to which we are exposed each day would "blow our minds." As a result, we must repeatedly judge what we will, and will not, allow ourselves to be influenced by. The difficulty, needless to say, is deciding what we should let influence us and what we should not. Such decisions are made on two planes: the emotional and the intellectual. Whereas the majority of people find themselves influenced on both levels, close observation will demonstrate that most people lean farther in one direction than in the other; that is, they either process new ideas from the brain downward or from the gut level upward.

There are several well-known reasons why people resist being influenced. These include: (1) the belief that it is a sign of weakness, (2) refusal to allow others to feel that they have power over them, (3) the notion that embracing a new idea necessarily makes an old one worthless, (4) unwillingness to "follow the leader," (5) fear that yielding to influence will lead to embarrassment or ridicule, (6) avoidance of possible risk, which they cannot or prefer not to take, and (7) a general distrust of others. Sherif, Sherif, and Nebergall, researchers in groupthink, have studied the question of how people handle being influenced by incoming messages. They suggest three basic categories or latitudes: (1) latitude of acceptance, (2) latitude of rejection, and (3) latitude of noncommitment.* Their meanings are straightforward. If you are a staunch believer in the concept of open marriage, not only will the latitude of acceptance enlist your support of statements in favor ot it, but you will also be receptive to such statements as, "Traditional marriage laws are obsolete," or "Divorce rates are now at an all-time high." In contrast, the latitude of rejection will take in not only those statements and positions directly contrary to what you believe, but all those indirectly contrary to it. To the religious person, a statement like, "God is dead," would immediately be rejected and, along with it, such other statements as, "Formalized religion is losing its relevance in the Atomic Age," and "The Bible is a science fiction novel of two thousand years ago," Finally, the latitude of noncommitment applies to those statements and positions which you neither accept or reject—a kind of fence-straddling maneuver.

How easily can you be influenced? Do you fancy yourself highly resistant, moderately resistant, or a hopeless capitulator? Research on the individual's susceptibility to influence or changes in attitude has introduced the role of the ego. The more ego-involved a person is, the more difficult it will be to change his or her attitude. Egoistic people seem to possess small latitudes of acceptance and noncommitment and large latitudes of rejection. People with moderate or low degrees of ego involvement are most susceptible to being influenced—being persuaded. They have large latitudes of acceptance and noncommitment and small latitudes of rejection. Naturally, there is some middle ground on which rational and mature people, having neither high nor low ego involvement, are open and willing to consider a number of different ideas about a subject. Once willing to listen to alternatives, these people become more susceptible to attitude change (Sherif, et al.).

Generally, you will find that people who are overly concerned with what others say and think about them have a rich imagination, are strongly empathetic (put themselves in other people's places), suffer from a lack of self-confidence, fear rejection, and are chronically insecure are more easily influenced or persuaded. On the other side, those who are extremely dogmatic, who cling to old values, are excessively committed to the opinions rendered

*Carolyn Sherif, Muzafer Sherif, and Robert Nebergall, *Attitudes and Attitude Change: The social Judgment Approach* (Philadelphia, Pa.: W. B. Saunders, 1965).

by authorities, have tightly closed minds, and who are impressed by power are more difficult to persuade or influence. Thus, to the former, believing comes easily; to the latter, believing comes hard.

> *Name at least six people whom you consider to be extremely influential or persuasive personalities. After each name, list your reasons for choosing them.*

Name of Exercise: The Carnival Midway

Purpose: Using a carnival setting, this exercise is designed to illustrate how varying persuasive appeals influence the people passing by.

Procedure:

Step 1. A few days before performing this exercise, each member of the class is to prepare a pitch that will draw people into one of those side-show acts (the smallest man in the world, the two headed cow, sword swallower, rubber man, fat lady).

Step 2. The day of the exercise, six chairs should be lined up at the front of the room, and six students selected by the teacher should be told to stand on them (carefully). At the teacher's signal, each student should begin to tout his/her side-show attraction in the most persuasive way possible. Costumes and props are permitted. Each hawker should try to out-do the others by using any and all verbal, nonverbal, and vocal techniques.

Step 3. While the students standing on the chairs are making their pitches, other members of the class are invited to mill around the room stopping and listening to whomever they wish on the basis of their appeal.

Step 4. After 12 minutes have passed, all pitches are to stop. Take a vote as to which pitchman was most persuasive. After a winner has been chosen, a general discussion should follow in which reasons are given for the choices that were made.

Motives Behind Influence

Real or imagined, rational or irrational, intentional or unintentional, legitimate or illegitimate motives can usually be found lurking behind a thousand-and-one attempts to influence others. Knowing why someone is trying to influence you or why you are trying to influence them can be very important. Such insight seems to provide a broader understanding of the influential process. For example, if you had a job and wanted a raise, you might try acting especially nice, offering to work a little overtime without expecting to be paid for it, or to do things you would not normally do during a typical work day. But, what would you do if, in the process, your employer became suspicious and asked why you were behaving so nicely? You could say that acting that way was a natural characteristic of your personality, or you could level with your boss by saying that you were bucking for a raise. Your boss' reaction to your motives would probably depend on his or her value system. It might also happen the other way around; your employer might treat you extra nice in order to get you to do something your job doesn't call for. For a wide variety of reasons, a substantial part of business and professional transactions involve trying to influence others by winning them over. Whatever the situation, knowing the reasons behind it can make a significant difference in the attitudes of the people involved.

In addition to winning people over, convincing them of something also qualifies as a popular mode of influence. A lawyer trying to convince a jury of his client's innocence, a physician trying to convince her patient to undergo a much-needed surgical procedure, an accountant trying to convince a client not to take certain questionable deductions, a guidance counselor trying to convince an undergraduate to major in a particular area of concentration—all are busily engaged exercising their influence upon others. Any evaluation of the degree to which they have succeeded should include their motivation.

Practical experience in any field quickly reveals how reluctant people are to disclose their true motives. Whereas, someone hungry for a promotion might display a number of familiar signs, asking outright whether his or her behavior is aimed at a promotion might be met with an emphatic, "No, of course not!" College students angling for an A in a course are quick to deny any effort to exert a favorable influence upon a teacher. It is the rare instance in which a person freely admits true motives. Consequently, most motives must be inferred from how people behave. It is interesting to speculate why this is so. Perhaps, it is because our culture frowns on open admissions of pursuits motivated by greed, power, position, and control, making those so motivated embarrassed to admit it. In certain circles, however, such motivating forces are not only held in high regard, they are enthusiastically bragged about at every opportunity.

A word closely related to motivation is *intent*. In any court of law, apart from the crime someone has committed and the consequences to which it has given rise, there is always an interest in why the person did it. Take the case of a man who shot and killed another for trying to rape his wife or daughter. Would knowing of his intent to protect his wife or daughter influence your judgment of his crime? To a far lesser degree than murder, there is the insurance salesman who joins a health spa under the pretext of building up his body when, in reality, his true intent or motive behind joining is to sell more insurance policies. Examples of telltale motives or intents abound in the business and professional world; the only problem in dealing with them is that all too often, they remain hidden from view. This, in turn, makes communicating with the people who sponsor them somewhat strained. Once their motives or intentions are uncovered, however, dealing with people can become more manageable.

Perhaps, the cardinal motive that prompts people to influence others is survival; not only personal survival, but survival in a business and professional context. A man who has built up a successful tool and die business that does $5 million dollars a year must be motivated not only to survive as its founder, but to see to it that the business survives as well. Behind these motives, one will usually find such values as growth, responsibility, ambition, loyalty, challenge, perserverance, and creativity. Each, in its special way, has exerted an influence both on the man and on the business he has built. Things don't just happen. People make them happen. To understand this phenomenon, you have to look behind the motives that influence them.

There is a legal expression, which reads *caveat emptor*, let the buyer beware. In plain language, if you buy something that turns out not to be what the person who sold it to you said it was, it's your own fault. Con games thrive on the ignorance and gullibility of the general public. The motive behind the influence of the con man is to get you to believe something that isn't quite what it appears to be. Here are a few con games. See how many of them you know.

Con Games

Balloon Con

The balloon con goes like this: A man stands on a street corner holding a spiral balloon that is at least 10 feet long. In his other hand, he holds a bunch of deflated balloons. Around his neck, he wears a sign reading: "Balloons–50 cents each." Anyone wishing to buy a balloon simply walks up to him and says, "I'll take one," and he promptly hands them one of the deflated balloons. If he is asked for the already inflated balloon, he glibly says, "They're all the same." Not until they get home and try to blow up the deflated balloon to the size of the big one, do they find that they were not the same. His customers all inferred that they were–and this was their big mistake.

Huge Duke

Huge duke is a short con game widely used by big-time con men. It usually takes place on a train or ocean liner. It is a card game in which there are three con men and a *mark*, who is the person they swindle. At first, they play any game for sociable items, such as cigars, or anything of little value. As they are playing, one of the con men happens to say that he wished they were playing poker because he had a swell poker hand. When he says this, one of the other con men bets him that he has a better poker hand. So they lay down their hands and deal again, except from then on, they jokingly bet on their hands as if they were poker hands, even though they are supposed to be playing another game.

They deal again, and this time, they deal the mark three aces. One of the con men says he's got poker this time, showing the mark his three queens. The mark knows he can beat three queens with his aces, so he says that he's got some poker too; so they bet a few dollars and the mark wins.

The plays have been so timed that the following deals fall to the mark. Furthermore, if the mark deals the cards himself, he knows there has been no manipulation. But, as the con man cuts the deck, he switches the deck without the mark's realizing it. The deck is set up so the mark deals himself four aces, and the hands of the other three members of the game is also prearranged. When the mark deals and sees he has four aces, they run him up as high as he can go and, perhaps, even get him to write a check if he doesn't have any cash. Then, one of the con men pulls a royal flush and takes all the mark's money.

Occasionally, to avoid suspicion, one of the con men speaks up for the mark, telling the others he really isn't a good poker player and it isn't right to take his money. The con man then takes the check and tears it up and burns it with a match right in front of the mark. The mark, believing he is off the hook really isn't because the check he saw burned was not the real check. It was a blank check about the same size and color, which the con man substituted for the real one. The mark doesn't realize he has been swindled until he gets his end-of-the-month bank statement.

Car Dealer Hustle

A hustling car dealer offered a customer a new car worth $4,000 for $2,000 if he could find two other people who would go for similar deals. The customer got two other people, and the dealer collected $2,000 from each of them, totaling $6,000. He told the first man that he would get his car in a few weeks and the other two customers to get two other customers apeice if they wanted their cars for $2,000. The dealer was really paying $4,000 for each car, but as long as his customers paid him in advance, he had enough money to buy one car at a time.

The dealer delivers the new car to the first customer and also got four more customers from the other two men. The dealer, now collecting $8,000 more, told each of the four men that they must find two people each in order to get their cars. He then gave the next two men their cars and continued promising cars to more and more people as he kept collecting his money in advance. After collecting more than $150,000, the dealer disappeared, leaving a great many people without their cars and $2,000 dollars poorer.

Lost Diamond Swindle

The lost diamond swindle is worked with two people. One of them claims to have lost a diamond ring in the rest room of a gas station and offers the attendant a reward if it is found. The second person comes along after the first one and claims to have found a diamond ring in the rest room. The attendant tries to buy it for less than the reward offered by the other party. As you might already have guessed, when he tries to claim his reward, the telephone number he was given to call doesn't exist.

The Hot T.V. Set

The person being "taken" in a hot T.V. set deal is told he can buy a hot (stolen) color T.V. set at half-price or less. He meets the seller and is given a sealed carton with apparent brand markings, indicating a color T.V. set. When he gets it home, he finds that he has purchased a carton with some weighted material inside. From the sound of this con, you probably are saying to yourself, "This could never happen to me." Perhaps not, but a great many intelligent people, with a touch of larceny in their souls (wanting something for nothing), are hoodwinked daily by this con.

Phoney Estate Claim

In the phoney estate claim, the con man reads the obituary column and sends some merchandise to the home of the deceased, claiming it was ordered before the person died. On the basis of this fraudulent claim, he seeks payment. It works on most next of kin, out of respect for the deceased.

Bait-and-Switch Advertising

A store advertises a product at a large discount. When the customer wants to buy it, she is told that they are out of stock, or that the product is inferior. The salesperson then begins a hard sell for some more expensive product.

Ring Toss

It is usually easy to win the cheap, plastic, inexpensive prizes at a carnival by tossing the ring around them. The more expensive prizes, however, are almost impossible to win because they are pitched at a particular angle. To persuade passersby that it is possible to win, they often toss the ring around one of the cheaper items, rarely one of the expensive prizes.

Veteran's Day

You will not believe this one. The Veteran's Day con: A woman in a large city on the East coast collected several thousand dollars soliciting donations in a tin can for the *widow of the unknown soldier.*

These are but a few of the many con games perpetrated upon the general public. All have one motive in common—deception. Whereas the majority are against the law, there are many similar practices which operate just barely within the law. Admonishing people with the phrase *caveat emptor* is not enough; they must be taught how to defend themselves against such deception. One way is to make them superconscious of the motive behind any of these con games. For example, "If this is such a good deal, why is this person telling me about it? I don't know him from a hole in the wall." Con games tend to make sense on the surface, but scratch away the surface and what is underneath usually wreaks of foul play. The motives behind them leave a great deal to be desired—by the con man!

Propaganda

The word *propaganda*, like the word *argument*, discussed in Chapter 7, does not have a very good reputation. A great many people quite innocently

assign negative connotations to these words. Even before we had a name for it, propaganda was one of the most widely used forms of persuasion—of influencing people to adopt a particular form of belief or action. For many, the word propaganda still brings to mind visions of spies and secret police, cynical reporters, biased magazines, and wartime aircraft dropping pamphlets from the sky. What they fail to realize is that propaganda can be used for a good cause, as well as a bad one.

> The motives and the ends are the important parts of any campaign; propaganda merely supplies the method of operation. Advertisements are propaganda for products. They are attempts to sell large quantities of shampoos and baby foods, automobiles, sheets, roofing and zwieback. But the same methods are used to sell war bonds, to win support for the Red Cross, to obtain help for crippled children. The aims are different, but the methods are the same.*

Although we have not developed any foolproof defenses against propaganda, it remains an integral part of our everyday life.

> Most of us know that the earth moves around the sun because we have accepted the propaganda of mathematicians and astronomers, or that vaccination prevents smallpox because we believe the persuasion of physicians and bacteriologists, but few laymen can produce adequate sceintific evidence to support these propositions . . . most of our essential information comes to us, at best, second hand."†

Propaganda has sold everything from sex, to toothpaste, to the Vietnam War. Nearly everyone, everyday, does something or thinks something partly because propaganda has urged them to do so. The list of propagandists include the author of this book, your parents, you, politicians, performers, editors, artists, teachers, preachers, and our immediate circle of friends. The original propagandists were Roman Catholic missionaries sent to spread the words of the gospel in other countries.‡ (*Propaganda* is an abbreviation of a Latin phrase, *de propaganda fides*, "of the propagation of the faith") In a sense, all propagandists are missionaries. They are missionaries for an idea, an action, or an attitude. They are in total control of whatever situation arises, owing to their prowess in the field of general knowledge. To be quite blunt, the removal of propaganda from any organization's bloodstream would soon lead to its demise. Every business and profession, if it is to survive, must grow. To do this, its protagonists are obliged to communicate its worth to others. They must "spread the word." To carry this notion a step further, every member of an organization should be a propagandist on its behalf. To accomplish this spirit within an organization is no easy task. Personnel must be influenced to believe that such behavior will stand them in good stead with the company in terms of getting raises, promotions, and vacations.

*William Hunnel and Keith Huntress, *The Analysis of Propaganda* (New York: The Dryen Press, 1949) p. 2.

†Ibid

‡"Propaganda," *The World Book Encyclopedia,* XV (Chicago, Ill.: Field Enterprises Educational Corporation, 1974), p. 725.

Brainwashing

Propaganda is child's play compared with brainwashing. Although both are used to change people's beliefs, the methods differ considerably. Brainwashing consists of removing all the necessary things from a person's environment. Techniques involving starvation, freezing, physical abuse, and isolation are not uncommon. Subjects are constantly annoyed and questioned and find peace only if they yield to their captor's will.

Without calling it brainwashing, it is practiced in many organizations on a much smaller scale. Privileges are removed from employees who misbehave and are extended to those who render the company some special service. Company policy is strengthened through emotional blackmail, by threats of dismissal, and tattling on a fellow worker is often rewarded. In a number of ways, by instilling propaganda, we all brainwash each other. This precipitates more propaganda, a vicious circle involving people influencing people in special ways through the process of communication. The following exercise has been designed to give you some practical insight as to how a knowledge of communication can be applied in an on-the-job situation.

Name of Exercise: Communications Department

Purpose: To experience what factors would be involved in the establishment and management of corporate communication guidelines where none had existed previously.

Procedure:

Step 1. In this simulation, imagine that an ad has appeared in a local newspaper for a director of communication for a large company which we shall the American Box Corp.

Step 2. The teacher should appoint one member of the class to represent the employment representative of the corporation whose responsibility it will be to hire the individual best suited for the position advertised in the paper; i.e., director of communication.

Step 3. Five students in the class should volunteer to apply for the position. One at a time, they will be interviewed by the employment representative. After all have been interviewed, one should be chosen for the job.

Step 4. The director of communication should now appoint six other members of the class to act as a committee to assist in the establishment and implementation of the corporation communications policy to be developed.

Step 5. Seated in a circle before the rest of the class, the committee will have its first meeting chaired by the newly appointed director of communication for the American Box Corporation.

Step 6. With a 25-minute time limit (which may be altered by the teacher), the committee should discuss the corporation's communication requirements. These should take in such items as: (1) intraoffice communication, (2) interoffice communication, (3) incoming communication, and (4) outgoing communication.

Step 7. After the meeting is over, the entire class should offer its criticism of what was observed in open discussion. Members of the committee are encouraged to defend/or explain their conduct, if necessary.

True or False

A great many people are preoccupied with whether things are true or false. When asked why it is so important for them to know the difference, they answer, "Because it helps me decide what to think and how to act." What they fail to realize is that most of the information concerning human interaction is based on folklore, assumption, presumption, inference, and faith. Most things are not testable like the temperature of water, the height of a structure, or the weight of a metal. What percentage of the information in the world dealing with such subjects as, religion, psychology, ethics, morality, nationalism, love, death, philosophy, and education do you think is true: 10 per cent, 25 per cent, 50 per cent, 75 per cent, or all of it? This question doesn't warrant an answer, but it does give one cause to wonder about the role played by "truth" in the universal communicative process.

The mainspring of influence, whether in the form of a con game, propaganda, brainwashing, or advertising, is what people believe—what they consider to be true or false. On this premise, people can be manipulated in a variety of directions and to varying extents. This book, for example, will only influence you to the extent that its contents find meaningful correlations for you. Although other factors are certainly at work, without these correlations, its influence on you will probably be minimal.

In the emotional sweepstakes of organizational life, the distinction between what is true and what is false is rarely clear cut. Countless actions and reactions are made on the basis of shaded versions of already biased perceptions of reality. If you are working for an employer whose notion of true dedication to your job consists of being punctual, your efforts to get a raise or to be promoted had better include punctuality. In spite of the fact that your work record is notably superior to that of your coworkers, if you aren't punctual, your employer will not consider your dedication to the firm "true." In short, your ability to influence your employer will hinge on the extent to which your view of true and false coincides with his or hers.

No respectable discussion of this subject should end without mentioning the pehnomenon of *lying*. To define a *lie* by saying that it is something that is not true is about as meaningless as defining a horse by saying that it is not a cow.

Define the word lie. Now, look up its definition in at least three different dictionaries.

An extraordianry number of people regard the act of lying as an extremely serious offense: Thou shalt not bear false witness. Some are preoccupied with the intent behind a lie, others with the act of lying itself, and still others with the consequence that results from telling a lie. Regardless of the aspect of lying they find offensive, all agree that it is wrong. Not only do our courts currently mete out punishment for perjury—lying under oath—but, many organizations have been known to dismiss an employee on the spot if caught in a lie. A less orthodox view divides the misrepresentation of truth into such categories as fibs, whoppers, white lies, black lies, or teany-weany lies.

Practically every culture maintains rather stern strictures against lying. From childhood, most of us have been told that it is wrong to lie. As a result, we have developed a kind of reflex or automatic signaling system that lets others know when we are not telling the truth. Such behavior as stuttering, poor eye contact, fidgeting, and talking too much often gives us away. Unfortunately, lying occasionally masquerades as business acumen, shrewdness, cunning, diplomacy, strategy, or gamesmanship. What do you call it when a manufacturer tells a customer that his order went out yesterday and it didn't? What do you call it when a diplomat from one country is having tea with a diplomat from another country Saturday afternoon, and the next day that country is attacked? What do you call it when an actor turns in an outstanding audition for a play, is told by the casting director that he will call the next day, and then doesn't? What do you call it when a teacher tells you not to worry about the material in a particular chapter, and that material is on the final examination? What do you call it when a president of a country flatly denies knowing something he knows? What do you call it when you go on a job interview and tell the employer that you did things you never did?

These adjustments of our communication happen every day. One might almost say that they play a principal role in influencing others in a wide variety of situations. This places upon each of us the responsibility of being able to distinguish between what is true and what is false. Perform the following exercise to find out just how good you are at this task.

Name of Exercise: Believe It or Not

Purpose: To provide the student with an opportunity to analyze the criteria different people use to distinguish between true and false stories.

Procedure:

Step 1. On an assigned date, each student is to think up a short story and come to class prepared to tell it. (*Time limit:* 2–5 min). The story should either be false or true. Because it is difficult to tell a story that is completely true or false, it should be predominantly one or the other. It may be drawn from life—something that really happened—or an outright lie.

Step 2: Seated in a circle, each student should take a turn telling a story. After it is told, the teacher should take a vote by asking, "How many of you thought the story was true, raise your hands. How many of you thought it was false, raise your hands."

Step 3. After each vote, students are asked to volunteer the reasons for their voting the story true or false.

Step 4. Following the voting on each story, the storyteller is to reveal whether it was, in fact, true or false.

Step 5. Depending on the size of the class, it may be necessary to carry this exercise over to another period. After all have had an opportunity to tell their stories, an open discussion should address itself to the following questions:

a. Are there any nonverbal characteristics common to most liars?
b. Do you think liars are born or made?
c. Describe the biggest liar you have ever known.
d. In your opinion, which is more important:
Why a lie is told?
The nature of the lie itself?
The consequences to which the lie gives rise?
Explain your answer.

From what has been said thus far, shaping the truth to meet various personal and public needs is not an uncommon means of influencing others. One of the most interesting of these tendencies in the organization is the proverbial grapevine.

Rumor Spreading

A grapevine is a human chain along which information travels rapidly, efficiently, and without regard for truth or consequence. Again, like propaganda and argument, rumors communicated by a grapevine are generally considered to have a negative reputation. This is not necessarily so. Rumors serve a constructive purpose in that they reflect an interest in work, the people doing it, and the organization for which the work is being done. They can be destructive, however, when they result in the betrayal of company secrets, poison someone's reputation, lower morale, or distract people from their work. In either case, whether they are constructive or destructive, they exert an influence within an organization.

When someone tells you a rumor, do you immediately search out someone else to whom to tell it? Probably not. Relatively few people make it their business to "spread the word." The average person on the job is a passive receiver of news. Those who harbor a special psychological need to spread rumors have also been referred to as "change agents." Their need apparently to center on influencing others by telling them things they didn't ask to hear. The role seems to elevate their self-worth and reinforce their feeling of involvement within the organization. It is important to note that rumor-spreaders are job-centered people and, as such, can serve a useful purpose to their employers. What they do can and should be converted into an asset to a company. Because they are usually intensely interested in what goes on in an organization, such interest can be harnessed. It would, therefore, behoove employers, supervisors, or administrators to make absolutely certain that the liaison people (change agents) within their organizations have their facts straight, rather than try to censor them.

There are several reasons why people are attracted to rumors. When they are anxious about the outcome of a particular event or action, they appear to be willing to accept practically *any* explanation or version of it. If the word is out that a company is being taken over by a conglomerate, not only do the rumors fly fast and furious, but the employees—hungry to know how the take-over will affect them personally—are quick to swallow any number of different interpretations of what will happen. Another reason why certain people find rumors appealing is that knowing something, even though that information might be inaccurate, is preferable to not knowing at all. Rumors function to reduce tension by satisfying the compelling curiosity so many people possess.

From a management standpoint, rumor control may be an objective. Some helpful hints for controlling the spread of rumors are: (1) make certain that all communication is as clear as possible, (2) be alert and responsive to what employees are saying, (3) keep the information on your desk up-to-date —delays cause dissonance, and (4) when a rumor comes to your attention, take immediate action by seeing that the information it contains is accurate.

Interview at least three people whose jobs are either managerial or supervisory in nature. Ask them how rumors manifest themselves in their organizations and how they deal with them.

Exerting an influence on others through the use of a grapevine generally involves a one-to-one interaction: Eric tells Danya, Danya tells Phil, Phil tells Cheryl, and so on down the line. Influencing many people at one time involves a somewhat different set of persuasive dynamics. For instance, communicologists agree that unless speakers know their audience, their chances of influencing them are slim. In the next section, you will find some of the things speakers should know about their audiences.

Audience Analysis

The need to know how to analyze an audience rapidly becomes apparent to anyone actively involved in a business or profession. Sales meetings, conferences, briefings, seminars, union rallies, training programs, and negotiations all require a knowledge of audience analysis. A good speech *per se* does not always yield successful communication, but a good speech buttressed by a carefully planned audience analysis frequently does.

In the earlier pages of this book, you were told that meaning is in people, not in their words or actions. Whether you will be required to influence a group of people or a single person with a persuasive speech, their response will usually be based on whatever meaning they assign to your words and actions. This factor alone makes audience analysis an invaluable tool for anyone seriously interested in the art of influencing others.

Many people believe that an audience is simply a collection of people assembled to see or hear others perform. This is a gross oversimplification. Not only do performers get feedback from an audience—those in the audience get feedback from each other. Inasmuch as an audience is a multidimensional unit, any one of a number of factors is capable of influencing it. These include such determinants as: size, intelligence, language, affiliation, sex, health, and time and place, which we will discuss subsequently. Although one may generalize about audiences in the broader sense, each audience should be analyzed on its own merits. Keltner makes these distinctions with reference to audience influenceability.*

> For those who are actively antogonistic or less active but opposed, one must first establish his own credibility and honesty. Whatever is said to these people, great pains should be taken to speak to them directly and tactfully; one should avoid in any way reinforcing their opposition. For the disbelievers and the doubters, one needs to assemble all the sound and reliable arguments and proofs possible to support one's argument. In speaking to this type of persuadee, one should document all information carefully and precisely and make every effort to answer all objections with clear and unequivocal reasons. One should appear easy and assured, and the discussion should remain calm, confident, and poised. For believers and those who accept the idea, one needs to provide the persuadee with strong motivation if the persuasive process is

*John Keltner, *Interpersonal Speech-Communication* (Belmont, Calif.: Wadsworth, 1970), p. 211.

one which is designed to bring about action of some sort. The matter should be discussed intensely and directly using more emotional and reaction-stimulating words than with others. The language used can be colorful and vivid.

There isn't always time for a speaker to research the character and temperament of an audience. Often, it is simply a matter of being able to quickly think on one's feet. It is also worthwhile to mention that audiences are not static, that is, they do not remain unchanged throughout a presentation. Some have been reported to start out in a quiet, attentive manner and, in a matter of moments, become extremely hostile right before a speaker's eyes. The reverse is also possible. An initially hostile audience may suddenly become quiet and attentive. The best insurance against either of these untoward shifts in audience behavior is to have a reasonably clear understanding of an audience's disposition and composition. But, realize that even with such an understanding, there are no iron-clad guarantees when it comes to predicting audience behavior. Your best bet is to become familiar with those external factors that *can* be controlled to a certain extent.

Size. The size of an audience can be important. An appropriate sound system is needed for an auditorium that seats 500 to 1000 people. With an audience of 25 to 50 people, this would be unnecessary. Also, the larger the audience, the more impersonal it will tend to be; the smaller it is, the more intimate. Body movements, facial expressions, and gestures will probably have little or no effect with a large audience, and a much greater effect with small ones.

Intelligence. The overall intelligence of an audience is an important concern to a good speaker. What level should be aimed at? Few things offend an audience more than being "talked down to" by a speaker. Equally offensive is the speaker who talks over an audience's head. Above all, intelligence and knowledge should not be confused. A person can be extremely intelligent and not very knowledgeable, or knowledgeable and not terribly intelligent. Whichever the case, it is essential that a speaker try to find out beforehand whether an audience is generally bright or dull, plain or sophisticated. In the event that this information cannot be ascertained, the wise course is to try to strike some middle ground that will offend neither type.

Language. Some audiences have a peculiar sensitivity toward the kind of language a speaker uses. It is not uncommon for one ill-chosen word or phrase to negate an entire speech. The use of dialect is also tricky business. In their attempt to ingratiate themselves with an audience, speakers have been known to use a local word or idiom that winds up alienating everyone in the room. The way a person speaks is an extremely personal matter. Humor, based on the language an audience speaks or obvious attempts to imitate it, should be avoided. This is particularly important with a bilingual audience. A speaker who is not reasonably fluent in the native language of the audience should refrain from attempts at being cute by casually uttering a phrase or two in that language. If not executed with great tact and precision, it will usually backfire and come off as presumptuous. The wisest course for a speaker to follow is to speak his or her native language in a simple and straightforward manner. Attempts at using language variations to influence an audience should be left to the more expert speaker.

Affiliation. No member of an audience lives in a vacuum. Most come from somewhere, have family roots, and belong to different organizations. Without prior checking, a speaker cannot possibly know the affiliation of the audience being addressed. Imagine the chagrin of a speaker who, after telling a joke about blood transfusions, learned that the audience was comprised predominantly of Jehovah Witnesses (their religion does not sanction blood transfusions). Audience affiliations could be political, racial, national, academic, cultural, or social. A negative remark or allusion to any of these affiliations could offend members of an audience to whom they apply. Tied in with affiliations are attitudes, values, and beliefs. Thus, the threat of offending becomes compounded for the speaker untrained or uninterested in audience analysis.

Sex. The sex distribution of an audience also warrants consideration. In an age when male and female roles in society are not only being challenged, but are also being significantly altered in a great many organizations, it is essential that a speaker know the male/female distribution of the audience being addressed. With the advent of such phrases as "male chauvinist pig" and "sexist," speakers (and writers) have suddenly become keenly aware of the need to monitor their arbitrary and capricious labeling of the roles played by men and women in society. For instance, a female sales executive addressing an audience made up predominantly of salesmen could easily fail to influence them unless she covers the necessary precautions at the beginning of her speech. Conversely, a male speaker addressing a predominantly female audience must also exercise care not to behave as if women didn't exist, or that those who do exist run second place to men.

Health. People who are not well are not really themselves. To a large extent, they are consumed by thoughts of dealing with their illness. Furthermore, in select cases, people in poor states of health tend to perceive their internal and external environments in terms of their particular condition. To the person with heart disease, there are only two types of people in the world: those with heart disease and those without it. Pretend you had to deliver a speech to an audience of disabled veterans. Would the fact that they were disabled alter your approach? How? What if you sold insurance and had the opportunity to address an audience of senior citizens in varying degrees of ill health? To influence them, would you organize your speech in any special way? In short, should a responsible audience analysis include knowing about the health of your audience?

Time and Place. When and where a speaker confronts an audience could be crucial to the influencing process. Adult education classes offered in the evening occasionally lose their ability to influence mature students who, in most cases, have just come from a full day's work By the same token, the teacher might also have put in a full day's work at a regular job. Here, because the course is given at the end of the day, both students and teacher may lack the vitality and interest they might have had were the course given at 10:00 A.M. Of comparable importance is where a speech is delivered. No speaker should accept an engagement without knowing exactly where it is to take place. Ignorance of this simple fact could find a speaker in a gymnasium, basement, hallway, parking lot, or even a condemned building. Although some of these examples are a bit facetious, they do drive home the importance of knowing beforehand where a speech is to be given.

You now have some idea of the factors to be taken into account in making an audience analysis, but this is by no means an all-inclusive list. What they should have done is make you aware of the pressing need every speaker should feel for audience analysis. To deliver any speech, without first making an audience analysis, is as dangerous as climbing into a cockpit without a map or a compass. Bear in mind that no one really persuades or influences anyone – all they can do is provide a vehicle with which audiences persuade themselves. Nevertheless, to do this, one must know something about an audience's likes and dislikes, interests and aversions, temperaments and idiosyncrasies. It is only *through* these traits that influence can be exerted. The prime mover is the audience; the speaker is only the instrument. Test your own ability to make an audience analysis in the next exercise.

Name of Exercise: The Auctioneer

Purpose: To determine an auctioneer's ability to influence his or her audience using audience analysis as a basis for the sales pitch. In the Midway Exercise you tried earlier, the product being touted was not seen by the audience. Here it is.

Procedure:

Step 1. On a pre-announced date, each member of the class is to bring three items to be put up for auction. The ceiling price is not to exceed $10; the opening bid is to be set by the auctioneer, and the bids are to progress in units of 25 cents each.

Step 2. Each student is to take a turn at being the auctioneer, coming to the front of the room and trying to sell the articles brought to class. Each auctioneer is permitted a time limit of one minute to "sell" each item before starting the bidding on it. If the item does not move within two minutes, it must be passed by and the next article put up for sale.

Step 3. Whenever an item is purchased, the auctioneer should take the buyer's name and complete the transaction after the auction is over.

Step 4. Post-auction assignment: Each student who acted as an auctioneer should write a brief description of the audience analysis used during the auction; that is, were the attempts to influence the audience based on price, appearance, utility, sympathy, status of the auctioneer? The audience analysis should not exceed one page in length.

Step 5. The day the audience analyses are to be handed in, the teacher should arbitrarily select five students to read their papers. A general open classroom discussion should then take place in which all members of the class should participate by reflecting the contents of their own audience analysis.

As an added test of your ability to make an audience analysis, here are some rather atypical audiences. See whether you can formulate a strategy of influence to use them. Enter your ideas for each audience in the spaces provided for them.

An Audience of Blind People

____

____

____

____

An Audience of Deaf People

____

____

____

____

An Audience of Psychiatrists

____

____

____

____

An Audience of Prison Inmates

____

____

____

____

____

An Audience of Teenage Retarded Children

____

____

____

____

____

Although organizing an approach to the average audience is not without problems, establishing an approach for the atypical audience often presents additional difficulties. The example of teenage retarded children illustrates such a difficulty. Not only does the average speaker suffer from a lack of knowledge about retarded children, but also probably suffers from a great deal of misinformation about them. Whatever the reason, there is a pressing need for finding out what method would be best in approaching an audience of retarded children. Some investigation along these lines should uncover information that will lead you to: (1) organize your speech into small individual units, because retarded children often have relatively short attention spans; (2) speak in short, uncomplicated sentences; (3) make use of a great many visual and auditory aids; (4) use analogies liberally so that meaning is sharpened wherever possible; (5) adjust the seating arrangement so that it is a little less formal, and so members of the audience enjoy a wider range of eye contact with each other and the speaker; and (6) use purposeful nonverbal communication freely.

Whereas on the surface it would appear that these atypical audiences would be harder to analyze, this is not necessarily so. Aside from the variations inherent in each group, all share a very conspicuous bond: Blindness, deafness, psychiatry, prison life, or retardation. As a result, a considerable part of their values and life-style is highly predictable. Their experiences are more alike than different from one another. The term *homogeneous* applies to such audiences. When dealing with an audience in which such a common bond does not exist, where considerable differences exist among its members, the term *heterogeneous* applies.

A conclusion that should follow from these statements is that homogeneous audiences are generally easier to analyze than are heterogeneous ones. Confronting a mixed audience, one in which there is a wide range of differences, creates the greatest difficulty for a speaker. An on-the-spot set of assumptions, presumptions, inferences, and intuitions must be made in order to arrive at a common denominator—a target a speaker can shoot at, with the highest chance of hitting a mark of influence. Although the fact that they are all human beings might, at first, seem a rather feeble target, it might turn out to be the only one available to the speaker.

> *Assuming you are that speaker, list as many generalizations as you can about an audience whose common denominator is simply that they are human beings, requiring love, self-respect, a warm bed at night, a job they don't mind going to each morning, and so forth.*

The process by which we influence others should, by now, begin to make more sense. You should appreciate the fact that people can be influenced through their emotions, by logic, and by the prestige exerted by a speaker. The importance of knowing why a particular form of influence is being exerted should also be apparent. Finally, in addition to becoming more aware of the role that audience analysis plays in the persuasive process, you should have a feel for why people believe the things they do. Now, to further round out your understanding of the process of influence, here are some of the ways we influence others without words.

Influencing Without Words

Thus far, we have been concerned with influencing others through the use of language. To what extent does influence occur without words? Obviously, to a much greater extent than many of us realize. A foundation for this belief was advanced in Chapter 2 (Interpersonal Self-inventory) and will be expanded here to apply more specifically to business and professional settings.

Are you influenced by the following?

1. Someone always walking off with the key to the men's or ladies' room.
2. Sitting at tables in a restaurant that are too close together.
3. Having an employer or supervisor stand and look over your shoulder while you are working.
4. People borrowing things from your desk without asking.
5. Working in an office that is kept too hot or too cold.
6. Being given a company car that needs repairs every Tuesday and Thursday.
7. Going to a doctor who is good, but who has bad breath or cold hands.
8. Sitting in a theater that has poor acoustics.
9. Being kept waiting.
10. Working in a place where things are poorly layed out, that is, you have to walk upstairs to get your supplies, downstairs to have something xeroxed, and two blocks to the parking lot in the rain.

List some of the nonverbal things that could have a negative influence on you in a work situation.

Researchers in the field of organizational communication have recently begun to take a closer look at the role body language and proxemics (spatial relationships) play on the job. As a result, the literature is beginning to accumulate. Companies specializing in communication are offering their services as consultants to business and industry. They will analyze an organization's operation from a communications standpoint—particularly, its human factors. In the past, such analyses consisted primarily of an organization's verbal communication: letter writing, interoffice memos, contracts, agreements, telephone transactions, advertising copy, and so forth. Today, the term *communication* has been expanded to embrace a whole raft of nonverbal considerations.

One of the most frightening aspects of organizational life is public speaking. Getting up on your feet and addressing your peers often strikes fear into the heart. Whereas public speaking would seem an almost exclusively verbal act, it consists of an incredibly wide assortment of kinesic and proxemic elements. In fact, a major part of stage fright is nonverbal (think of the palpatations of the heart, sweaty palms, trembling knees, dryness of the mouth, light-headedness, and purposeless movements). Many of these symptoms are perfectly normal, unless they become seriously exaggerated, or a speaker becomes abnormally preoccupied with them. It is the exceedingly rare person who never experiences any of them. Let us take the time here to talk about a few ways of how we influence others nonverbally when delivering a speech.

One of your best nonverbal assets is eye contact. Learn to look your audience in the eye; scan it like a television camera—from left to right, front to back. By engaging your audience with your eyes, you put them on notice that they are your target—that your message is for them. Catching their eyes will not only make them feel that what you have to say will be of interest, it will also alert them to the fact that their opinion may be solicited. To forfeit eye contact is to invite boredom and apathy.

Another nonverbal method of holding your audience's attention is to lessen your distance from it. Attention levels seem to perk up when a speaker steps out from behind a lecturn or moves to the front of the dais. The inexperienced or insecure speaker frequently takes refuge behind a lecturn or desk. To step out from behind such barriers is to assume a certain amount of risk and, at the same time, responsibility. You are exposing yourself to your audience in full view. Behind a lecturn, your audience gets to see only half instead of the whole you. Nightclub performers (the more accomplished ones) occasionally employ this technique in their act. They will either sit on the edge of the stage and talk or sing to their audience, go out among them, or ask people to join them on the stage. Whatever their practice, it succeeds in making other members of their audience feel more a part of what is going on. They tend to empathize with those taking part on the stage. Apart from *what* you may have to say, manipulating the distance between you and your audience inclines to make them more sensitive both to you and your message. It makes them "feel," and that is good. People tend to remember more how they felt than what they thought.

The use of *paralanguage* (a subset of nonverbal communication) is another technique you might want to consider. Audiences are generally sensitive to the pitch and rhythm of a speaker's voice. Knowing this, experienced speakers can quickly get an audience in the mood "to feel." By cleverly manipulating the pitch of their voices and the rhythm of their speech, they can begin to move an audience in a number of emotional directions. This does not mean that an impact cannot be made intellectually. It should be taken to mean that audiences are often more dramatically moved through their emotions than through their intellect.

One more thing about audiences is that they are a curious lot. If you stand before them with your hands behind your back, they want to know what's going on back there. If you appear with a brown bag or a black box, place it on the desk, they won't rest comfortably until they know what is in it. This characteristic of being nosey can be used to your advantage. Without an audience's attention, little can be accomplished. Therefore, why not include some nonverbal article with which to trap their attention? Consider the following list of speech topics. Next to the first two topics, you will find specific articles intended to trap an audience's attention. Complete the list by inserting an appropriate article next to the others.

1. Capitol punishment a length of rope.
2. The problem of being overweight several packages of cakes and candy.
3. Tax reform ______________________
4. Abortion ______________________
5. Drunk driving ______________________
6. Obscenity and the law ______________________
7. Pollution ______________________
8. Medical abuses ______________________
9. Consumer fraud ______________________
10. Communication ______________________

Whether you will, one day, be addressing a board of directors, members of your staff, a federal commission, collection of stockholders, or a committee of lay people, bear in mind that what they hear and see nonverbally often exerts a greater influence upon them than what you have actually said. There is a positively charming Vietnamese folktale that proves this point.

It seems a young Buddhist monk found pleasures of the flesh more interesting than those of the spirit. Hearing rumors of his indiscretions, the pagoda's elders decided that the young monk's fitness should be tested by a famous holy man whose pilgrimage would soon bring him to their village. Terrified of such an examination, the monk changed clothes with a cobbler friend who, for some reason, was confident of his ability to pass the test.

Thus, the holy man, though he had taken a vow of silence and communicated only through gestures, appeared at the appointed time ready to examine the young monk. He, then, turned to the young monk and touched his forehead with the palm of his right hand. The monk replied by stamping his left foot several times. The holy man smiled and touched his armpit. The young monk immediately patted himself on the back. The holy man's smile grew wider, and he raised the first three fingers of his right hand. The young monk replied by stretching all five fingers as high and wide as possible.

After the examination, the holy man rejoined the elders who were anxiously awaiting his verdict. The holy man then asked for a brush and paper on which he wrote the following impressions: I have visited many pagodas between here and Siam, but never did I meet a monk as learned in doctrine as your young bonze. He not only answered my questions perfectly, but he responded with the subtle parable that shows great learning. I said to him: "We must always cherish the Buddha image in our head." And he replied: "We must fiercely stamp out the illusions of Mara, the Tempter." Then, I showed my armpit to indicate: "The prayers of the just mount to heaven as if tucked by the stork under his delicate wings." He replied: "The stork disappears in the clouds, but the dependable tortoise stays on to carry the heavy stele of remembrance on his rounded back." I then quoted the phrase: "The stars of the faith shine under the celestial arch." And immediately, he replied: "The five joys enter the home of the faithful." These citations are all taken from the holy writings, and they form parables worthy of a great master. Your young monk has gone far in the ways of faith. I congratulate you on your choice. After hearing such a glowing report, the elders quickly returned to the pagoda, prostrated themselves before the young monk asking his foregiveness for ever doubting his worthiness.

Later in the day, the two friends embraced and congratulated each other. "But what in the world did you do?" asked the young monk of his friend. "Your holy man is nothing but a fraud," replied the cobbler. "As soon as he saw me, he asked if I was a hatmaker. I stamped my foot on the ground to show that I make shoes. Then he pointed to his armpits to let me know he wanted a pair of sandals cut from the supple flank of the beast. I showed him my back to explain that the leather from that part is tougher and better adapted to the dusty trails of a pilgrimage. He offered me three piasters for a pair. But I asked for five and he left. Perhaps he found my price too high."*

A brief classroom discussion should address itself to the meaning of the story as it relates to the understanding of communication in business and the professions. Efforts should be made to cite specific examples.

How beautifully this story illustrates that *how* we perceive the world is the world in which we live. Neither the holy man nor the cobbler monk had the slightest suspicion that what he was communicating through his gestures had absolutely nothing to do with what the other had in mind. But each seemed thoroughly convinced that the other was making perfect sense. How often do you think this happens in your daily life? Do business people tend to communicate with others as if they were prospective customers of clients? Do teachers tend to lecture others in casual conversation? Do actors tend to behave as if they were always on stage? If these tendencies are even moderately true, we must gesture "beyond each other" more often than we are aware. And, if personal nonverbal experience does shape the reality of

*From *Playboy Magazine*, March 1968, excerpted from *The Boisterous Bonze Thich Xuan,* retold by G. W. Victor from a Vietnamese folktale. Copyright © 1968 by HMH Publishing Co.

the world in which we live, it is to that experience that we must look if our goal is to influence others. You not only influence others without words, you, yourself, are "an influence." (Go back to the section on The Silent Self in Chapter 2.)

Resisting Influence

Thus far, the emphasis in this chapter has been on influencing others. But what about your ability to resist being influenced? Is such resistance something you develop, or are you born with it? Are those who are skillful at influencing others equally capable of resisting being influenced? Although a glib answer to these questions is not readily available they have the capacity to generate some rather interesting discussion on the subject of influence.

In most cases, the die with regard to your influenceability, has already been cast by the time you arrive for work on your first job. Literally, thousands of situations have already borne witness to whether you possess a high or low level of resistance to the influence of others. Those endowed with high resistance are fortunate. Those with low resistance must work to increase it. This can be done with a little effort, and the balance of this section will attempt to show you how. Before getting into specifics, however, it should be mentioned that, in the majority of instances, appealing to someone's feelings is generally more effective than appealing to their intellect. Naturally, there are circumstances where influence derives exclusively from an appeal to the intellect. These, in the more commonplace run of things, are in the minority. Feelings are tools of communication which, if properly manipulated, can influence the most prestigious executive as well as the hard-working stock clerk. What any conscientious influencer must do, therefore, is to find ways and means of getting at people's "feelings." Words are but one means of getting at them; wordless methods must, likewise, be sought out. You, in turn, must develop defenses against such attempts, if you are to resist them.

Everyone is selling something, whether it is themselves, a product, service, or an idea. Using the term "salesman" or "saleswoman" in its broadest possible sense, let us consider all others as consumers. What are some of the ways they can resist being influenced? Persuasion expert, Gary Cronkhite, suggests the following means people use to exercise such resistance:*

1. *Avoiding dissonant information:* Simply steering clear of any information with which you disagree or prefer not to expose yourself.
2. *Misperceiving or forgetting dissonant information:* Twisting what you see or hear according to what you already believe through a process called selective perception.

*Gary Cronkhite, *Persuasion* (New York: Bobbs-Merrill, 1969), pp. 156–158.

3. *Deprecating opposing arguments.* Taking whatever arguments are being used to support a point of view and attempting to shoot them down as either illogical or irrelevant.
4. *Seeking information to refute it.* Raising information conflicting with that being used to influence you.
5. *Devaluating its importance.* Labeling the information being used as unimportant and valueless.
6. *Deprecating the speaker.* Attempting to put down the person trying to influence you.
7. *Differentiating the information.* Breaking down the information or message into smaller units and assigning them different values. For example, hearing something toward which you are unfavorable (Unit A) followed by information about Unit A, toward which you are favorable would cause you to break it down into Unit A^1 and A^2 – one toward which you are unfavorable and the other toward which you are favorable.

To further enrich your resistance, here are some additional techniques you might want to try.

Proxemic Technique

Notice how near or far someone who is trying to influence you is standing. As soon as you have established the person's "influencing distance," alter it. Some people, when trying to influence others, prefer to stand close to them; others prefer to maintain a liberal interpersonal distance. Compromising the distance may serve the purpose of disturbing their train of thought, thereby, upsetting their psychological balance. A similiar end can be achieved by noting whether someone's preference is to influence you in a seated position. A popular technique among many successful persuaders is to get their subjects into as comfortable a position as possible. Sitting is generally considered more comfortable than standing, so they will try to get you to sit down. Parry this technique by remaining in the upright position. One other reminder of a proxemic nature: If you must sit when given the choice, sit directly opposite the person, rather than next to him or kitty corner. It has been suggested that sitting face to face with someone trying to influence you conveys a greater resistance than other sitting relationships.

Eye Contact

An age-old and well-respected resistance to being influenced is direct eye contact. Excluding the highly talented and experienced persuader, the amateur persuader does not handle direct eye contact too well. Whereas, such a person may have mastered the verbal side of influence, the nonverbal side involving eye contact is not so easily managed. The novice who tries to persuade you will often betray himself by looking away periodically.

Safety in Numbers

A good salesperson will try to get you alone. The fewer people involved in the persuasive process, the better they like it. The more people involved, the more opinions there will be. From their point of view, this is bad. Consequently, you resist being influenced by taking a friend along or having one or two of them present while someone is trying to influence you. This is particularly good if the person with you is a talker and you are not. It will tend to stack the chips in your favor. Furthermore, it will act as a source of intimidation to the persuader.

Ask More Questions Than You Answer

The single greatest drawback to successful persuasion is insufficient knowledge of the subject being persuaded. Nine times out of 10, the person doing the influencing has only a limited amount of information about the person to be influenced. The bulk of it must be extracted during the actual interaction. This means you will be asked questions. Your answers will then be used as sales ammunition against you. The less information you divulge, the greater will be your resistance. You cannot, however, just sit or stand there like a bump on a log. Your best course of action is to ask more questions than you answer. Keep redirecting the subject matter raised by the persuader into the conversation by asking for clarification, expansion, examples, and restatement of what has already been said. By doing this, you will prevent the persuader from breaking any new ground,and, thereby,confine the interaction to a very narrow frame of reference. Whenever asked about people, places, or things, plead ignorance, if at all feasible.

Avoid Personal Pronouns

You have already been alerted to the fact that more influence is effected through feelings than through the intellect. What better way should a persuader use to get at your feelings than through your emotions? And what better route is there to your emotions than through the use of personal pronouns? Block this endeavor by omitting the words *I–me–my* from your vocabulary during a persuasive attempt. Let's say a persuader asks: "How do you feel about life insurance? Why do you think you would do well in this position? When do you think a person should retire?" Don't answer any of these questions with the personal pronouns *I–me–my*. They constitute egocentric language which, if cleverly manipulated, could lead directly to submission. Egocentric language is "self-talk" and is is considered by some to be the backbone of the persuasive process. In short, the less you say about yourself, the more difficult you will make it for someone to influence you on any subject.

Do Your Homework

Those whose business it is to influence others count heavily on your ignorance. This is particularly so when it comes to the topic of influence.

An East Coast firm has recently jarred the advertising world with the slogan, "An educated consumer is our most valuable asset." This simple phrase has come to represent the bane of many businesses' existence. No longer could they market their products without worrying whether or not they will be taken to task with regard to such things as content, packaging, advertising, and pricing. The citizens in this country have been shaken out of their complacency to blithely accept what they are sold or told. It becomes increasingly difficult to influence people who know something about the product or service in question. In this regard, your level of laziness or apathy, when it comes to whatever you anticipate being influenced about, will represent in direct proportion your level of resistance against it. You simply cannot afford the luxury of not doing your homework.

The Good Ol' Days

All forms of influence deal with either the here and now or, what is going to be—the present or the future. People who cling to the past, who continually relive the events of yesterday and yesteryear, make up the sum of those who are most difficult to persuade. Their values are locked into a kind of historical vault, well out of reach of most persuaders. The chances are good that if you organize your resistance around a strategy of constantly dwelling on what used to be, you will be successful in warding off most persuasive attempts.

Conducive Environment

Beware of soft background music, a sumptuous meal, and beautiful surroundings. Any one of these could lower your resistance. If you hear soft music playing, go somewhere else to talk, if you're asked to dine, say you've just eaten, if the surroundings are beautiful, relocate your conversation to a less attractive place. The clever persuader knows one thing: to get the subject comfortable and content. Realizing this, make sure you don't allow yourself to get too comfortable or content. If possible, try to arrange things so the transaction occurs in your home (on your own turf), rather than on the outside. Also, if you are in your own home, avoid the comfort of the living room by heading for the kitchen.

Commit Yourself Beforehand

Plan in advance exactly what you are going to say and do. Tell someone exactly where you plan to draw the line on how much you will pay for something before confronting a salesperson. The important thing is that you commit yourself to someone (the more people the better) before you expose yourself to being influenced. It seems that a prior commitment tends to act as a form of resistance.

Sleep on It

It is very important to avoid reaching a decision on the spot. Tell the person that you will have to sleep on it. Although there are undoubtedly those who will argue that some decisions must be made on the spot or an opportunity will pass you by, the wiser rule of thumb is to sleep on it. There are also those who will argue that opportunity is always knocking. The problem is more a question of who is ready, willing, and able to move on it. In any case, the wiser course is to make it an iron-clad rule to go away from a persuader with a mind that is still not made up. Taking one's time in the decision-making process is a form of resistance you should give serious consideration.

Name of Exercise: Try to Influence Me

Purpose: To test a person's ability to resist being influenced by others in a variety of social situations.

Procedure: Students will be selected by the teacher to dramatize several scenes. They will be unrehearsed and spontaneous. Each will be limited to 5 to 10 minutes of class time.

SCENE I

The Restaurant

PLAYERS: Customer, waiter, chef, owner

Scene opens with a customer seated at a table waiting to be served. The waiter approaches to take the order. It consists of a medium steak, baked potato, and salad with Russian dressing. The waiter disappears and returns in a minute with the steak. The customer tastes the steak and complains that it isn't the way it was ordered, medium. The waiter takes it back to the kitchen and returns with another steak. Again, the customer complains that it isn't right. The waiter and customer argue about the steak. Finally, the customer, without having gotten satisfaction, asks to see the chef. The chef appears and the argument continues. Unable to satisfy the customer, the chef suggests that the customer speak to the owner of the restaurant. He appears, and the argument continues. Essentially, the customer tries to influence the owner, chef, and waiter that the steak he ordered is not medium. They, in return, insist that it is.

SCENE II

The Chinese Laundry

PLAYERS: Shopkeeper, customer

Scene opens with the shopkeeper behind the counter ironing a shirt. The customer gives his name and proceeds to explain that he needs his shirts, but has lost the ticket. The dialogue ensues over the shirts and the lost ticket. The shopkeeper explains that he cannot release the shirts without a ticket. The customer, in turn, frantically explains that he must have his shirts tonight. The customer tries to influence him to release the shirts, and the shopkeeper tries to influence him that he cannot do it without the ticket.

SCENE III

The Receptionist

PLAYERS: Receptionist, visitor

Scene opens in a typical office. The receptionist is seated at a desk and a visitor approaches her. He asks to see Mr. Grauling, the boss. She leads with the usual question, "Do you have an appointment?" He answers, "No." The dialogue continues with the visitor trying to see Mr. Grauling without having an appointment and the receptionist trying to keep him out.

SCENE IV

The Raise

PLAYERS: Employer, employee

Scene opens with the employer seated at her desk. A knock at the door is answered, and an employee enters. The employee has worked for the firm for a year and a half and wants a raise. The dialogue involves the employee's argument as to why a raise is warranted, and the employer's argument as to why it is not.

After all the scenes have been enacted, the entire class should engage in an open discussion, wherein the various types of resistance to influence are recounted. The scenes should then be judged as to which one contained the most effective form of resistance. Reasons should accompany such a judgment. Finally, each member of the class who acted in these scenes should make a self-judgment as to how well they each resisted the influence of others using a scale of Good, Fair, Poor, Bad. Again, reasons should accompany these judgments.

Write a one-page essay on the importance of resisting the influence of others in the business world.

SELF-EXAMINATION QUIZ

Having read this chapter, my answers to the following questions reflect my understanding of its contents.

1. In terms of "influence," what is the relationship between you and the society in which you live?

2. What is the importance of influence in your life with regard to business and the professions?

3. How does what people believe influence their behavior?

4. Why do people believe the things they do?

5. Explain why people resist being influenced.

6. Identify some of the common motives behind the process of influence.

7. Name theree examples of con games and briefly describe the principle behind each of them.

8. What is the rationale of propaganda and brainwashing?

9. How does one differentiate between what is true and what is false?

10. How do rumors spread through the grapevine?

11. What is the value of a thorough audience analysis?

12. Give three examples of how people are influenced without words.

13. Tell some of the ways people resist being influenced.

Suggested Readings

Aurbach, Joseph, "Social Dimensions of Cross-Cultural Name Calling," *Media Ecology Review,* 3-6 (1976).

Bennis, W. G., E. Schein, D. Berlew, F. Steele. *Interpersonal Dynamics* (Homewood, Ill.: Dorsey Press, 1968).

Bogart, L. *Strategy in Advertising* (New York: Harcourt Brace Jovanovitch, 1974)

Cronkhite, Gary, *Persuasion: Speech and Behavioral Change* (New York: Bobbs-Merrill, 1969).

Davis, K., "Management Communication and the Grapevine," *Harvard Business Review,* 31, (5), 43-49 (1953).

Dillehay, R. C., "Judgmental Processes in Response to a Persuasive Communication," *Journal of Personality and Social Psychology,* 1, 631-641 (1965).

Goodstadt, B., and D. Kipnis, "Situational Influences on the Uses of Power," *Journal of Applied Psychology, 54* (3), 201-207 (1970).

Herzberg, F., "One More Time: How Do You Motivate Employees?" *Harvard Business Review,* 53-62).

Knapp, M., "Public Speaking Training Programs in American Business and Industrial Organizations, *Speech Teacher,* 18, 129-134 (1969).

Larcom, J., "The Grapevine: How to Beat It or Join It," *Personnel Management and Methods,* 22-23 (1963).

Megargie, E. I., "Influence of Sex Roles on the Manifestation of Leadership," *Journal of Applied Psychology,* 53 (5), 377-382 (1969).

Myers, Robert J., "Fear, Anger, and Depression in Organizations: A Study of the Emotional Consequences of Power." Unpublished doctoral dissertation, St. John's University, 1977.

Singer, J. E., "The Uses of Manipulative Strategies, Machiavellianism and Attractiveness," *Sociometry,* 27, 128–151 (1964).

Sutton, H., and L. Porter, "A Study of the Grapevine in a Governmental Organization," *Personnel Psychology,* 21 (2), 223–230 (1968).

Walton, E., "How Efficient is the Grapevine?" *Personnel,* 38, 45–49 (1961).

WORK AREA FOR CHAPTER 8

Chapter 9

Instructional Communications

It does not follow that if you know the letters of the alphabet, you can spell; if you know words, you can write; nor does knowing how to do something qualify you to instruct others how to do it.

TO: Reader

FROM: Author

MEMO

After reading this chapter, you should have a better understanding of:

1. How important a role instructional communication plays in our lives.

2. Why there is a pressing need for additional study in the field of instructional communication.

3. Why knowing how to do something doesn't automatically qualify an individual to teach or instruct others to do it.

4. Why certain people block to taking instruction.

5. How many instruction writers feel toward the people for whom they write.

6. What theory underlies instruction.

7. What types of people write instructions and who hires them.

8. What are the dynamics of written, oral, and nonverbal instruction.

9. How to perform instructional analysis.

10. How to write your own instructions.

11. How signs regulate our lives.

Chapter 9

Personality traits may have a marked influence on how people react to various types of instructions.* Individual differences dealing with knowledge, perception, and understanding of materials at various levels of sophistication have probably been [more] responsible for the difficulty most of us have understanding instructions. Instruction is, after all, an effort to assist or to shape growth.†

Beginning with our earliest remembrances of toilet training, life could be viewed as an uninterrupted chain of learning how to do things—how to read, ride a bicycle, pour a tall glass of milk without spilling it, tie shoe laces, and drive a car. The one thing we all seem to have in common is "learning." Through learning, we conserve and pass on what we have learned; not an easy task. We have to be shown or instructed how to do things. This raises certain questions; such as, Who will do the instructing? What form should the instructions take? Who is to be instructed? This chapter charges itself with the task of bringing to light some of the difficulties often associated with instructional communication.

Strange as it may sound, there are people in business and professional circles who know about a great many things, but who cannot communicate these things to others. Simply because someone knows how to operate a cash register or typewriter doesn't automatically mean they can successfully instruct others how to do it. Even more peculiar is the fact that there are people instructing others to do things that they, themselves, cannot do—the overweight physician whose practice is limited to reducing, the bald barber who instructs his clients in methods of growing hair, the voice teacher who cannot sing. What we seem to have here are two categories: those who know, but cannot instruct, and those who instruct, but cannot do. Although both phenomena appear to be a contradiction in terms, they make up a sizable part of the working population. And, in the form of rationalizations, they are often accompanied by certain clichés: "You don't have to have cancer to treat it" (cancer specialist), "Do not do as I do, do as I say" (psychiatrist) "those who can, do; those who can't, teach" (people in the field). You have probably experienced both sides of this instructional dilemma and will be able to clearly identify with many of the situations described in this section. The result should be an extended appreciation of the need for further study in this area.

Overview

Value

Organizations cannot survive without instructional communication. Older members must pass on their knowledge, understanding, and skills to

*Walter A. Wittich and Charles F. Schuller, *Instructional Technology* (New York: Harper & Row 1973), p. 3.

†James S. Bruner, *Toward a Theory of Instruction,* (Cambridge, Mass.: Belnap Press, Harvard University, 1966), p. 38.

younger members. Without the benefit of this time-binding process, not only would businesses and professions cease to grow, they would perish.

During the first half of this century, before there were such things as training programs, newcomers to a field learned from the more experienced members in it. Like folklore, those who knew told those who didn't. Without any well-developed system, plan, or procedure, instructional know-how was casually passed from person to person. One of the shortcomings of this

laissez-faire method involved the question of competence. People shown how to perform a task and, for any reason, unable to catch on were often taken to be incompetent. Rarely was the instructor suspected of incompetence.

It has since been discovered that knowing how to do something and being able to communicate that knowledge to another person are two separate and distinct processes. Insight like this has given rise to streamlined training programs, sophisticated methods of screening applicants, and the hiring of administrative personnel who are both sensitive to, and qualified in, the field of organizational communication. In short, instructional communication has itself become big business. Millions are spent yearly on the training of personnel. The effectiveness of this training is determined by how well the trainees perform their jobs.

In addition, there seems to be a growing awareness on the part of manufacturers and distributors of the importance of the instruction leaflet. It is not something to be used only after a purchase is made. Rather, the instruction leaflet is one of the things a potential consumer might consult before buying an item. Then, if the item is bought, the leaflet (more commonly referred to as a booklet) has the continuing job of helping the consumer use the product to its best advantage. The literature should also encourage the customer to buy accessories, supplies, and related products. Hence, the instruction booklet is of value before, during, and after the purchase of the item for which it was written.

Instructions, whether directly labeled or not, play an important role in our lives in the public as well as the private sector. These include instructions on buses informing us that exact fare is needed, no pennies are accepted, no smoking, spitting, or littering allowed. Street signs instruct us to stop, go, wait, and so forth. Newspapers tell us how to dress by giving the weather report, where to find a job or apartment, where to find sales in local department stores and supermarkets. Only if all these sources of instruction were to suddenly disappear would we be able to fully appreciate the vital function they perform in our lives.

Attitudes

People not only learn differently, they also tend to harbor different attitudes toward learning. There are those, for instance, who have difficulty getting past the first stage, that is, admitting that they don't know how to do something and therefore have to be shown. Surely you have been in a car with someone, gotten lost, and had the driver stubbornly refuse to ask for directions. Then, after driving in circles for almost a hour, the driver asks for directions and refuses to believe them. Being open and willing to accept instructions is perhaps the first major step toward understanding them.

The process of unlearning creates still another set of difficulties. For psychological reasons, there are people who, having learned to do something one way, find it almost impossible to do it another. Does the phrase, "Well, the last place I worked at did it this way" have a familiar ring? Few things irritate a new employer more than having a new employee recall how things were done at a previous place of employment. An attitude such as this could easily constitute an obstacle to advancement on any new job. It could also stand in the way of learning new methods of doing things.

From the standpoint of the person giving instructions, another set of attitudes must be taken into consideration. Most important is the manifestation of genuine patience and concern for the welfare of the person being instructed. Too often, there is a failure on the part of the instructor to appreciate the difficulties experienced from the learner's perspective. It is almost as though, metaphorically speaking, the instructor is farsighted and the instructee, nearsighted. To work harmoniously, each must be aware of how the other sees things. When you want to convert someone to your point of view, you must start where he is and work from that position. That is an effective way to get him to change.

To give you an idea of how one authority recommends approaching the writing of instructions for any type of merchandise, note his attitude:

1. The reader is absolutely at the bottom level, so far as a mechanical or procedural grasp is concerned.
2. The consumer may not even read the instructions, or, if he does, he will not read them thoroughly and carefully.
3. The chances are, he will not keep the instruction booklet in a convenient place to refer to it as often as necessary.
4. The consumer is apt to begin assembling or using the product before he actually reads the instructions.
5. The consumer will have no sense of need for current maintenance.
6. The consumer may try to tinker with the product when he should not.

What this boils down to is that one should write instructions with the assumption that they are to be interpreted by the semiliterate who has never before worked with mechanical gadgetry or complicated devices in his hands.* Although this attitude may seem a little harsh and heavy-handed on the general public, it doesn't stray too far afield from the attitudes held by many who write instructions. Suffice it to say that whatever attitude a person holds toward the performance of a specific task, it has the potential of influencing its course, character, and outcome. In this case, it happens to be the task of writing instructions for the average customer.

Theory

A theory of instruction is *prescriptive*, that is, it sets forth rules that deal with the most effective way to achieve knowledge or skills. It also provides an excellent means of criticizing or evaluating a particular way of teaching learning. The distinction to be made here is between learning theory and instruction theory. Theories of learning are *descriptive*, that is, they tell us what happened after the fact. Theories of instruction are prescriptive in that they concern themselves with how what one wishes to teach can best be learned; also, with improving rather than describing learning.

Instructional theory embraces four main features. First, it should identify those experiences a subject possesses making that individual favorably disposed toward performing a given task. Second, it should spell out the manner in which the material should be structured so that it can most

*Joseph D. Cooper, *How to Communicate Policies and Instructions* (Washington, D.C.: BNA, 1960), pp. 131–132.

readily be grasped by the subject. Third, it should advance the most effective sequence in which material should be presented to the learner. Fourth, it should apprise the subject of what is to be gained (the rewards) and what is to be lost (the punishment) by performing the task.*

Instructions come to us in basically three forms: (1) *verbal,* written and spoken, (2) *nonverbal,* body movements and gestures, and (3) *visual aides,* pictures, diagrams, graphs. Whereas each has its separate assets and liabilities, most instructional communication attempts to maximize its effectiveness by incorporating all three forms. For example, while written instruction allows learners to re-read what has been said at their own rates and as many times as is necessary, they lack the benefits to be derived from a good picture or diagram. Conversely, a learner suffers equally from the shortcomings of pictorial or diagrammatic instructions that are not adequately explained.

Oral or spoken instructions represent a substantial part of business and professional activity. People are forever telling others what they should do and how they should do it. It generally occurs in a face-to-face situation in which the learner and instructor are able to experience both the advantages and disadvantages of the other's paralinguistic and kinesic behavior. In this form of instruction-giving and instruction-taking, there is usually immediate feedback enabling the learners to know whether they are on or off target.

Any theoretical approach to learning which assumes that everyone learns best in the same way is doomed to failure. For instance, there are people who simply cannot follow instructions from a piece of paper, they must be allowed to actually observe someone perform the task being described. Others require personal involvement on a physical basis—being permitted to touch, feel, or handle whatever articles or tools a task demands. Some cannot learn if the person instructing them stands too close, uses a harsh tone of voice, or goes too quickly. This and more points to the need for reliable instructional theory to consider not only the different ways people learn, but also those factors which prevent them from learning.

Who Writes Instructions?

Have you ever seriously wondered who writes the instructions that accompany various items you find on the market? In an effort to discover an answer to this question, many firms were either called directly or written to by this author. The replies were extremely interesting. First of all, you would be surprised at how uptight many of these companies were when it came to revealing information about who writes their instructions. Aside from those who said the person who writes the instructions is "out to lunch," they offered the following answers: (1) designers, (2) engineers, (3) outside consultants, (4) home economists, (5) psychologists, (6) technical writers,

*Jerome Bruner, *Toward a Theory of Instruction* (Cambridge, Mass.: Belnap Press, Harvard University, 1966), p. 40.

(7) copywriters, (8) production managers, or simply (9) people with a college education. Here is an actual letter received from a national firm:

Dear Sir?

Other than a good background in English and an ability to understand what's going on, the people who write game instructions do not require special skill or qualifications. Working together with researchers, the person in charge of instructions must be able to say as much as possible in a few words, find and stop misconceptions before they happen, and use illustrations whenever possible.

Sincerely,

Director of Research and Product Development

Among the more responsive replies was this letter:

Dear Sir?

Thank you for your recent letter with reference to your interest in the qualifications for people who write instructions for the assemblage of toys and the rules for the games.

A degree in technical/journalism is most helpful. If the toys are more complex, an engineering degree.

Sincerely,

Assistant to the Vice President
Research and Development

Essentially, these two replies represent the general tone of the inquiries made by telephone and letter. Together, they appear to raise a most important question, "What qualifications, if any, should the people who write instructions have?" Is it sufficient that they have a command of the English language, a working knowledge of the product, or perhaps a flare for merchandising?" List in the spaces provided below the qualifications *you* think such people should possess:

In a way, the qualifications you have just written supply a clue to how difficult you think it is to write instructions. Like so many other things, they "look easy" until you try to do it yourself. This chapter will provide you with an opportunity to try your hand at writing instructions. For the moment, however, let us concern ourselves with those who do, actually, write them.

People who tell others how to do things often suffer from a peculiar sickness called COIK. It stands for CLEAR ONLY IF KNOW. It's easy to do something that you already know how to do. To the person who has never done it before, it is not so easy. Imagine you have just met someone from the tropics who has never seen or heard of an overcoat. Make an attempt to write instructions on how to put it on in the spaces below:

Larry Barker, in *Communication Vibrations,** illustrates how we all suffer from COIK in his description of a conversation between an avid baseball fan and an Englishman seeing a baseball game for the first time. The Englishman asked, "What is a pitcher?" "He's the man down there pitching the ball to the catcher." "But," said the Englishman, "all of the players pitch the ball and all of them catch the ball. There aren't just two persons who pitch and catch." Later, the Englishman asked, "How many strikes do you get before you are out?" The baseball fan said, "Three." "But," replied the Englishman, "that man struck at the ball five times before he was out."

These answers, given to the uninitiated, are CLEAR ONLY IF KNOWN, Actually, if a single barrier to effective instructional communication had to be identified, COIK would indeed be a most compelling choice. More than

*Larry Barker, *Communication Vibrations* (Englewood Cliffs, N.J.: Prentice-Hall, 1974), p. 100.

any other shortcoming, those who write instructions tend to assume that those for whom they are writing know certain things which, in fact, they do not.

If this chapter has given you the impression that very few of the people who write instructions are qualified in the area of human communication, you have correctly gotten its meaning. As you shall soon discover, there is considerably more to transmitting accurate images from writer to reader unless both minds are tuned in to the same organizational plan. As unbelievable as it may seem, instructor and learner seldom operate from the same perceptual perspective—that is, they rarely see eye to eye. One major reason for this is that an instructor usually sees the larger picture of the task at hand while the learner, only a small piece of it. Another difference which separates instructor from learner is the fact that the former comes to the situation with the benefit of experience, the latter without any. These are but two of the more important considerations which should be embraced by any responsible study of instructional communication. In this next section, you will find others.

Written Instruction

Before anyone attempts to write a single word of instruction, that person must ask and answer these three critical questions:

1. Who is going to read these instructions?
2. What are they supposed to enable the reader to do?
3. What must I do in order to make myself understood?

Instructions are frequently given with complete disregard for proper audience identification. Too often, one set of instructions is available for seasoned executives, sales personnel, distribution dealers, college students, property owners, young mothers, etc. There can be no doubt that a proper audience identification is essential in designing an effective message, and insuring maximum acceptance."* A perfect illustration of this shotgun approach to audience identification comes to us once a year in the form of income taxes. As you know, the instructions are easy to follow. That's what you think! One professor of education at a west coast university struck a blow for the kind of tax reform tax payers would like to see most, *clarity*! Using 12 excerpts taken from a 1973 Form 1040, he asked 35 graduate students to apply the principles it advanced to 12 sample situations. The average student got less than 6 of the examples right. If you are interested in testing your skill against theirs, here is the actual excerpt:

> It may pay you to use the "averaging method" if after subtracting 3,000 dollars from your 1973 taxable income [line 48], the balance is over 30% of the total of your taxable income for the last four years (1969 through 1972).

*M. St. John, *"Do You Get Your Message Across?"* Nations Business (Aug. 1972), pp. 66–67.

One other more personal abuse of audience identification occurs when you are invited to a party and given instructions on how to get there. Regardless of who has been invited, they all get the same directions. Here are two paragraphs of such directions.

> Follow the signs to East Meadow. If there aren't any, look for signs to Canyon or Valley Junction which are bigger but you don't want to go as far as Canyon or Valley Junction because you want to make a sharp left near East Meadow onto Route 122 (or 221?) It's one of those funny towns you can go through without knowing it but you'll see a funny old store with a wooden Indian outside–or is it a totem pole? Anyway, ...

The only thing more amusing than these confusing instructions is the fact that the person who gave them almost invariably closes with, "It's really easy to get here, really."

Both illustrations–the tax form and the directions to the party–demonstrate the chaos that can result from a faulty audience identification: For whom are these instructions being written? The second question raises still another brand of difficulties. By asking what a reader is supposed to be able to do as a result of reading certain instructions, one must also be prepared to be asked, ". . . supposed to do according to whom?" Individual standards of expectation vary. What you might consider completely unacceptable, another person might find terrific. Have you ever found yourself in an instructional situation where you thought you were doing just great and the instructor thought you were screwing up everything? Those who know how to do things often seem to impose high standards of excellence on those who don't know how to do them. Perhaps, it has something to do with their ego. This tendency, however, appears to be less prevalent among instructors who possess greater empathy–an ability to feel with and for the problems being experienced by the learner. Put another way, the instructor with empathy is able to communicate to the learner that "we've got a problem" rather than "you've got a problem."

People who write instructions are prone to make assumptions of various kinds. They might assume, for example, that everyone is right handed, reads and writes English, is reasonably coordinated, has either experienced or heard of certain things, possesses average intelligence, or is endowed with a moderately respectable attention span. The ability of a reader to perform the task for which the instructions are intended will often rest heavily upon the correctness of these assumptions made by an instruction writer.

The answer to question three is crucial; "What must I do in order to make myself understood?" Actually, this question is incomplete. In addition to asking, "What *must* I do?" it should also ask, "What *can* I do, and am *willing* to do?" Those who find themselves in positions of instruction generally can boast a great deal of experience with the subject. As a result, they often have become somewhat set in their ways of doing things. This particular phenomenon is frequently noticed when experienced individuals move from one firm to another. Accustomed to doing things in a certain way, and doing them successfully, they are inclined to resist change. Frequently, and not because of any downright pigheadedness, they feel more comfortable doing things the "old way." This characteristic in an instruction writer can occasionally present problems. Take a recipe that has been on a box of cake mix for a half century. If it has sold well all these years, it is reasonable to assume that those who bought it and followed the instructions, made and ate cake. Then, why change the instructions? Well, if the company continues to sell cake mix, there's no need to change the instructions. But, what if the sales on such a product fell markedly and they could be traced to customer dissatisfaction? It is a provable fact that baking practices have undergone some radical changes in the past 50 years. We have gone from wood-burning stoves to gas, electric, and microwave ovens; fresh vegetables, homemade butter and preserves to frozen foods, margarine, and synthetic eggs. Cooking and baking times have changed. Today, practically everything you buy in the supermarket comes with instructions on its label telling how to prepare it. All of this means one thing—those who write these instructions must keep abreast of the times if their instructions are to be understood.

Having discussed the broader implications of these questions, it is now fitting that mention be made of the more specific essentials associated with successful instruction writing:

Stages

Instructional communication involves three stages:

Preparation. This stage is designed to make sure that all of the information and practice necessary to successfully perform the task is included in the instructions.

Development. This stage draws a bridge between what we have and what we want by outlining directions so that after each step, the reader is able to do something he couldn't do before. Then, the outcome of each step is analyzed for effectiveness.

Improvement. This stage should see to it that the instructions keep up with the changing times; that is, outdated techniques, obsolete vocations, passé expressions.

Language

In order to put your ideas across effectively, you must recognize one thing from the start: "all forms of . . . communication involve not merely words, but words and pictures. The two fit together neatly and interlock as closely as two sides of a zipper. This means that the words you write or speak must create pictures in the minds of your readers.*

*Lou Richardson and Genevieve Callahan, *How To Write For Homemakers* (Ames, Iowa: The Iowa State University Press, 1974), p. 3.

Instructions, if they are to be easily understood, should not contain abstract words or phrases (disseminate, negate, articulate), foreign phrases (*raison d'etre, sine qua non, per annum*), technical jargon (fulcrum, cranium, bushing), or the names of people a reader is not likely to know (Cashmir Funk, Ray Birdwhistell, Alfred Korzybsky).

Geography and culture are of equal importance. The migration of people from all over the world to the larger cities in the United States often compounds the difficulty of instruction writing. Many of these people, at best, possess only a sketchy ability to read or write English. Therefore, it is necessary to not only use visual aides liberally (pictures, diagrams, color coding), but also to realize that people from other cultures carry different pictures around in their heads. The word *house*, for instance, might conjur up an igloo to an Eskimo, a grass hut to an African, or a teepee to an American Indian.

Similar attention should be given to regional dialects within the United States. Whereas the word *pop* would mean a type of soda that you drink to someone from down South, it may be taken to mean ice cream on a stick by someone up North. Recognizing these differences, many larger cities in this country have already converted much of their public instructions (signs on buses, trains, railroad stations, telephone booths, and rest rooms, etc.) into two languages and many more use pictures and line drawings.

Grammatical considerations should also include the avoidance of: (1) incomplete sentences (leaving out a subject or predicate, the object of a transitive verb, or a definite or indefinite article), (2) sentences longer than

17 to 20 words, (3) excessive colons, semicolons, dashes, parentheses, commas, and underscoring of words, and (4) beginning sentences with conjunctions such as "and or" but."

Sequence

Paying strict attention to the order in which instructions are given can make a significant difference in how well they are understood. Experienced individuals, as stated previously, are occasionally observed to alter the sequence in which they do things. When they are asked why they do one thing before another, they blithely answer, "Because I have found that it works better for me." Learners who see that such casual departures from rules or instructions are likely to think that they can do it, too. What they fail to realize is that the experienced individual has earned the right to deviate from conventional instructional sequence.

Sequence refers to whatever order best enables an individual to achieve an objective with the least possible expenditure of resources and energy. It would be a more serious mistake to leave out an essential step than to present essential steps in an awkward order. Sequence should lead learners through a series of statements and restatements of a problem or body of information that increases their ability to transfer what they are learning. Other advantages of sequencing is that it: (1) helps avoid haphazard, hit-or-miss type of instruction, (2) enables the learner to progress according to his/her own capabilities, and (3) makes broad areas of content or complex skills easier to manage if they are broken down into smaller, subordinate parts.

A friend of mine was so hooked on sequencing that it almost rendered him immobile. Having lived in Brooklyn, New York, for 35 years, his world suffered a rather telling blow when he moved his family to Long Island. Addicted to sequence, whenever he wanted to go somewhere, he first had to drive back to his old neighborhood in Brooklyn, and then, on to his destination. He was one of those people who preferred to think his way of doing things was the "only way," rather than admit the existence of alternatives.

Sequence is an important factor deliberately built into any set of instructions. Learners, in particular, must respect it because it invests instructions with both reliability and predictability. From a psychological and mechanical point of view, sequence generates stability in learning and doing. Perhaps the most enjoyable anecdote illustrating the importance of sequence is the one about a gullible college student. One evening, while studying at home, he heard the front doorbell ring. Answering it, he was met by a salesman selling the big Webster's dictionary for a mere $3 apiece. Overwhelmed by the ridiculous price, he bought one, thinking he really got a fantastic deal. On closer examination (after the salesman had left), he discovered why it was so cheap—IT WASN'T IN ALPHABETICAL ORDER!

Feedback

A common question asked by people following instructions is, "How am I doing?" They seem to have a definite psychological need to know whether or not they are doing things right. The phenomenon in the field of communication referred to as *feedback* fills such a need. It acts as a signalling device designed to let the learner know what is going on during the instructional process. An example of such a feedback device can be found at many amusement parks. It is a machine which simulates driving an automobile. You sit down at a steering wheel and in front of you is a course marked out which represents a roadway. As soon as the machine begins, the operator's objective is to keep the little toy car on course. When it is on course, a little "green light" goes on; when it goes off course, a little "red light" goes on. These lights represent feedback mechanisms.

Instructions that lack feedback mechanisms reduce their chances of being understood. Whereas it is not necessary to overload a set of instructions with feedback, an occasional usage is valuable. If you are giving someone traveling instructions, you might wish to say that seeing a fruit stand and a big Shell Gas Station on the right means that they've gone too far. Or, if you are teaching someone how to drive a car, that smelling something burning might mean that the emergency brake was not released. Both are excellent means of suppling a learner with feedback.

Time Allotment

Everyone knows that people do things at different rates of speed. The more experienced they are, the more quickly they are apt to do things. Though this is certainly commonsensical to most of us, it is occasionally overlooked when giving instructions. There is absolutely no way for those who write instructions to know how patient or impatient a reader will be. Realizing this, they field test their instructions on subjects whom they consider to be "average" and know nothing about the task for which they are writing their instructions. From these tests, they arrive at estimates as to how long or how rapidly a particular task should take to perform. Having done this, you would think that no one would ever have any difficulty following instructions in which "time" is a factor. Unfortunately, the reality is that people do have such difficulties, occasionally As a rule the difficulty stems from the fact that words, rather than numbers, are used to denote time intervals. For example, instead of writing: Let it boil for a little while, they should say: Let it boil for 10 minutes.

Another problem associated with time allotments and instructional writing is related to assumptions about a reader's manual dexterity. Some people have a flare for doing things with their hands; whereas, others foul up everything they touch. The latter are those who, in spite of the fact that the instructions were as clear as crystal, the product was in perfect working order, appear at the store from which they bought the product complaining, "There's something wrong with this darn thing. It doesn't work!" What they usually mean is that there is something wrong with them and they can't make it work. In any case, whereas instruction writers cannot be responsible for such people, they must, nevertheless, make every effort to protect these people from themselves. This can be done only by making the instructions as clear and simple as possible and hope for the best.

Malproportionment

Another hindrance to understanding instructions concerns the use of diagrams. We have all received directions to someplace in which the sender drew a line representing a distance to be traveled on a certain avenue. This line is proportionately twice as long as the actual distance to be traveled! Without providing the reader with some accurate means of knowing how to interpret the construction of the diagram, it can—instead of making things easier, make them more difficult.

The risk of malproportionment is also associated with the use of pictures. Whether the task relates to cooking, baking, tuning an automobile engine, or sewing a button on a vest, pictures of the items involved can be confusing, at times. Take the picture of an egg which, to the reader looks *small*, is referred to in the instructions as *large*. Although most people might not think this is too important, a young baker anxious to please his new boss by having his batch of pasteries come out beautifully might become somewhat confused.

The use of pictures and diagrams in instructions requires accuracy with respect to relationships; proportions must be preserved, or confusion will surely result. An annoying example is the menu furnished in certain restaurants designed to instruct their patrons how to order a meal. In addition to the written description of various foods, pictures are used. A beautiful salad is shown in which the tomatoes look gigantic next to the hamburgers except, when the actual salad arrives, they are half the size. The opposite may also happen—the tomatoes are pictured small next to an oversized-looking hamburger. Again, upon arrival, the tomatoes are big and the hamburger small. Obviously, "one picture is not worth a thousand words" in this case.

Layout

How instructions are organized is extremely important to effective communication. As instructions are vehicles of change or innovation, they start with a handicap of spontaneous resistance to what they say. The reader tends to be automatically predisposed against them. The psychological mood seems to say, "The people who write these things know something and I don't." This resistance can, however, be reduced by laying out instructions in such a way as to make them as understandable as possible in the least amount of time.

The size of the sheet or booklet of instructions can vary. Naturally, the complexity of the item will dictate, in part, its size. Instructions on how to assemble a giant computer will necessitate a more elaborate treatment than how to use a bottle opener. The usual instruction booklet may be 6 X 9 inches or 8½ X 11 inches, depending on how the product is to be packaged and to be stored away. Smaller products packaged in small cartons will generally make use of smaller pamphlets because of the inherent size limitation of the packaging itself.

The instructional layout must also take into account the colors to be used, arrangement of written material on the page, whether the copy will be large or small—in printed form or script, contain illustrations, diagrams, graphs, or miscellaneous cardboard and paper gadgetry. A decision must also be made as to the title of the instructions. It must be short and positive. Each and every one of these layout determinations must be made with this thought in mind: "Will it help the reader understand what is being communicated?" Unless the answer to this question is an unequivocal *yes*, the choice under consideration should be bypassed.

Style

The element of style when it comes to any form of writing, whether it be instructional, technical, literary, academic, or fictional, becomes a problem. Why? Because the very term "style" has yet to be satisfactorily defined. According to one expert, "Style signifies the manner in which a man expresses himself, regardless of what he expresses, and it is held to reveal his nature, quite apart from his actual thought—for thought has no style."* Can style be applied to the writing of instructions? Does the fact that most instructions tend to be rather dry and to-the-point make them ineligible when it comes to style? Couldn't instructions be prepared so as to reflect creativity, with, charm, and interest? After all, if people write these instructions, and those very same people possess varying degrees of style, why shouldn't it come through in the instructions they write?

If, as suggested by Paul Valéry, "thought" has no style, perhaps it comes through nonverbally in a set of instructions. Surely, if size, shape, color, texture, and line all contribute to the style of an automobile, evening gown, or a piece of statuary, why couldn't it also apply to instructional communication? Wouldn't instructions written on a high quality of paper, in elegant type, and carefully layed out in a neat and orderly manner elevate its style? From any point of view, the question of style always seems to invite controversial discussion. When applied to instructional writing, this discussion should be even more controversial simply because the area has received so little attention from communicologists.

Safety

Instructions associated with potentially dangerous materials require special care, precision, and responsibility in their preparation. Appropriate

*Paul Valéry, "Style," in J. V. Cunningham, editor, translated by Eugenia Hanfmann and Gertrude Vakar, *The Problem of Style* (Greenwich, Conn.: Fawcett, 1966), pp. 18–19.

safeguards must be taken when inexperienced individuals are exposed to handling chemicals, electronic and electrical materials, or sharp objects. Not only must they be forewarned of existing dangers, they must also be told WHY they are dangerous and exactly what must be done (or not done) to avoid being injured or injuring others.

Three things are usually responsible for accidents related to instructions working with potentially dangerous materials: (1) people don't read instructions carefully, (2) they tend to underestimate the importance or seriousness of warnings, and (3) they are convinced that whatever they are being warned against will not happen to them. Countless personal injuries may be traced to one or a combination of these causes.

Whereas it is essential that instructions contain warnings, they should not be exaggerated so as to frighten people half to death; for example, BE EXTREMELY CAREFUL WHEN MIXING THESE CHEMICALS. IMPROPER MIXING CAN CAUSE EXPLOSIONS CAPABLE OF RESULTING IN SCARRING, MUTILATION, DISMEMBERMENT, OR SUDDEN DEATH BY SUFFOCATION. By the same token, warnings are not to be underplayed.

One other reminder about communicating safety measures should be mentioned. Since people "think in pictures," word warnings should, whenever possible, be accompanied by a picture or line drawing illustrating what will happen if that warning is not heeded.

Sense Appeal

We learn through our senses: by seeing, hearing, tasting, touching, and smelling. Certain individuals can read a set of instructions on how to replace a roll of toilet paper in a dispenser over and over again and never be able to do it. Yet, it is conceivable that such a person could do it rather easily if, instead of reading instructions, someone *tells* them how to do it. They learn better by hearing than seeing. Others may have difficulty doing it, regardless of whether it is read or heard. Their need is to actually take the roll of toilet paper and dispenser in their hands and "feel" what they are doing. One's sense of smell and taste might play an important role in following cooking or baking instructions. For such people, seeing the written words on a recipe or hearing someone say them has little meaning until they actually smell or taste the ingredients involved.

A rule of thumb for those writing instructions is to bring into play as many of the learner's senses as possible. If the subject is making drapes, one might include pieces of fabric; if the subject is baking, packettes of spices can be made available. *To repeat:* the objective is to reach the learner's brain through as many of his senses as possible. The comprehension and execution of any task seems to be positively reinforced by such a multichanneled approach.

Environment

Most instructions overlook this factor. Seldom do they mention the surroundings in which learning and concentration operate best. Some people require absolute silence in order to figure out a set of instructions, others have the uncanny ability to filter out both people and noise. Then, there are people who function better indoors than outdoors, in warm rather than chilly rooms, with bright rather than dim lights, before rather than after eating. While these preferences may differ widely, all forms of instructions should consider the learner's environment. Instructions which say, for example, REMOVE YOURSELF TO A PLACE WHERE YOU CAN CONCENTRATE could make a significant difference in how well they are comprehended. The nature of the task to be performed will also dictate the type of environment best suited to it.

Although only a small percentage of the instructions on the market are completely foolproof, an awareness of language, sequence, feedback, time allotment, layout, style, safety, sense appeal and environment have been found to increase their efficiency.

Oral Instruction

Thus far, we have been talking about the written form of instructional communication. But what about its oral counterpart? Does it warrant a separate treatment? The answer is an unequivocal "yes!" The reason for such an enthusiastic response is because, while reading instructions from a piece of paper, you are wholly deprived of any vocal qualities (paralanguage) or body language (kinesics). Both these sources of information, as you shall soon see, could make a significant difference in the way you respond. This is particularly true when, as you were told in earlier pages, a contradiction occurs between what is said, how it is said, and how one looks while saying it.

The most commonplace method of telling people what to do is to give them either orders or directions. Although orders and directions are basically very similiar, there is a slight difference. Giving someone orders seems to suggest that they haven't any choice in the matter–they must do what they are told. Directions, on the other hand, suggest a somewhat more democratic situation; the person being given directions still enjoys the freedom of choice. The idea of "giving orders" to another human being appears to be more charged with psychological risk than "giving directions." It is far less prevalent today; but, not long ago, certain members of society were reared to accept the fact that they would be given orders and be expected to follow them without registering any mental or physical resistance. One possible reason why this attitude has diminished so markedly is that many Americans are not working at jobs they enjoy doing or, to which they feel they are suited. As a result, they tend to be a bit thin-skinned and somewhat uncomfortable taking orders from people whom they do not respect. This lack of respect may involve such things as attitude, competency, prejudice, rank, and seniority.

In most organizations, management is responsible for all aspects of production. If things are to get done, it must decide what needs doing, who should do it, how it should be done, and formulate appropriate orders to be given by the appropriate people. The successful completion of any task will usually depend on how efficiently orders are conceived and delivered. Here are some of the more important considerations to be made if successful order-giving is to occur:

1. The spoken message must be understandable.
2. The person(s) taking the orders must pay attention to what is being said.
3. Good eye contact should be maintained throughout between those giving orders and those taking them.
4. Most people are more responsive when taking orders than those who can themselves perform the task in question.
5. Purposeless gestures, body movements, and facial expressions can sometimes act as interference to meaningful order-giving.
6. The tone of voice of the person giving orders should be monitored for such characteristics as patience, understanding, confidence, and respect.
7. Repeat orders as many times as necessary.
8. The person taking the orders should be asked to repeat them back to the person who gave them.
9. Establish the willingness of the person taking the orders.

10. State the results expected to be derived from the orders being successfully carried out.
11. Briefly explain why the orders are being given. (This advice has been debated.
12. Follow up the order. Don't assume that it will be done and the work it is intended to provoke will be done.
13. Watch for any nonverbal signs of confusion or misunderstanding. Invite questions.
14. Don't give too many orders at one time.
15. Allow a reasonable amount of time for the orders to be carried out.

One might add to the preceeding considerations the different types of order-giving. First, there is *calling for volunteers*, a technique popular in the armed forces when an order came down from headquarters. It is still used in many civilian organizations. Then, there is the *implied order* "That truck out back is still waiting to be unloaded, men. It sure would be nice if some of you decided to do it this afternoon." Next, is the *request approach*: "Would anyone like to unload that truck out back?" And, finally, the *direct order*: "You, unload that truck!" Generally, the type of order used will depend upon the situation at hand and the preference of the person giving the order. But, whatever the method selected, it should be noted that giving orders orally is frequently considered to be slightly more complex a procedure than doing it in writing. This is because oral communication operates on a verbal, nonverbal, and vocal level, whereas, written communication operates only on a verbal level.

Nonverbal Instruction

In a face-to-face situation, it is virtually impossible for someone to give an order that is strictly oral in nature. It must have its nonverbal content. The question is to what extent does it influence the delivery, comprehension, and execution of the order? Will the fact that a person ordering you to straighten up your work area does it with an accusing finger, a wrinkled brow, and tightly closed lips affect your reaction? Would a smile, a comforting pat of the back, and a wink of the eye make the same order more palatable? Probably. There is little reason to doubt that any order will not be influenced by the positive or negative nonverbal language that attends it.

Another consideration is the extent to which seeing someone actually do what they are telling you to do affects your comprehension. Surely, you've heard the expression: "Don't tell me, show me!" There are a great many of us who must see what we are being told to do; hearing it is not enough. Instructors who cannot actually do what they teach, place the learner at a disadvantage. In the field of Judo, for example, there are two ways of teaching it. One consists mainly of showing the student how to perform various moves and having the student imitate them. The other involves demonstration, but a great deal more explanation of how and why the moves are made. Naturally, the ideal way would be to blend the two in accordance with how a particular student learns best.

What is even more interesting about the nonverbal aspect of instructional communication is its contagious nature. Have you noticed that students usually adopt the body language of their teacher? This is especially true if they like the teacher very much. Students are, in effect, great imitators and, as such, are easily turned off or on by those from whom they are obliged to learn. This is very important because in the organizational community, everyone is essentially involved in either instructing others or being instructed, formally and informally.

Consider the retail selling situation where one particular individual trains the majority of new sales personnel. Granting, that each new employee brings to the position a specific style and character of kinesic behavior, not having any nonverbal reference for the job, there is a definite tendency to emulate the person training them (e.g., approaching a customer, manner of carrying an order book or a piece of merchandise, bagging or boxing an item).

Body language, unlike words with which we try to make pictures, is, in itself, a series of pictures. When you tell someone how to tighten a bottle top with your hands, you are providing your subject with a positive "nonverbal picture." These pictures can, however, work in reverse during an instructional transaction. Negative signs of instructional resistance to learning also make pictures. Take the case in which an individual who, for some reason, finds himself in a learning situation he does not like. Afraid or unwilling to express his lack of interest or apathy orally, he does it by generating negative nonverbal pictures. These might include: (1) nail or lip biting, (2) head scratching, (3) backing off, (4) day dreaming, (5) shifting his weight from one foot to another, (6) yawning, or (7) a blank stare.

There is one other tremendously powerful nonverbal force which you know as *silence*. Not talking or, as it is known in the vernacular, "clamming up" can act as either a positive or negative influence upon others. It can be interpreted as annoyance, hostility, boredome, recognition, rejection, peacefulness, indifference, vindictiveness, and so on. Having to sit still and be taught how to do something makes a number of people feel very uncomfortable, a trait common to many extroverts. Their nervous systems seem to experience difficulty when required to play a *passive role* in any situation. One of their favorite nonverbal retreats is silence. Its meaning, however, should not be judged in isolation, that is, by itself. "The meaning ascribed to silence, or the interpretation of a person's silence, very much depends on the context in which it occurs and behaviors that accompany it."* Instructional communication is one such context.

*Dennis R. Smith and L. Keith Williamson, *Interpersonal Communication* (Dubuque, Iowa: Wm. C. Brown, 1977), p. 207.

Regardless of whether your approach to instructional communication is written, oral, nonverbal, or a strategic blend of all three, it remains an art form that requires a great deal of thought, imagination, creativity, patience and practice. And, to begin such practice, here are some sample instructions you can sink your teeth into.

Instructional Analysis

Based upon what you have read in this chapter so far, here is an opportunity to test what you have learned. A series of instructions written by college students will be presented. Your objective will be to analyze them carefully. Try to search out both their good and bad points, those which are clear, and those which are unclear. Criticize each set of instructions on the basis of your ability to follow their meanings, plus your estimation of how you think others would react to them. Speculate as to what would happen if they were given orally instead of being written. What visual aids would you recommend to further clarify their meaning? In short, allow your mind to explore these instructions from every conceivable angle.

INSTRUCTION I – How to Construct a Cube.

Step 1. Construct a straight line along the horizontal 4 inches long.
Step 2. Label the end point 1 and 2 and label the line A.
Step 3. From point 1 construct another straight line 4 inches long vertically at an angle of 90 degrees from line A.
Step 4. Label this line B and its end point 3.
Step 5. Locate end point 2 and construct a line 4 inches long vertically at an angle of 90 degrees from line A.
Step 6. Label this line C, and its end point 4.
Step 7. Connect end point 3 to end point 4 with a straight line 4 inches long.
Step 8. Label this line D.
Step 9. From end point 2 construct a line 4 inches long at an angle of 45 degrees from line C.
Step 10. Label this line E and the end point 5.
Step 11. From point 4 construct a line 4 inches long at an angle of 45 degrees from line D and 135 degrees from line C.

Step 12. Label this line F and its end point 6.
Step 13. From end point 3 construct a 4 inch line 135 degrees from line D at an angle of 135 degrees from line B.
Step 14. Label this line G and its end point 7.
Step 15. Join point 6 to 7 with a straight line 4 inches long and label this line H.
Step 16. Join point 5 to 6 and label this line I.
Step 17. From end point 5 construct a horizontal line 4 inches long at an angle of 90 degrees from line I and 135 degrees from line E.
Step 18. Label this line J and its end point 8.
Step 19. Join point 8 to point 7 and label this line K.
Step 20. Join point 8 to point 1 and label this line L.
Step 21. Erase all the letters and numbers. This should now be a perfect cube and, with practice, you should be able to construct many more cubes of various sizes. Eventually, you should be able to draw houses, buildings, tables, chairs, and so forth.

ANALYSIS:

INSTRUCTION II – Quick and Simple Way to Start a Car.

Step 1.	Insert car key into lock and turn key until lock releases.
Step 2.	Open the door and sit behind the wheel.
Step 3.	Move rear view mirror, which is located on the center of your windshield, so that you are able to see the reflection of everything behind you from the center of the rear window to the right of it.
Step 4.	Roll down window to the left of you and adjust the side view mirror, which is located on the outside of your door. You should be able to see everything from the center of the rear window to the left of it.
Step 5.	Fasten your safety belt that is found on your seat to the right of you and on the floor of the car between the seat and the door to the left of you.
Step 6.	To do this, you must take the piece on your seatbelt, pull it across your waist, and insert it into the piece on the floor.
Step 7.	Stick the key into the key hole, found either on your dashboard, which is directly in front of you, or, on the steering wheel.
Step 8.	On the floor under the steering wheel, you will find two pedals. The one to the right is the gas pedal and the one to the left, the brake pedal.
Step 9.	Turn the key to the right and, at the same time, step on the gas pedal until the car starts.
Step 10.	You are now ready to drive away.

ANALYSIS:

____

____

____

____

____

____

INSTRUCTION III – How to Walk.

Step 1. Start with feet shoulder width apart facing forward.
Step 2. Then move left foot about 6 to 9 inches ahead of right foot landing heel, then toe.
Step 3. When this is done, pick up right foot and place it ahead of left foot about 6 to 9 inches.
Step 4. Gradually, continuing this pace, increase the distance between the feet to a full 12 inches.

ANALYSIS:

____

____

____

____

____

____

____

____

INSTRUCTION IV – How to Change a Tire.

Step 1. Pry off the hubcap with a screwdriver.
Step 2. Loosen, but don't remove, all the nuts that hold the wheel on the axle.
Step 3. Place the bumper jack under a part of the bumper near the flat tire. Make sure that the hand brake is set and the base of the jack is on solid and level ground.
Step 4. Crank the jack until the bottom of the tire is several inches off the ground.
Step 5. Remove the loosened nuts and carefully take off the wheel.
Step 6. Put on the spare in such a way that the bolts sticking out show equal length.
Step 7. Attach the nuts as tightly as you can by hand.
Step 8. Finish the job with a lug wrench, going from one nut across to its opposite, until all are tightened.

Step 9. Replace the hubcap by fitting its edge into the wheel groove and hitting it with the heel of your hand.

Step 10. Pray the tire doesn't fall off as you drive away.

ANALYSIS:

INSTRUCTION V. – How to Tie a Tie

Step 1. Lift the collar of the shirt up. Then, place the tie around neck so that the wide side is on your right and the thin side, on your left side.

Step 2. Bring the wide side to the left side making a X across the chest. Then, wrap the wide side around the thin side.

Step 3. Bring the wide side under and up through the loop and down.

Step 4. Place the wide side down through the knot.

Step 5. Finally, pull the short end while guiding the knot to the top of the throat. Then, place collar down, covering the tie around the neck.

ANALYSIS:

Analyzing or, if you prefer, criticizing other people's instructions is one thing. It is quite another to conceive and develop them yourself. The following classroom exercise will convince you of this truth.

Name of Exercise: "It's Easy, All You Do Is . . . ."

Purpose: To allow students to see what happens when others are obliged to follow their instructions.

Procedure:

Step 1. As an assignment for a future date set by the teacher, each member of the class is to prepare a set of instructions for some specific task which can be performed in the classroom.

Step 2. Whichever task the students choose, they must bring to class, along with the instructions, the appropriate materials that will be required. For example, if the instructions deal with how to put on false eyelashes, that student must bring to class false eyelashes and the materials necessary for putting them on.

Step 3. Students should rehearse their instructions at home to make absolutely sure that they are clear and to the point.

Step 4. On the day the exercise is to be performed, the teacher should select a student (or one may volunteer) to go first. That student should select another student to carry out the instructions that were developed. The instruction-writer should then be seated and remain completely silent. There is to be *no communication*–verbal or nonverbal–between the person performing the task and the one who wrote the instructions.

Step 5. Every effort should be made during this exercise to have people perform the instructions who have never done it before. For example, men should be chosen to perform such tasks as: How to put on lipstick, mascara, hair rollers; women should be selected to use an electric razor, tie a tie, wire a household plug, and so forth.

Step 6. If someone following a set of instructions is having difficulty, it shall be the privilege of the person who wrote them to select a consultant from the audience to assist the person following the instructions. If difficulty is still being had with the project, one more consultant can be sent to the rescue.

Step 7. After each performance, members of the class are invited to make comments on what they thought was wrong, could have been done better or differently, and so on.

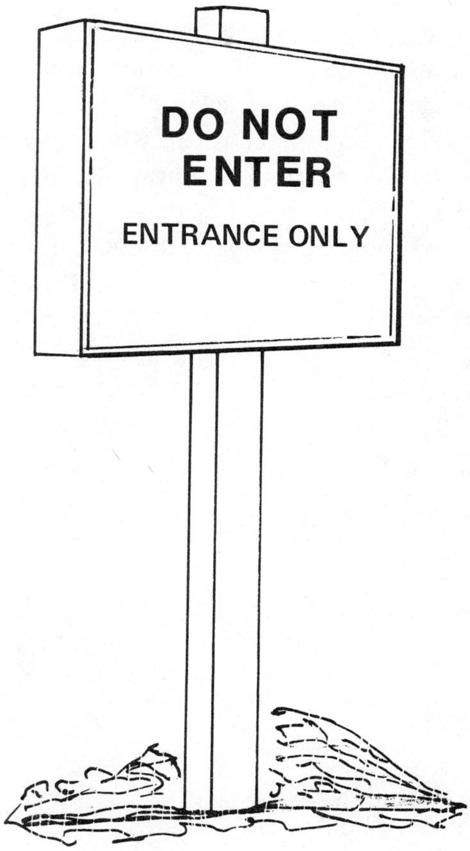

This is but one of the millions of signs which attempt to regulate our lives. The word "attempt" is being used here because they do not always succeed. How many times have you *pushed* when a sign said *pull,* gone *in* through a door which read *out*, boarded an elevator going *up* when you wanted to go *down?* Although disobeying most of them is relatively harmless, it can be dangerous, at times. For example, such signs as HIGH TENSION WIRES, ONE WAY STREET, BRIDGE WASHED OUT, or KEEP OUT–BUILDING CONDEMNED could represent a matter of life or death. It would be difficult to imagine the consequences if all the signs in the world were to suddenly disappear by magic.

Write a one-page essay on what you think would happen if all signs in the world were to suddenly disappear. Give examples.

Signs come in all sizes, shapes, colors, and design. Basically, they fall into two major categories: (1) those whose meanings are clear, and (2) those whose meanings are unclear. Because the meanings of those that fall into the first category speak for themselves—they can be understood by practically everyone—our attention here will be focused on those signs which are unclear or ambiguous.

As we move along, you will discover that a distinct line of demarcation between clear and unclear signs is almost nonexistent. To repeat a warning mentioned several times throughout this text: *meaning is in people, not words.* What a sign actually reads and what a person perceives it to mean can, at times, be worlds apart. The phrase, "Didn't you see the sign?" is as much a part of Americana as apple pie, bacon and eggs, bread and butter.

The signs you are about to read are real, not imagined, or made up. They have been observed in a variety of places, by a great many people, and have elicited numerous different types of reactions. After reading each sign, do three things: (1) tell what you think it means, (2) speculate as to where such a sign might be found, and (3) rewrite it so as to convey the meaning you think it should communicate. Use the spaces provided for your responses.

NOT A MEANS OF EGRESS

Meaning: ______________________________

____

____

____

Location: ______________________________

Rewrite: ______________________________

____

SNOW EMERGENCY STREET
NO STANDING IN
EMERGENCY

Meaning: ______________________________

____

____

____

Location: ______________________________

____

Rewrite: ______________________________

____

____

ALL COTTON MADE IN INDIA

Meaning: ______________________________

____

Location: ______________________________

____

Rewrite: ______________________________

____

____

CURB YOUR DOG–
NO DOGS AT LARGE

Meaning: ______________________________

____

Location: ______________________________

Rewrite: ______________________________

SKIRT STEAKS

Meaning: ______________________________________

____

Location: ______________________________________

Rewrite: ______________________________________

DISABLED VEHICLES–
DRIVE OFF RAMP

Meaning: ______________________________________

____

Location: ______________________________________

Rewrite: ______________________________________

BUS STOP–
NO STANDING

Meaning: ______________________________________

____

Location: ______________________________________

Rewrite: ______________________________________

EAT AT AL'S
AND GET GAS

Meaning: ______________________________________

____

Location: ______________________________________

Rewrite: ______________________________________

STAIRS SLIPPERY
USE HANDRAIL

Meaning: ______________________________

____

Location: ______________________________

Rewrite: ______________________________

YOUR SHIRTS NOT TORN BY MACHINERY
WE DO IT CAREFULLY BY HAND

Meaning: ______________________________

____

Location: ______________________________

Rewrite: ______________________________

FINE FOR HUNTING

Meaning: ______________________________

____

Location: ______________________________

Rewrite: ______________________________

BABY SALE
4th FLOOR

Meaning: ______________________________

____

Location: ______________________________

Rewrite: ______________________________

MAIN ENTRANCE AT REAR

Meaning: ______________________________

____

Location: ______________________________

Rewrite: ______________________________

PLEASE RING BELL IF NO ONE ANSWERS

Meaning: ______________________________

____

Location: ______________________________

Rewrite: ______________________________

SALE QUART ICE CREAM 14 FLAVORS

Meaning: ______________________________

____

Location: ______________________________

Rewrite: ______________________________

OUR COFFEE COMES IN A BOTTOMLESS CUP

Meaning: ______________________________

____

Location: ______________________________

Rewrite: ______________________________

PLEASE REMOVE ALL YOUR CLOTHES
WHEN MACHINES STOP WORKING

Meaning: ______________________________

Location: ______________________________

Rewrite: ______________________________

OUR MOUSTACHES HAVE MORE MILK
AND LESS CALORIES

Meaning: ______________________________

____

____

Location: ______________________________

Rewrite: ______________________________

____

____

Each and every one of the signs you have just read was perfectly clear, if you had a reference for it. If not, you probably scratched your psyche and said, "I don't get it. What does it mean?" Going back to that sickness called, COIK—CLEAR ONLY IF KNOWN, suggested by Larry Barker, you made sense out of the sign only if you could bring meaning to it from your memory banks. After all, signs, by themselves, are nothing more than ink marks on pieces of paper or paint strokes on pieces of board. Their meaning comes from without, not from within.

Communication, through the medium of signs, is not always bland. Some are extremely imaginative and creative. Here are some samples:

In front of a clock shop:

THERE IS NO PRESENT LIKE THE TIME

On the window of a fish store:

OUR FISH COME FROM THE BEST SCHOOLS

On a front lawn:

YOUR FEET ARE KILLING ME

In the window of a shoe store:

COME IN AND HAVE A GOOD FIT

Above a hardware store:

LET US REMOVE YOUR SHORTS

In the window of a wig shop:

LOSING YOUR HAIR IS NO EXCUSE FOR BEING BALD

In a pizzeria window:

EAT AT TONY'S PIZZERIA
(we knead the dough)

Because a significant number of the verbal signs with which we come into contact tend to be somewhat ambiguous, communicologists recommend that, wherever feasible, they be replaced or supplemented by pictures, diagrams, or line drawings. Such changes on highways throughout the country, on telephone booths, at airports, railroads, and bus terminals have already implemented some of these changes.

> *To derive the full impact of converting word signs into nonverbal signs, go back over the ones you have just read and try to communicate the same message by using pictures, diagrams, or line drawings. If you are completely lacking in artistic skills, merely indicate what you would use if you could draw.*

SELF-EXAMINATION QUIZ

Having read this chapter, my answers to the following questions will reflect my understanding of its content.

1. What role does instructional communication play in our lives?

2. Why is there such a pressing need for additional study of instructional communication?

3. Why doesn't knowing how to do something qualify a person to teach someone else how to do it?

4. Give some reasons why certain people block to taking instructions from others.

5. What is the attitude many instruction-writers have toward the people for whom they write?

6. Simply state the theory behind instruction-writing.

7. Describe the types of people who write instructions and the people who hire them.

8. Differentiate oral, written, and nonverbal instruction.

9. What are some of the elements to be looked for when performing instructional analysis?

10. Evaluate your own ability to write instructions.

11. How do signs, as instructions, regulate our lives?

Suggested Readings

Bruner, Jerome, *Toward a Theory of Instruction* (Cambridge, Mass.: Belnap Press, Harvard Unviersity, 1966).

Cooper, Joseph, D., *How to Communicate Policies and Instructions* (Washington, D.C.: BNA, 1960).

Fergason, G., Giving, Getting and Understanding Instructions," *Best's Insurance News*, 61 (4), 39–41 (1960).

Indik, B. P., B. S. Georgopoulos, and S. E. Seashore, "Superior-subordinate relationships and performance," *Personnel Psychology*, **14**, 357–374 (1961).

Meyer, F. F., and F. J. George, "Transmitting Company Policy Through Employee Manuals," *Personnel Journal,* **42**, 329–335 (1963).

Richardson, Lou, and Genevieve Callahan, *How to Write For Homemakers.* (Ames, Iowa: The Iowa State University Press, 1974).

St. John, M., "Do You Get Your Message Across?" *Nations Business* (Aug. 1972), 66–67.

WORK AREA FOR CHAPTER 9

Chapter 10

Mistaken Meaning

Definitions, like road signs, keep drivers and communicators on course.

MEMO

TO: Reader

FROM: Author

After reading this chapter, you should have a better understanding of:

1. *How a subjective and objective communication breakdown differ.*

2. *How a communication breakdown may turn out.*

3. *The nature of a communication breakdown.*

4. *How a breakdown in communication manifests itself in a field-related situation.*

5. *Why guarantees and warranties are not what they appear to be.*

6. *How to go about diagnosing a communication breakdown.*

Chapter 10

As you near the back cover of this book, a reasonable question could be raised, "What does it all mean?" How does your conception or understanding of business and professional communication differ from when you started? In any discussion of this subject, it soon becomes apparent that it can be approached from several different perspectives. The preceeding nine chapters each represents one of these perspectives. Having read them, it is possible that you now have developed a few perspectives of your own on the subject.

This last chapter differs from the others in that it represents a kind of outgrowth of those elements involved in the process of communication. It should enable you to see more clearly how and why organizational communication can go astray. Once you are out in the field, you will soon come to realize how sadly inept the majority of people are when it comes to figuring out a breakdown in communication. You will hear complaints like:

> I don't understand what's wrong with George. Every week I have to explain the same things over and over again.
>
> What do you mean, you don't understand? You understand English, don't you?
>
> I will say it for the fourth time, Jean, not this week, NEXT WEEK!

These are but a few of the more typical remarks you will hear. The tragedy is that many of these breakdowns remain unresolved and continue as company jokes, such as, "Guess what? They screwed up again and labeled the cartons upsidedown!" or "Here we go again, gang. Ole absentminded Phil has gotten Tuesday's and Thursday's assignments turned around." Instead of trying to mend such mistaken meanings, they are often treated as routine, everyday occurrences.

This chapter makes the assumption that practically everyone who works for a living has, at one time or another, suffered the personal frustration of a breakdown in communication. Whether it is the president of a large corporation having difficulty communicating with stockholders or the chairman of the board, a teacher with students, or a national sales manager with field representatives, they all seem to have essentially the same problem—getting others to understand what they think, feel, and mean.

Breakdown in Communication

Types

Subjective The subjective type of breakdown is people-oriented; it involves those misunderstandings in which the nature of the breakdown is limited to how people think, feel, and behave toward themselves and others. For example, a department store manager might experience a breakdown with a buyer on the basis of prejudice. Ofttimes, such a breakdown is one-sided with one individual being unaware of the other's frustration. Then, again, the feeling might be mutual. In either case, it is referred to as a subjective breakdown because its basis cannot be confirmed or denied by a third party; it is a matter of one opinion against another—a stalemate.

Objective The objective breakdown differs from the former in that it is object-oriented, that is, it involves things in relation to people, not people exclusively. Examples of such things might include statistical data, merchandise, handling equipment, modes of shipping, etc. Take the case of the section manager and buyer just mentioned. If a breakdown in communication occurred between them concerning a specific date on which a shipment of goods was supposed to have gone out, and such a date could be verified, the breakdown would qualify as objective. So, a subjective breakdown deals with the internal or psychological aspects of the human condition while an objective one, those things with which they work.

Other Terminology Tubbs and Moss* approach a breakdown from a slightly different perspective, classifying it as being either *primary* or *secondary*. On the basis of the established premise that understanding plays an important role in the communication process and that such understanding refers primarily to the accurate reception of the content of an intended stimulus, they offer the following example of a failure to achieve content accuracy:

> The Service Manager of an oil company had a call one winter morning from a woman who complained that her oil burner was not working. The manager then asked her how high her thermostat was set. She returned several minutes later and replied, "Four and one half inches."

Here was a situation typical of failure to achieve understanding. Like most primary breakdowns though, it should be relatively easy to remedy through clarifying feedback and restatement.

A secondary type of breakdown involves a much deeper understanding of the communication process. Some individuals believe that if a person selects the right words and states them precisely, communication will be ensured. This is a wrong assumption for "total effectiveness requires a positive and trusting psychological climate." Secondary breakdowns, then, are disturbances in human relationships which result from misunderstandings. They stem from frustration, anger or confusion (sometimes all three) caused by initial failure to understand.

A breakdown in communication, in addition to being either subjective or objective, primary or secondary, also occurs on horizontal and vertical planes. When it occurs between people whose positions in an organization are essentially equal, it is considered horizontal. If it takes place between persons of high and low status, it is to be regarded as vertical. In both instances, aside from the position a person holds in an organization, the fact that they are both human beings must never be ignored. Each, to varying degrees, is prone to such emotions as depression, alienation, embarrassment, humiliation, and ridicule. True, there are some people who, because of their thick skin, can withstand a great deal of abuse growing from a communica-

*Stewart L. Tubbs and Sylvia Moss, *Human Communication* (New York: Random House, 1974), pp. 7-11.

tion breakdown. By the same token, there are those who, at the slightest hint of a misunderstanding, immediately begin to manifest mental or physical symptoms, or both. Stated plainly, it is quite possible for a comparatively innocent breakdown in communication to have some rather far reaching effects. The reason for this is that the effects of a breakdown are usually determined by the personality and character traits of the people involved. In one situation, a major breakdown might be very casually dismissed with a wave of the hand and a smile; in another situation, it might precipitate some rather dramatic consequences. Hence, when dealing with either minor or major breakdowns, it is essential to remember that the nature of the breakdown, along with the people involved, exert a definite influence on the events which follow.

Consequences

Resolution

Obviously, the most desirable outcome of a breakdown in communication is for those involved to work out their differences. Unfortunately, as suggested earlier, most people are not too adept at working out their misunderstandings constructively. It is the exceptional person who can take what would appear to be a negative situation and turn it into a positive one. An interesting side effect (a positive one) of being able to manage a communication breakdown successfully is that it tends to strengthen the inner workings of any organization or profession.

Dismissal or Resignation

Less desirable among the consequences of communication breakdowns is to have an employee "be fired" or "quit." Whereas, there are most certainly situations in which there are no viable alternatives to such courses of action, it does not speak well for any department or firm to have its people quit or be fired. It represents a definite flaw in the communications system of any organization if these consequences happen too often.

Bearing Grievances

Few things do more damage to an organization than to have members of its personnel grieve. Grieving or brooding (as it is sometimes called) can destroy morale, incite conspiratorial activity, and lessen productivity. Aside from badmouthing an organization or members of its staff, there are numerout nonverbal ways grievances are expressed: (1) giving someone the silent treatment, (2) taking extended coffee breaks, (3) sloppiness, (4) excessive absenteeism, (5) abuse of safety regulations by taking needless risks, and (6) disinterest in work.

Management that is sensitive to these consequences can do something about them. By discovering who the individuals are that are grieving and what they are grieving about, the difficulty is often on its way to being solved. Once the grievant is revealed, an open flow of communication must be established in which all aspects of the perceived problem (real or imagined) from both points of view are given a thorough airing. What the proper handling of this situation entails is attending to the grievance promptly, getting all of the related facts, taking the necessary action, and following it up after a reasonable amount of time has elapsed.

Dynamics

One of the most unforgivable mistakes you can make when approaching a breakdown in communication is to think that it must be "rational." In truth, the majority of misunderstandings which occur in organizational circles are more inclined to the "irrational." If you are now thinking to yourself, "I agree, but the distinction between what is rational and what is irrational is not always that clear," we are thinking in tune with each other. A further sign of being in tune is that you realize that while hardware, jargon, and organizational structure may differ, people remain essentially the same—the bigot will be a bigot whether in sales, manufacturing, accounting, or driving a bus. Laziness, aggressiveness, ethics, a sense of humor are all portable—people take them with them wherever they go. This admonition cannot be emphasized enough!

Role Behavior

A basic principle of communication in administration is that role behavior prescriptions, descriptions, and expectations should be closely related to each other. People should (a) be told what they are to do, (b) be given an accurate prescription, and (c) be led to expect what will happen—*before* it happens. When prescriptions, descriptions, and expectations differ significantly, communication breaks down. One of the frequent complaints heard in a system is "I never know what's expected of me." People need to reduce uncertainty. This carries over into their own role behaviors. Failure to do this increases tensions, increases uncertainty, and reduces accuracy of prediction.*

Every role has a position within the system, with a given amount of authority, power, prestige, and rank. Ignorance of the importance of position has the capacity to cause serious breakdowns in communication. When individuals feel that their positions are under attack, they often react negatively. Ambiguity interferes with communication fidelity, ambiguities in authority structure increase tensions within the organization and reduce the satisfactions that members get from belonging to the system.

Too much ambiguity as to who is in charge causes trouble, but no ambiguity may also cause difficulties. As communication channels become increasingly complex, as more and more group members get involved in

*Charles V. W. Brooks, *Sensory Awareness* (New York: Viking, 1974), pp. 213-214.

decision-making or approving and relaying messages that were sent to someone else, efficiency within the organization is strained.*

Routinization

Lest it be forgotten, we spend the majority of our business lives in a routine. Day after day, we do essentially the same things, with the same people, within the same environment. Once a routine is broken, so are communications. To put it more simply, take two people who are completely different, with different job routines, and put them together. Because they have little or nothing in common, they will have no meaningful communications.† It would be foolish to say that they could not engage in "any" meaningful communication, but it would be more reasonable to suggest that a basis for such communication between them would be highly unlikely.

Predictability

Any one of us can cite a number of illustrations of difficulties in communications that can be traced to ambiguities or conflicts in the expectations of the source and the receiver in a communication situation. If we operate from conflicting expectations, we will make conflicting predictions. People will not behave as we predict, and communication will breakdown.‡ If an employee is asked to work overtime and, on the basis of being asked, expects to be paid time and a half, he will be furious if he is paid only straight time. Conversely, if an employer expects an employee to put in overtime only to find that the employee has left for the day, he too will be upset. In both cases, expectations of another person were not realized. Each had predicted the other would behave differently. Result: A communication breakdown.

Fault-finding

A large proportion of the communications which break down turn up one factor in particular, the compelling tendency so many people have to criticize, judge, and evaluate others. Perhaps, they believe that by showing up the the faults or shortcomings in others, it will elevate their own status. Such people seem to subscribe to Murphy's Law: *If something can go wrong, it will.* They thrive on negatives instead of positives. The keen eye of management should make a special effort to uncover such individuals. By so doing, they will have an advantage when a breakdown does occur in their midst.

An Example Occasionally, a breakdown in communication comes along that really tops them all. Although reading it might cause you to think that

*David K. Berlo, *The Process of Communication* (New York: Holt, Rinehart, and Winston, 1960). pp. 150–152.

†"Cognitive differences as impediments to communication, with some uneasy hindthought of the questions What and When," Joseph Church, *Communication, Theory and Research*, Lee Thayer, ed. Ph.D. (Rochelle Park, N.J.: Hayden Book, 1967).

‡Cornelis, B. Bakker and Marianne K. Bakker-Rabdau, *No Trespassing* (San Francisco, Calif.: Chandler & Sharp, 1973), pp. 209–210.

it goes a little too far, you can rest assured that the more experience you have in the field, the more inclined you will be to say that it could happen.*

Colonel communicates to Major:

> At 9 o'clock tomorrow, there will be an eclipse of the sun, something which does not occur every day. Get the men to fall out in the company street in their fatigues so that they will see this rare phenomenon, and I will then explain it to them. Now, in the case of rain, we will not be able to see anything, of course, so, then, take the men to the gym.

Major passes message to Captain:

> By order of the Colonel tomorrow at 9 o'clock, there will be an eclipse of the sun. If it rains, you will not be able to see it from the company street, so, then, in fatigues, the eclipse of the sun will take place in the gym, something which does not occur every day.

The Captain then said to the Lieutenant:

> By order of the Colonel in fatigues tomorrow at 9 o'clock in the morning, the inauguration of the eclipse of the sun will take place in the gym. The colonel will give the order if it should rain, something which does not occur every day.

The Lieutenant then told the Sergeant:

> Tomorrow at 9, the Colonel, in fatigues, will eclipse the sun in the gym, as it occurs every day if it's a nice day. If it rains, then, this occurs in the company street.

The Sergeant then instructed the Corporal:

> Tomorrow at 9, the eclipse of the Colonel in fatigues will take place because of the sun. If it rains in the gym, something which does not take place every day, you will fall out in the company street.

Finally, one Private said to another:

> Tomorrow, if it rains, it looks as if the sun will eclipse the colonel in the gym. It's a shame this does not occur every day.

While such a foul-up in communication might be tolerated in a peacetime Army, its consequences might not be quite so amusing if it happened during wartime around an operating table during brain surgery, on a space probe with live passengers, or during the building of a giant bridge, tunnel, or skyscraper. Remind yourself constantly that to fully appreciate the dynamics

*Joseph P. Zima, "The Organization: A Communication System," Unpublished manuscript, 1976.

of any breakdown in communication, it must be analyzed in a given context—breakdowns never occur in a vacuum. To give you some idea of how communication breakdowns occur in context, here are two examples from the fields of health care and education.

Breakdowns in Context

Health Care

> *Write a short essay in which you describe, in your opinion, the breakdowns in communication arising between, nurses, patients, and doctors.*

Regardless of what business or profession you should soon find yourself, there is a chance you might need to visit a doctor or be admitted to a hospital. At such a time, it will be necessary for you to communicate with various members of a health team—for example, a doctor and nurse. Unlike a routine business meeting where you would be in a sound state of mind and body, communicating while you are physically ill and emotionally upset is not always easy. To give you some idea of the kinds of communication breakdowns that are associated with health care, read the following description.

Doctor, nurse, and patient are the three leading players in life's dramatization of health and disease. Survival, individually and collectively, depends on how well these three characters communicate with one another. To illustrate how they do it, here are their respective role perceptions.

From the Nurse's Point of View You will recall that how people think and feel about themselves and others strongly influences their behavior. This applies to the nurse. The lowly status for the nurse in the hospital has been characterized as a "bargain" which she has struck with the physician; the physician has the "scientific" responsibilities, while the "nonscientific" responsibilities are left for the nurse. Part of the bargain is that the nurse not only helps the physician in his scientific tasks, but also helps overcome inadequacies in the scientific method of practicing medicine. She does this by helping to prevent knowledge concerning errors, ambiguities, and uncertainties from reaching the patients and their families.* Historically, the nurse has been in a clearly subordinate position in relation to the physician. She has frequently been described as his "handmaiden." The nursing orders of ancient and medieval times emphasized selflessness, self-sacrifice, and unending services to others, usually together with rigid military discipline and strict obedience to those in a position of authority.†

*Fred E. Katz, N*urses, in the Semi-Professions and their Organizations* (New York: The Free Press, 1969), p. 56.

†Helen Nahm, "*Nursing Dimensions and Realities*," American Journal of Nursing 65 (pp. 96–98 (1965).

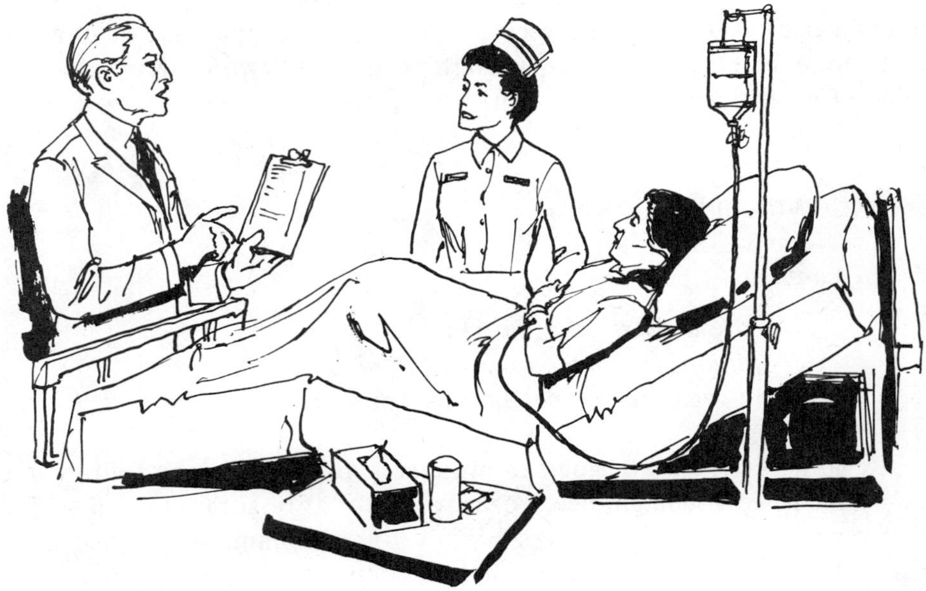

Ray Birdwhistell, some thirty years ago, advanced some rather definite views of women in nursing; he suggested that our culture usually refers to women when the symbol *nurse* comes to mind, despite the presence of men in the profession. Men in the nursing profession are often faced with disapproval. Nurses are not stimulated by others to gather information and make decisions on their own. They are present not to interpret, but to carry out orders and directions.* Some of this grows out of the difference between how nurses and physicians are educated. Medical education, for example, focuses upon teaching *how to know* rather *than how to do*. Instruction provided medical students is aimed at helping them develop their powers of critical thinking; the programs are rigorous and scientific in their orientation. In contrast, the emphasis in nursing education traditionally has been learning how to do rather than how to know.†

This caste-like separation of nurses from doctors suggests that nurses are not really part of the scientific-based clinical fraternity that is the basis of the hospital setting. Is it any wonder that communication breakdowns frequently occur? As long as the primary role of medicine is characterized as the "cure" process, the primary role of nursing, the "care" process, doctor-nurse communication will encounter difficulty. According to Barbara Bates, neither role is an exclusive domain, and there is a feeling of responsibility of both professions to attempt to meet the patient's psychological needs.‡

*Ray L. Birdwhistell, "Social Science and Nursing Education: Some Tentative Suggestions," NLNE 1949, Fifty-fourth Annual Report, p. 316.

†Rozella Schlotfeldt, "A Mandate for Nurses and Physicians," *American Journal of Nursing,* 65 102 (1965).

‡Barbara Bates, "Doctors and Nurses: Changing Roles and Relations," *New England Journal of Medicine,* 283 p. 129 (1970).

Unfortunately, the difference between what *should* be and what *is* continues to leave a great deal to be desired.

Perhaps the most striking piece of evidence of how brainwashed certain nurses are comes from an experiment cited by Barbara Bates. It illustrated the willingness of nurses to accept medical orders. When a telephone order for an unknown drug in twice the maximum dosage was given to each of 22 nurses by an unknown voice, identifying himself as a doctor, 21 of the nurses set out to administer the medication.*

While a study like this, if generalized out of proportion, is frightening, it should serve as a warning of what can happen when communication breaks down with human life at stake. Fortunately, educators in the field of nursing are aware of this inclination and working hard to graduate nurses with a well-developed sense professional communication. These same educators fully realize that doctors and nurses, as Stein points out, communicate via an indirect system in which nurses, who really believe they have something to contribute to the care of a patient, present their suggestions in an indirect fashion so that the physician appears to be the decision-maker. He refers to their relationship as the "doctor–nurse" game. A factor perpetuating this game is the sexual identity of the players. Doctors are, for the most part, men, and nurses are, almost exclusively, women. Thus, the "game" reinforces the roles of male dominance and female passivity that seem to be prevalent in our society. Part of the "doctor–nurse" game is that it has an inhibitory effect on open dialogue which, in effect, is both stifling and anti-intellectual.†

Enough of the reasons why certain nurses have difficulty communicating with physicians. Let us now turn to some specific examples of nurse–doctor breakdowns in communication. The most common of these involves the message that is sent and received but, for some reason, either not understood or misinterpreted. To be effective, a message must be sent in a way that will be correctly interpreted by the receiver.

Example No. 1

A doctor's written order states: Give 1 oz. of MO at H. S. This could mean 1 oz. of mineral oil or Haley's Milk of Magnesia, since the abreviation for both of these is MO. In a case like this, it is up to the nurse's subjective thinking to give what she feels is the correct medication. For instance, if the patient has had a hemorroidectomy (the removal of hemorroids), it will be up to the nurse to realize the patient just needs mineral oil to make the passage of stool softer so it won't hurt the operation. Conversely, if the patient has had abdominal surgery,

*Ibid., p. 131.

†Leonard I. Stein, "The Doctor–Nurse Game," *The Archives of General Psychiatry*, **16** 699–703 (1967)

the doctor will never give Milk of Magnesia because it would generate too much abdominal activity, and might tear the sutures.

Example No. 2

A doctor calls the nursing station and tells the nurse to give a patient, who has just been admitted, MS Stat: Since the doctor did not indicate the dosage or write out the order completely, the patient may receive Morphine Sulphate which is a narcotic or Magnesium Sulfate, a laxative. The danger is obvious to those who know better. If the patient is diagnosed as a cardiac, the nurse will assume MS to mean Morphine Sulphate, since a cardiac patient should be sedated immediately on arrival to her unit. But, if there is no diagnosis, as is usually the case, the nurse has to wait for written orders and then have them verified before giving medication.

Another source of misunderstanding involving the nurse occurs when a message is interpreted on face value. Imagine a patient who is feeling afraid and lonely. Having had no visitors, he may stop a passing nurse and ask her what the weather is outside. His real motive may have nothing whatever to do with the weather; he may simply want to strike up a conversation—to have someone to talk to for a couple of minutes. If the nurse fails to grasp the "real" meaning of his question and interpretes it literally, she might reply, "It's raining outside and about 75 degrees." This, of course, is not the response the patient wanted and did little or nothing to relieve his feelings of loneliness and apprehension.

Another case is the patient who is scheduled for surgery in the morning who asks the nurse, "Is this a difficult or dangerous operation?" The message is in reality a plea for reassurance and not just a request for information. If the nurse is not perceptive enough to realize this, she might reply, "Don't worry, this is routine surgery." Although the intent of the nurse's reply was well-meaning, it did little to allay the patient's anxiety." The patient could take her answer to mean, "My gosh! They aren't taking any precautions. I am just being treated routinely."

Then, there are the nonverbal messages nurses send to patients, consciously and unconsciously. The nurse who works rapidly, walks down the hall briskly, closes doors emphatically, is likely to be seen by the patient as an angry person who is unapproachable. The nurse who smiles as if she were happy, speaks in a warm and friendly manner, and seems to approach her work calmly, conveys to the patient an acceptance which prompts him to turn to her for help. Patients in a hospital are usually sensitive to the nonverbal messages sent out by nurses, doctors, aides—anyone around them. Too often, nurses forget that their smiles, frowns, body postures and even their touch transmit messages. Touch, one of our most primitive modes of communication, tells so much. The nurse who comes to the bedside of a patient, male or female, adult or child, and takes their hand is doling out one of the more effective healing agents we have at our disposal. The tightly clasped hand relieves tension and instills courage. This kind of contact is telepathic—it communicates understanding, a desire to help. It is a universal language—often more meaningful than words. The perceptive nurse communicates her feelings with her hands.*

From the Patient's Point of View Few things in life produce greater frustration than being sick and having to go into a hospital. Aside from being ill, frightened, and in a completely unfamiliar set of surroundings, the patient is confronted by a language barrier—"hospital talk." And, as though this were not enough, there is also a nonverbal language barrier—doctors, nurses, aides, orderlies, and therapists hovering over the patient doing a variety of strange things. These include inserting needles through which substances are pumped in and pulled out of the body, applying different medications and salves to the skin, putting tubes into various openings, wrapping and unwrapping sections of the anatomy. The procedures are not only alien to the patient, they seem to be practiced as if they were some cultic rites whose nature must be kept secret. When a patient asks a nurse or doctor what one of these procedures is or what it is supposed to do, they often get, "It will help you, make you feel better, or make you more comfortable," as an answer. Regardless of how intelligent or learned a patient is, there is a distinct inclination for hospital personnel to treat that person as one would a child. Expressions like, "It's time for our bath now," or "Well, I see you ate all your cereal and drank all your juice," and "Did we have a good bowel movement today?" are not alien to the hospital ward.

Another source of confusion for patients is the use by staff members of various abbreviations such as: EKG, EEG, CBC, WBC, IM, IV, etc. Patients, on hearing these terms used in connection with their condition, seem to get even more upset and confused. Unfortunately, doctors and patients seem to share different perceptual and cultural worlds. It takes some time for patients to learn the expectations, values, beliefs, and ways of behaving in hospitals. Their perception of their situation are different than the doctor's perception of their situation. "The doctors are frequently not aware of their perceptions, and they often imply that they should be aware . . . ."† What happens is that patients often simply do not know how they are supposed to behave in a hospital. Many have the misguided notion that remaining silent and accepting all treatment without comment is the best way to get well quickly and be discharged. What they fail to realize is the importance of feedback. Doctors and nurses are not mind readers; they cannot know what a patient is feeling without verbal or nonverbal feedback. Such information is carefully charted, and it gives the doctor, at a glance, an idea of how a patient's condition is progressing.

*Florence K. Lockerby, *Communication For Nurses* (St. Louis, Mo.: Mosby, 1963), p. 107.

†Mary Myers, *The Effects of Communication on Patient's Reaction to Stress* (Nursing and Doctor Research, Spring, 1969)

Occasionally, patients tell lies, or do something which they honestly believe will help their condition. There was a young woman in the hospital receiving intravenous glucose for a number of weeks. Because she had a heart condition, the glucose was administered slowly. As her heart condition improved (which they did not tell her), the drops per minute were increased. Thinking there was something wrong when she noticed a change in the rate of flow of the drops, she proceeded to press the tube against the side of the bed to lessen the flow. When discovered, she was scolded and told to stop. Fortunately, she was told that her heart condition was better and that she was to get an increased rate of fluid flow through the tube. She, verbally, expressed relief and no longer attempted to regulate the flow of fluid through the tube. One can only wonder why the improvement in this patient's heart condition was not communicated to her. Imagine, an entire treatment procedure could have been altered at the expense of discomfort to the patient, had the information not been provided. What patient does not want to know that she is better? In this instance, the young woman was being blamed for her behavior, when, in realty, her behavior was due to a lack of communication by the staff.

A patient's ability or willingness to communicate with hospital personnel, generally, is influenced by such things as prior experience, basic personality, fear, pain, or difficulty with the language. Any one of these factors, or a combination of them, could result in a communication breakdown. Although, it is certainly the responsibility of the health profession to prepare its personnel to cope with these problems, the patient is, likewise, obliged to share some of the responsibility. A first step in this direction is for staff and patient to become more familiar with the objectives of the other. It is amazing how much better patients progress when they know (even on a simple and non-technical level) what is going on. If there is anything that can destroy a patient's hope of recovery, it is a breakdown in communication with those administering health care.

From the Doctor's Point of View To the dismay of many doctors, patients occasionally have a tendency to misunderstand what they are told. An unbelievable example of this involved a fifty year old man who went to his family doctor because he wasn't feeling well. Returning home, he immediately got into bed and told his wife, "The end is near." When she asked him what the doctor said was wrong, he replied, "I have a flucky." Having never heard of a "flucky" before, she, too, was convinced that it must be a rare and serious disease. Bracing herself for the inevitable, she called her children, who were away at college, telling them to come home at once—that their father was dying. Arriving home, the son and daughter insisted on knowing what fatal disease was going to snuff out their father's life. The mother finally told them, "Your father has a *flucky*." Also stunned by the name of this unfamiliar disease, the son decided to call the doctor and get more specific information. On talking with the doctor about his father's "flucky," the physician said, "What flucky?" I told your father, "*He got off lucky*!"

Less amusing is the fact that certain doctors are not overly concerned with the meanings their patients attempt to convey to them. They tend to assume that situations which are usual and comfortable to them have the same meanings for their patients. In reality, what is meaningful to their patients should also be meaningful to them. Even the term, *surgery*, carries a different meaning to the patient. Whereas surgeons speak of minor and major operations, patients tend to regard *all* surgeries as major when it involves their own bodies.

In order to communicate effectively with patients, a doctor must make a decided effort to know (1) how patients see themselves, (2) how they see the situation in which they are involved, and (3) the interrelationship of the two. An unawareness of these considerations was observed when a doctor said to Mr. Jones, "It seems to me, you are not cooperating. You interrupt everyone when they speak and try to be funny about everything." The patient replied, "No one listens to me when I get serious and everyone laughs and listens when I joke. I just decided that it is the only way I get heard around here." The doctor, after giving the matter some thought, realized that, while not all patients would be this frank, Mr. Jones was able to perceive himself and the situation in which he found himself and verbalized his perception.

"Because doctors are human, some of them allow their bias about divorce, illegitimacy, religion, and social values to influence their attitudes, which, in turn, in some cases influences their care of patients, particularly those who did not fit their stereotypes of proper social and moral values."* References to patients as, "The Greek man in 711–that lawyer in 402 thinks he knows everything–Mrs. Gotrocks is up to her old tricks again," illustrate how a doctor might use personal information about a patient, not as a means of improving communication, but in a manner that implies judgments against the person.

Another pitfall of communication among some doctors is the tendency "to develop the false notion that patients always mean something else than what they say."† This is definitely a barrier to effective doctor–patient communication. Although it is true that for a variety of reasons many people do not clearly state what is on their minds, doctors make a definite error when they arbitrarily decide that the person means something other than what he/she says. When doctors are in doubt as to what a patient means, they should ask for clarification: "Did you mean . . .?" "I'm not certain what you meant to ask me."

Then, there are doctors who think the patients will not understand what they are saying when they use medical jargon. As a result, they will talk about a patient's condition quite freely, right in front of them. While medical vocabulary is not everyday language, with the advent of so many

*Leo Strauss, A. Schatzman, Social Class and Modes of Communication (New York: Holt, Rinehart, and Winston, 1966), p. 178.

†Ibid., p. 186.

television shows dealing with medical themes, health-oriented articles in popular magazines, books, and newspapers, patients often understand much more than doctors realize. Doctors should, therefore, be careful not to assume too much about a patient's ability to understand.

There is also the matter of how some doctors give patients orders: Turn over! Don't move your arm! Lie quietly! Eat your breakfast!" All these seem to be commands rather than requests. Since patients are people, they are apt to take offense at being spoken to in such a manner. Doctors are very quick to react when it happens to them. A patient says, "Bring my medicine! Bring my medicine! Send over the nurse! Get me a drink of water!" They, frequently, will parry such demands from a patient with, "You could at least say, "please."

Other sources of breakdowns in communication from the standpoint of the doctor concern nonverbal cues. Although facial expressions can sometimes be excellent indicators of a patient's disposition, one must guard against making inaccurate generalizations or stereotypes that are not based on the evidence at hand, but on one's own past experiences with various individuals. Not all patients who look grumpy *are* grumpy; a frown on one person's face may mean something entirely different on another person's face. Doctors must become sensitized to the fact that not only are patient's faces sources of information (fear, anger, surprise, relief, distrust, annoyance, confidence), their faces, likewise, communicate these same emotions. By the same token, the length of time a doctor spends at bedside, the number of times a doctor sees a patient, and the tone of voice that is used, all constitute forms of nonverbal information to the patient. And, since most patients are information-starved, they tend to grasp at straws; a wink, a smile, a nod, a wave of the hand, might be invested with a wide variety of meanings.

Perhaps, the most difficult aspect of communication for the physician is understanding the relationship between verbal and nonverbal messages. One perceptive young doctor suggests that we become cognizant of the fact that patients literally see differently when lying prone (face down) in their beds, and that their vision is further hindered if they wear glasses. While making his rounds one day, the young doctor came upon a patient who, while lying prone, complained she could not find her wristwatch. Although it was lying right on the table next to her, her position in bed restricted her range of vision, making it impossible for her to see it. Had the young doctor not realized the reason why she could not see her watch, he might have interpreted her behavior as a bid for attention, forgetfulness, or a simple case of laziness.*

Whether the communication breakdown is verbal, nonverbal, or vocal, or involves the nurse, patient, or doctor, the problem is usually one that must be analyzed in context. Seldom is the blame rightfully placed on the

*Jurgen Reusch and W. Kees, *Nonverbal Communication* (Los Angeles, Calif.: University of California Press, 1956).

shoulders of one individual; in most instances, if there is blame, it is collective in nature. To understand and correct it, one must take a comprehensive rather than an isolated approach.

This next classroom exercise, by having you draw upon your own conceptions about how doctors, nurses, and how patients think, feel and behave, is but one example of such a comprehensive approach.

Name of Exercise: Therapeutic Stimulation.

Purpose: To make the student experientially aware of how it feels to assume the various roles active in the traditional health care situation. From doing this, the student should become alerted to some of the more common causes of breakdowns in communications.

Procedure:

Step 1. Members of the class should divide themselves into triads (groups of three).

Step 2. Once in triads, each member is to decide which role he/she will play in the first round. There will be three rounds and, in each one, a member will play a different role; i.e., doctor, nurse, patient.

Step 3. In each round, using the principles of sociodrama, each member will improvise a dialogue according to the role that has been assumed. If you are not familiar with sociodrama, it is a technique in which people act out various real-life situations on the basis of specific roles played in society. Here, the situation is health care.

Step 4. According to the time limits for each round set by the teacher, students will begin the first round. It should be unanimously agreed upon beforehand by each triad as to whether the round will be held in a doctor's office or a hospital ward.

Step 5. After all three rounds have been completed, one large circle should be formed by all members of the class. In an open discussion, the following questions should be fielded:

a. In which role were you most comfortable psychologically? Why?
b. In which role were you most uncomfortable? Why?
c. What specific communication breakdowns did you encounter? Explain.
d. Of what particular nonverbal activity were you aware in each role? Explain.
e. In each of the roles you played, what was the relationship, if any, between what was said and how people behaved? Explain.

It is hoped that you will never be subjected to a communication breakdown with doctors and nurses. If circumstances should dictate otherwise, perhaps, what you have just read will stand you in good stead.

Yielding now to the lure of generalization, let us turn to various other fields and see what kinds of communication they are apt to incur.

Education

> *Make a list of as many types of communication breakdowns between teacher and student, student and teacher, teacher and teacher, and student and student as you can.*

Teacher to Student Two-thirds of classroom time is spent talking, the chances are two out of three that the person talking is the teacher; the teacher spends two thirds of his/her time expressing facts, opinions, giving directions or critizing students.* Educators, for some time–now more than ever–question whether the notion that "Teachers talk and students listen" truly constitutes classroom communication. According to Flanders, teachers influence students directly and indirectly. Included under the heading of direct influence are such things as: (1) lecturing, (2) giving directions, and (3) criticizing or justifying authority. Under indirect influence, there are: (1) accepting and clarifying student's feelings in a nonthreatening manner, (2) praising and encouraging student action and behavior, (3) accepting and using the ideas which originate from students, and (4) asking questions about content or procedure with the intent that a student answers.

Serious doubt exists as to whether there is a "right" way to communicate with students. Teaching philosophies vary from teacher to teacher, school to school, state to state, culture to culture. Essentially, all are represented by Flander's direct and indirect *teachers talk.* Differences are usually dictated by style, substance, sequence, students, and social order. The threat of a breakdown in communication between teacher and student is always there; all that differs is one's level of awareness of such a threat. Take the question of nonverbal communication in the classroom. Where, on a student's report card or transcript, is there a space provided for nonverbal communication? The truth of the matter is that, up until rather recently, student's nonverbal behavior has been sadly neglected or, in some instances, entirely ignored. The meaning invested in nonverbal communication here goes beyond something loosely referred to as *conduct*. This oversight is reinforced by the opinion of psychologist Ross Stagner. "The importance of certain kinds of defense mechanisms and personality traits early in life can be a major step toward helping a child improve his personality. Obviously, this function depends on

*N. Flanders, "Teachers and Classroom Influences on Individual Learning," in A. H. Passow, *Nurturing Individual Potential* (Washington, D. C.: Association for Supervision and Curriculum Development, 1963), pp. 57–65.

whether teachers agree with mental health experts as to what constitutes undesirable pupil behavior."* In support of his view, some teachers were asked to check from a list of child behaviors those which they felt were most indicative of emotional disturbance. The teachers' judgments resembled those of conservative parents rather than those made by child psychologists. The most serious problems, according to the teachers, were those student acts which they considered to be upsetting. They failed to become alarmed by those students whose passivity and withdrawal are often considered prognostic of neuroses and psychoses. In fact, some of the most withdrawn and disturbed individuals were rated, "perfect little boys and girls." Although teachers should, by no means, be expected to possess the critical eye of the psychologist or psychiatrist, as professionals charged with the responsibility of shaping young minds, they should, at least, be trained to recognize certain nonverbal signs as danger signals. For instance, teachers should recognize that: (1) a student's nonverbal behavior in school may not be indicative of that student's general psychic state, (2) there is often more than one motivation behind a particular nonverbal act, (3) nonverbal behavior should be interpreted in healthy rather than unhealthy terms (e.g., "There must be something terribly wrong with a child who is so active," and (4) it is an error to judge a student's nonverbal behavior on the same basis as he judges his own.

Student to Teacher These same silent messages also apply to student evaluations of their teachers. Surely you have had teachers who "looked mean" and, when engaged in a conversation outside of the classroom, turned out to be perfectly delightful people. In contrast, you have also encountered teachers who presented a very positive nonverbal impression at the beginning of a semester, only to become unbearable bores two weeks into a course. The nonverbal interaction between student and teacher is a continuous process, from the first to the last day of class. Have you ever noticed that whenever you don't know the answer to a question, the teacher calls on you; or, could it be that you sent out some kind of nonverbal signal by your facial expression, posture, or body movements? How about your nonverbal messages to the teacher, if you hate the course, or are bored to tears—do you think it shows? Body language experts would say that it does. Apparently, there need not be a word spoken between student and teacher in order for a communication breakdown to occur.

Consider, if you will, the traditional classroom arrangement; teacher sitting at a desk at the front of the room, students sitting in rows facing the blackboard. Whereas the teacher can see every student's face, students can only see the backs of their classmates' heads. This proxemic classroom arrangement, because it seriously reduces the student's source of feedback

*Ross Stagner, *Psychology of Personality,* 3rd ed. (New York: McGraw-Hill, 1961)

(eye contact, body movement, gestures), tends to decrease their level of attention. This, in turn, increases the probability of a communication breakdown.

Placement of the teacher's desk at the front of the room, because it symbolizes authority, tends to intimidate many students. Some become positively paralyzed when circumstances beyond their control cause them to take a front-row seat in class. Others love front-row seats. Seating preferences seem to correlate with performance; that is, classroom participation. Figure 1 shows that participation is greatest in the front row as well as the center section of each row. These figures were drawn from observations based on 10 sections analyzed.

INSTRUCTOR

57%	61%	57%
37%	54%	37%
41%	51%	41%
31%	48%	31%

Figure 10-1 Ecology of Participation in Straight-Row Classrooms

Paralanguage, poaching on the outskirts of nonverbal communication, is another source of breakdown. Students answering questions asked by teachers are occasionally penalized for such things as: (1) not answering quickly enough, (2) sounding unsure, (3) speaking too softly, (4) having an argumentative edge to their voice. Any one of these paralinguistic behaviors, coupled with some inadvertant nonverbal action, could easily spark an avoidable misunderstanding between student and teacher. Prevention would seem to lie in a mutual awareness of the communication process.

Another stumbling block concerns words and their meanings. Students, and, perhaps, because they are students, often fail to say what they mean. Ideas that seem perfectly clear in the mind, at least one thinks so, often suffer dreadful distortion when they leave the mouth. As with giving instructions discussed in the preceeding chapter, those who know how to do things are expected to be able to instruct another in doing them. This same myth crops up here; students who know what they mean should be able to say what they mean. Nothing could be further from the truth, especially among students.

*Robert Sommer, *Personal Space* (Englewood Cliffs, N.J.: Prentice-Hall, 1969), p. 118.

Also worthwhile mentioning is *silence* as an instrument of communication. Through the process of trial and error, certain students have learned that "keeping their mouths shut" often spares them a great deal of pain and suffering. To ask a question, to volunteer an answer, to agree or disagree with a classmate is to take a risk. Many have decided that the rewards are not worth the risk and, as a result, sit through entire semesters uttering but a handful of words. Although such a communication strategy might work with some teachers, it fails miserably with others. With the teacher who delivers an uninterrupted lecture for an entire period and has to be reminded when the class is over, student silence could be an asset; with the teacher whose presentation demands feedback in the form of classroom participation, silence will be a liability—it will run the risk of being interpreted as disinterest, boredom, apathy, stupidity or intimidation.

Jensen assigns five functions to silence. Each can be applied to a student–teacher relationship. First, he speaks of linkage—an invisible bond between people. The tightness or looseness of this bond between student and teacher is often established early in a course. On both a conscious and subconscious level, students manifest a degree of *linkage* between themselves and a teacher who, incidentally (if he or she is sensitive), is quick to detect. The character of this bond often acts as a catalyst in the event of a breakdown in communication. Second, silence serves an *affective* function in that it has an impact on any emotional interaction. For example, not answering back while being reprimanded by a teacher can prevent even greater friction. Similarly, giving a teacher who gave you a poor grade the "silent treatment" might cause her to be even more hostile toward you. Third is its *revelational* function, which can either reveal or keep something hidden. When a teacher asks a class, "Which of you read the entire chapter I assigned last week?" Half of them respond in the affirmative, the other half remain silent. What conclusion do you draw with regard to those who remained silent? They obviously preferred to remain silent rather than admit that they had not done their assignment.

The fourth function is *judgmental.* Students frequently use silence to suggest good or bad, agreement or dissent. If they do not complain about an unusually demanding homework assignment over the Christmas vacation, a teacher might very easily interpret their silence to mean consent. Then, again, silence could convey a negative judgment—like nobody responding to a request by a teacher for volunteers to remain after class to sweep out the gymnasium.

Finally, silence serves an *activating* function. The familiar phrase, "Let's stop talking and start working," implies that silence may better activate physical effort than continued oral communication. The student who says, "Let's take a break!" and is met by silence from his classmates may be prompted to continue studying.*

*Vernon J. Jensen, "Communicative Functions of Silence," *ETC: A Review of General Semantics,* 30, 249–257 (1973)

Teacher to Teacher Basic to the effective functioning of any professional staff are the available means used to exchange ideas. Faculty, departmental, committee, and PTA meetings are but a few of the occasions in which teachers come together to exchange ideas. In written form, they exchange ideas through bulletins, special bulletins, announcements, handbooks, manuals, lesson plans, reports, reports, and more reports on practically everything that goes on at school.

Most meetings are of little effect in communication. Supervisory meetings of the staff turn into announcement sessions at which the higher officials do most of the talking. Teachers meetings are often resented. Teachers are not usually asked to evaluate other speakers, or ask questions. They frequently go to these meetings with resentment and often "closed minds." One method of improving these meetings comes from Kimball Wiles: "The meeting must be structured so that there is time for teachers to talk together about the input the speaker has made. The minimum type of interaction should be a program with a presentation, discussion groups, and reaction panel, or question-clarification period.*

Perhaps, more than any other single factor responsible for breakdowns in communication among teachers is perception of roles. "The existence of a hierarchy produces restricting forces against communicating criticisms of persons at another level, and hostility develops as a result of perceiving persons at another level as threats to one's own position or as occupants of a coveted but unattainable position."† The implication is that people don't take criticism well. They tend to resent their critics. Only those who are extremely secure psychologically can accept criticism with grace and dignity.

Student to Student Oddly enough, students tend to experience more communication breakdowns among themselves than with their teachers. Psychologists tells us that peer-group pressures can, under certain circumstances, produce serious emotional strain.

The fact that a student is surrounded by other students does not automatically mean that such an individual cannot feel alone and threatened. This is especially true if that student has just transferred from another school.

Aside from differences in ability, personality, and character traits among students, differences of a special nature arise when numbers of them are collected and arranged in classes. Each class, according to some educators, has a specific "chemistry." Add a particular teacher and that chemistry can be altered again. What this all means is that a student may communicate one way in Class A and quite differently in Class B. Except in unusual cases, students rarely have a very close friend in every class they take. More often, they find themselves in classes with students they barely know by sight. This feeling of strangeness is frequently a key factor in most communication

*Kimball, Wiles, *Supervision for Better Schools* (Englewood Cliffs, N.J.: Prentice-Hall, 1967), p. 69.

†Ibid., p. 57.

breakdowns. Why? Because effective communication generally requires a common bank of information and references from which the people involved draw the raw material to construct their ideas. Understanding and misundering tend to pivot on the commonality of these references.

Have you noticed that, more often than not, bright students, dull students, and trouble-makers seem to search one another out? Seldom will the outstanding and the borderline students pal around together, well-behaved ones with troublemakers. This tendency of students to associate with those who are most like themselves generally makes for superior communication between them. The better the lines of communication between students, the better adjusted and productive they will be. Without a personal identification, a feeling of belonging, and a sense of "being liked," the risk of individual student breakdown in communication is increased.

So much for health care and education. But, what about all of the communication problems indigenous to other fields? To get at them, here is another useful exercise.

Name of Exercise: Field Specific Breakdowns in Communication

Purpose: To bring to the discussion level, problems in communication experienced by representatives of various businesses and professions.

Procedure:

Step 1. Have the following fields written on the blackboard:

Law	Social Services	Religion
Transportation	Funeral Services	Accounting
Stocks and Bonds	Politics	Mass Media
Law Enforcement	Engineering	Hotel Management
Public Utilities	Import–Export	Entertainment

Step 2. In teams of three, members of the class are to select one item from the offerings in Step 1. Over a period of time designated by the teacher, teams are to research their topic in the literature and on the job. Using source materials and personal interviewing techniques, they are to discover three things: (1) The problems with communication characteristic of the field, (2) how they are dealt with by members of the field, and (3) the methods of prevention used to reduce their frequency.

Step 3. On the day the exercise is to be performed in class, each team should be prepared to make a presentation to the entire class. It should last no more than 10 minutes and no less than 5 minutes. It should, as concisely as possible, present its responses to the assignment. All presentations should be made before any discussion is to take place. Students are encouraged to take liberal notes of what is said by other students.

Step 4. After all presentations have been made, the entire class is to form one large circle wherein an open discussion will take place. The overall objective of the discussion will be to compare and contrast the nature of the communication breakdowns unique to the various fields investigated.

Step 5. The discussion should be followed by a brief summation by one spokesperson from each team in which the derived significance of the exercise is expressed.

Communication Breakdown Checklist

As with the practice of medicine, it is an advantage to know what is wrong with a patient before prescribing a remedy. This same rule of thumb applies to a breakdown in communication; one must know what has gone wrong before it can be properly managed. Unfortunately, to the regret of both physician and communicologist, most breakdowns in communication are treated without knowing what caused them. Obviously, discovering the cause in either case makes everything easier.

It is one thing to recognize a communication breakdown, but quite another to repair it. Whereas, it is commonly agreed that every breakdown has a cause, or a combination of causes, the greatest difficulty appears to be getting at its cause(s). If two people are involved, chances are there will be at least two causes; if four people are involved, four causes, and so on. In short, the number of possible causes often appear proportional to the number of people involved in the breakdown.

You will now be supplied with a checklist consisting of 6 CHECKPOINTS. Each focuses on one common cause of a breakdown—*who, what, where, when, how,* and *why.* Hence, whenever you become involved in a misunderstanding, carefully analyze it against a background of each checkpoint for possible relevance.

Checkpoint 1 (Who)

Most breakdowns, except those which are intrapersonal in nature, involve a sender and receiver, and, as the process of communication is circular; rather than linear, one person generally talks while the other listens, and vice versa. This checkpoint suggests that a conceivable cause of a breakdown might be some mental or physical characteristic possessed by either a sender or receiver. Surely, you have met people who, because you couldn't stand their attitude or appearance, caused you to have misunderstandings with them. People have demonstrated the capacity to turn others *off* and *on.* Hope for mending a communication breakdown between people who can't stand each other is extremely guarded. Naturally, in business and professional situations where no alternatives exist, a special effort must be made by all concerned to keep the lines of communication open. Keep in mind that the essence of this checkpoint is to distinguish a breakdown caused by the actual people involved from what they are communicating about.

Blame has been leveled for more communication breakdowns at this checkpoint than at any of the others. For some strictly human reason, most of us have difficulty separating people from the views they hold. Rather than saying, "I disagree with the position you have taken," they tend to say, "I disagree with you!" The tendency is to attack people, rather than their ideas.

The value of knowing why you have had a communication breakdown can reduce your frustration. Realizing that it is not *what* you have said, *how* you said it, or *why* you said, it enables you to keep a breakdown in good perspective. It is not knowing why another person is angry or upset that can be nerve-wracking. This checkpoint will help you determine whether the breakdown at hand is solely a result of an individual, a *who*. If so, there is one course of action open to you. Avoid them like one who is allergic avoids certain foods, fabrics, and flowers. Perhaps, people can be allergic to certain other people. This checkpoint allows for the possibility.

Checkpoint 2 (What)

Having dealt with the *who*, your next consideration should be the WHAT. It refers to the verbal and nonverbal elements involved in a breakdown. Have you ever been lured into an altercation by someone who completely misunderstood what you said? While they may have heard the words you spoke, the meanings they assigned to them were markedly different from your own. Individuals like this have been known to lash out at a word or phrase, regardless of the context in which they were said, or who said them. Blinded by any qualification whatsoever, people like this are to be watched. The moment one of them picks up on something you have said, takes it out of context, or makes an irrevocable judgment against it, beware! They are often either uneducated, ill-mannered, not too bright, or have an ulterior motive for doing it. Phrases for which they are well known are: "I don't care what you meant, You said it and that's enough for me, "or" If there is anything I can't stand, it is language like that." Rest assured, people having this narrow view of language could not, if there was such a thing as communication insurance, get a policy. The risk would be too great.

Experienced members of any business or profession can probably recall numerous incidents where breakdowns were caused by this type of "tunnel vision." What salesperson has not come to grips with a customer who seizes on a particular word or phrase and works it to death? Mind you, this compulsion is not limited to customers; it happens on all levels of the organizational heirarchy.

Of equal importance in managing a breakdown is the nonverbal dimension of the *what*. To the exclusion of all other aspects of an interaction, there are people who are over-responsive to facial expressions, body movements, and gestures. Without fully realizing it, you might become the victim of a breakdown because someone can't stand the way you gesture when you speak. Thinking their reaction is based on something you said, it may have absolutely nothing to do with it. The list of nonverbal behaviors capable of triggering a breakdown is long. Try to think of some of your own.

The objective of this checkpoint is to help you detect people who deal with words and gestures apart from their contextual meanings. Managing such people becomes considerably easier, once you have discovered their method of communicating. Most of the difficulty is a result of not knowing what they are doing and being unable to respond appropriately. Proof of this is that many people have the same breakdowns over and over again, with the same people, and with the same outcome. Breakdowns over a *what* seem to be habit-forming. Avoid becoming similiarly addicted by realizing that words and phrases, by themselves, go nowhere and rarely serve useful purposes.

Checkpoint 3 (Where)

Also taxing the reasonable mind are those individuals deeply affected by where they communicate. To them, location is everything. Executives, keenly aware of this phenomenon, make every effort to select the best possible places to hold their business meetings. They know that the most persuasive argument is apt to fall on deaf ears if the other person is uncomfortable with the surroundings. Management has also found that, on occasion, moving its home office to another city has affected its employees' interpersonal communication.

Since meaning is in people and their communication is influenced by atmosphere, this checkpoint encourages you to consider the location when dealing with a case of mistaken meaning. Its remedy might amount to little more than relocating the transaction.

Checkpoint 4 (When)

Though you, personally, might not regard timing as essential to effective communication, some people do. In spite of the fact that every breakdown in communication involves the element of timing, the importance assigned to it varies. For example, it comes as no news to you that tomorrow morning, millions of people in this country will be unfit for meaningful conversation until they have had their coffee. Newcomers to an organization are quick to learn when and when not to talk to certain people in authority. How unfortunate it would be if someone approached a boss for a raise for the "right reasons," but at the "wrong time." People are creatures of habit; i.e., they eat, sleep, work, and play by the clock. Consequently, they are often highly predictable. When someone asks, "When would be a good time for us to get together?" don't be hasty and assume that anytime would be O.K. Sensitive field representatives rarely call on their customers or clients indiscriminantly; they know which ones to call on in the morning, which ones in the afternoon, and which ones to wine and dine in the evening.

Overlooking the time factor when analyzing any breakdown in communication would be viewed by this checkpoint as unforgivable. As difficult as it may seem to believe, most people search for the reasons communications breakdown in *what* was said, rather than *when* it was said. Think back for a moment to some of your own communication breakdowns. What was the relevance of the time factor? The importance of its role might come as somewhat of a surprise.

Checkpoint 5 (How)

In an effort to determine the cause of mistaken meaning, we have, thus far, inquired *who* communicated, *what* was communicated, *when* and *where* the communication took place. We must now ask how the people involved communicated. This raises two considerations: (1) manner of speech, and (2) channel.

Certain individuals have an edge to their voice that offends. They can make the most innocent remark sound angry, annoyed, or bored. While the consequences of such speech may be tolerated among friends or colleagues, it can be extremely misleading with strangers or newly made acquaintances. At the other extreme, there are those whose speaking voices are so charming that whatever they say is wholly incapable of offending. In most instances, if a priority had to be established, how a person speaks would have a slightly greater impact than *what* they actually say.

The channel through which someone communicates could also have a bearing on the outcome. There are some business and professional transactions which must be done face-to-face, others by letter, and still others by phone. It is a mistake to think that any channel of communication is appropriate, as long as the information it carries reaches its source. Someone who has been with a company for twenty years and who receives a dismissal notice in the morning mail is justified in being outraged. Such long service deserves the courtesy of a private conversation in which the issues are discussed. The type of channel used, whether it be a letter, telegram, telephone call, or a personal meeting, could make a great deal of difference in how the message is interpreted.

In practical terms, it is usually easier for someone to change channels than their tone of voice. Therefore, communication breakdowns in which the latter is found to be the cause are generally more difficult to correct. In either case, all breakdowns are to be screened for these two characteristics as possible direct or indirect causes.

Checkpoint 6 (Why)

Rational or irrational, people communicate for reasons. When those in communication know why the other is saying something, the flow is apt to be much smoother. It is when they don't know that things get rough. Any psychiatric jargon by a patient, if understood, makes some sense. The objective of this checkpoint is to draw attention to the fact that knowing *why* someone says something will throw some immediate light on most breakdowns. Unfortunately, finding out why people say things is often easier said than done. They frequently conceal their true feelings beneath layers of psychological armour that is difficult to penetrate (especially by the non-professional). The main thing to be borne in mind is that, behind every case of mistaken meaning, there are reasons. Just knowing that these reasons exist will often pave the way to greater understanding.

Guarantees and Warranty

Second in ambiguity only to contractual agreements and medical prescriptions are guarantees and warranties. If the phrase, "let the buyer beware," ever applied, it applies full force to the mystical world of guarantees and warranties. Millions, at this very moment, are thoroughly convinced, beyond a reasonable doubt, that the guarantee they get with the purchase of any item possesses some special power. This belief is borne out by observing the confidence with which they return defective articles to the dealer from whom they bought them. Convinced that their rights are fully protected by that piece of paper, their faces fall down into their shoes when they find out to the contrary.

For openers, let us see what Mr. Webster says about these two terms:

GUARANTY:

1. a pledge by which a person promises to pay another's debt or fulfill another's obligation in the event of default. 2. an agreement that secures the existence or maintainence of something. 3. something given or held as security.

WARRANTY:

1. official authorization. 2. justification, as for an opinion or action. 3. in Law, a guarantee—a covenant by which the seller of real estate, gives assurance of and binds himself to defend the security of the title.

Since the two terms (in a nonlegal sense) appear to be similiar in meaning and popular usage, *guarantee* will be used to represent both in this section. Before looking at some actual guarantees, notice that the definitions of these terms are, themselves, rather ambiguous. For example, what meanings do you assign to such words as: promise, obligation, maintainence, justification, assurance, and defend? It would be interesting to see how closely your definitions correspond to those advanced by your classmates. Withholding the names of products and manufacturers, and using the designation ABD instead, here are some sample guarantees for your examination:

> ABD Corporation warrants the parts, transistors and tubes (including television picture tubes) in any ABD color television receiver or ABD color television receiver or ABD color television combination receiver to be free from defects in material arising from normal usage. Its obligation under this warranty is limited to replacing, or at its option repairing such parts, transistors or tubes of the receiver which, after regular installation and under normal usage and service, shall be returned within one year from the date of the original consumer purchase of the receiver to the dealer from whom the purchase was made and which shall be found to have been thus defective in accordance with the policies established by ABD Corporation.
>
> ABD Corporation assumes no liability for failure to perform or delay in performing its obligations with respect to the above warranty if such failure or delay results, directly or indirectly, from any cause beyond its control including but not limited to acts of God, acts of government, floods, fires, shortage of materials, and labor and/or transportation difficulties.

This guarantee is about as clear as, "Tomorrow if it rains, it looks as if the sun will eclipse the Colonel in the gym. It's a shame this does not occur every day." The above guarantee is filled with semantically contaminated words and phrases which you are now challenged to define.

1. Free from defects ______________________________

2. Normal usage ______________________________

3. Regular installation ______________________________

4. No liability for failure to perform ______________________________

5. Directly or indirectly ______________________________

6. Acts of God ______________________________

Central to all of these ambiguous terms is the one overriding factor: who makes the determination as to what they mean? Does the customer or the manufacturer decide what is normal, regular usage, a defect? What better example of grounds for a communication breakdown is there than a guarantee like this? Here is another:

> We warrant each new ABD product to be free from defects in material and workmanship under normal use and service for a period of one year. Our obligation under this warranty is to replace any parts which upon our examination shall disclose to our satisfaction to be defective, provided the product is delivered prepaid to ABD Corporation, factory, or the nearest authorized service station. This warranty does not apply to any product that has been subject to accident, abuse or misuse and expressly does not cover parts or the labor of installing such parts that are subject to wear through use.

Again, semantic gobbledegook. This time, however, we are graced with a few new phraseologies: (1) our examination, (2) accident, (3) abuse and misuse, and (4) our satisfaction.

You must not get the impression that all guarantees are this weighted against the consumer. There are those which are quite straightforward and refreshingly reassuring to the consumer. Here is one such guarantee:

> Thank you for selecting this ABD product, designed and manufactured to the highest standard of quality and workmanship. ABD takes pride in guaranteeing this fine product for a period of 5 years from the date of purchase. The guarantee covers the cost of parts and repair service, excepting cords, bowls, and damage due to misuse. The guarantee is invalid where the product is used for commercial or institutional purposes. In order to exercise the guarantee, bring in or mail the product to the ABD factory or any authorized service station listed on the back of this certificate with your claim. It will be returned with the unit.

At least, this guarantee comes with some common courtesy and customer recognition: "Thank you for selecting this product," and "It will be returned with the unit." It clearly has fewer ambiguous terms and a more pleasant tone. Although the manufacturer does protect himself, he does it with psychological *finesse*; that is, with tender, loving care.

Though it would serve no useful purpose to present additional samples of guarantees in this chapter, it would be worthwhile if the reader were to examine a variety of them. Time should be taken to read the fine print and, wherever possible, underline words or phrases whose meanings are muddled. Having done this, the reader will have experienced the full impact of the type of communication breakdown a skillfully conceived guarantee can deliver.

P.S. For what it is worth, here is a guarantee that comes with this book. Read it carefully and decide its value.

GUARANTEE

> The author guarantees that each chapter in this book is sound, meaningful, and designed to serve a useful purpose. The author accepts no

responsibility for any failure in comprehension or misunderstanding of its content. The information carried by its pages is guaranteed not to offend the sensibilities of the average reader. This guarantee is rendered invalid if the reader, intentionally or unintentionally, misquotes, misreads, or in any way, shape, or form compromises the intended meaning of the work. Absolutely no liability is accepted by the author for examinations failed through the use of this book unless the purchaser can prove that it was used in a normal manner, approached with appropriate diligence, and afforded customary scholarly consideration. This guarantee is null and void if the book has been exposed to coffee or soda stains, shared by more than one person, or read by someone without a thorough gramatical knowledge of the English language. If these requirements are met, satisfaction is guaranteed for 1 year from purchase of any portion thereof.

SELF-EXAMINATION QUIZ

Having read this chapter, my answers to the following questions will reflect my understanding of its contents.

1. What is the difference between a subjective and an objective breakdown in communication?

2. List several different outcomes of a communication breakdown.

3. Explain the nature and characteristics of a communication breakdown.

4. Why is it so important to study breakdowns in communication in context rather than in isolation?

5. How can guarantees and warranties be deceptive to the buyer?

6. List the checkpoints mentioned in this chapter and briefly explain the function of each.

Suggested Readings

Argyris, Chris, "Interpersonal Barriers to Decision-Making," *Harvard Business Review,* **44**(2), 84–97 (1966).

Athanassides, J. C., "The Distortion of Upward Communication in Hierarchical Organizations," *Academy of Management Journal,* **16** (2), 207–214 (1973).

Boyd, B., "An Analysis of Communication between Departments-Roadblocks and By-passes," *Personnel Administration,* **28**(6), 33–38 (1965).

Braden, F. W., and J. T. Trutter, "Why Communication Goes Haywire," *Supervisory Management,* 12(1), 9–12 (1967).

Gibb, J., "Defensive Communication," *Journal of Communication,* **11** 141–148 (1961).

Hess, Sidney W., "Communicating with physicians," *Journal of Advertising Research,* **14** (1), 13-18 (1974).

Korman, A. K., "A Cause of Communications Failure," *Personnel Administration,* 23, 17-21 (1960).

Mayer, D. P., "But I Thought You Said . . . ." *Supervisory Management,* **11**, (12) 15–19 (1966).

Seiler, J. A., "Diagnosing Interdepartmental Conflict," *Harvard Business Review,* 121–132 (1963).

Debriefing

To orient you to the style, direction, and content of this book, it opened with an introductory briefing. It seems fitting that it close with a debriefing.

Understanding any subject rarely derives from memorizing facts, figures, names, dates, and places. Rather, it derives from the acquisition of an approach to the subject—a perspective, an attitude, a set of principles. It is hoped that this book will have supplied the reader with such points of reference. One way of making such a determination is to review the feedback given in each self-examination quiz.

As I have suggested, no reader comes to a book with a blank mind—without prior experience on a number of levels. It is against this background that all impressions are formed. The theme of this text is communication—communication in business and the professions. If it has been even modestly successful, the reader will have come away from it convinced that there is no such thing as a business or profession, only people who, because of their mutual interests and training, have come together for some common purpose. Thus, whatever the field, the common currency of exchange is communication—the sharing of meaning. The sense of this book, therefore, is contained in the knowledge that, as human beings, we all share a mutual psychobiology that enables us to anticipate what others think and feel rather accurately by looking more deeply into ourselves. That, in effect, is what communication is all about. If the proper line of communication is selected, every member of an organization should become accessible to every other member.

WORK AREA FOR CHAPTER 10

Name Index

Subject Index

Exercise Index